The Oxford Gui

Effective Writing
and Speaking

The Oxford Guide to

Effective Writing and Speaking

How to communicate clearly

Third Edition

John Seely

OXFORD
UNIVERSITY PRESS

OXFORD
UNIVERSITY PRESS

Great Clarendon Street, Oxford, OX2 6DP,
United Kingdom

Oxford University Press is a department of the University of Oxford.
It furthers the University's objective of excellence in research, scholarship,
and education by publishing worldwide. Oxford is a registered trade mark of
Oxford University Press in the UK and in certain other countries

First edition 1998
First published in paperback 2000
Second edition published 2005
Third edition published 2013

Impression: 1

Published in the United States of America by Oxford University Press
198 Madison Avenue, New York, NY 10016, United States of America

British Library Cataloguing in Publication Data

Data available

ISBN 978–0–19–965270–9

Printed in Great Britain by
Ashford Colour Press Ltd, Gosport, Hampshire

Preface to first edition

A book like this, which covers a wide range of topics, has to draw on the knowledge and experience of many different advisers. I have been fortunate to receive the help of readers who have given great time and care to commenting on early drafts of the manuscript and advising how it might be improved. In particular, I should like to thank Brigid Avison, Alison Baverstock, Tim Cracknell, David Elsmore, Jacky Hart, Caroline Hartnell, Andrew Heron, and Samantha Manning in the UK, while Dr Nelson Ong of New York offered an American perspective. They will probably recognize where their advice and comments have produced changes in the final text. For this I am deeply grateful, but, of course, the final responsibility is my own.

I should like to thank the staff at Oxford University Press who have patiently supported this project, in particular Kate Wandless and Kendall Clarke, for their encouragement and advice.

Closer to home, Katherine and Timothy Seely gave excellent and critical 'consumers' comments', especially about the communication needs of students and those seeking and gaining their first jobs. (I knew those long years of parenting would pay off eventually!) My debt to my wife, Elizabeth, is immeasurable. Although we have both worked as writers and editors for many years, I can only say that this time I was even more vague and abstracted than usual, but she bore it with great good humour. As ever, she read the manuscript with a critical eye and made many trenchant and invaluable comments, and it is with gratitude that this book is dedicated to her.

Preface to second edition

I have taken the opportunity of this new edition to make a number of changes. I have added a new chapter on emails, and have made extensive revisions to the chapter on job applications reflecting current practice. In addition, there are numerous small changes throughout the book designed to bring the text up to date.

Preface to third edition

In the revisions and additions for this edition I have focused on two areas in particular. The use of digital media for both informal and formal communication has taken over much of the territory where print media once held sway. This edition aims to reflect these developments, especially in Chapters 3, 24, and 27. I have also taken the opportunity of this new edition to rework the whole of Section D, with the aim of providing a more thorough and, I hope, realistic perspective on the processes of writing. Elsewhere, numerous changes have been made to update advice and examples.

Contents

① Introduction

At times the process of communicating with other people in speech or writing can seem straightforward and simple. At other times we may find it difficult and complicated. *The Oxford Guide to Effective Writing and Speaking* is organized so that readers can look at writing and speaking in four different ways. Three of them are shown in the diagram below:

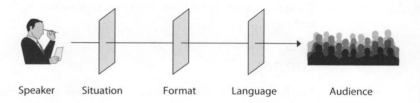

Speaker   Situation   Format   Language   Audience

At one end we have the speaker (or writer), with ideas to communicate. At the other is the audience—the people who are waiting to receive the speaker's message. In between are three screens through which the message has to pass. Each of these screens corresponds to a major section in this book.

Situation

Speaker   Situation   Audience

Before we can begin to frame our message effectively we have to consider the situation within which we are communicating. In particular we have to find answers to these questions:

- **What?**

  Exactly what is my subject matter?

- **Who?**

  With whom do I wish to communicate?

- **Why?**

  What is my purpose in communicating?

- **When and where?**

  Are there features about the place and time which affect how I should write or speak?

- **How?**

  What type of communication am I aiming at—narration? description? exposition? argument?

These five questions are the subject matter of section B, *Getting the message across.*

Format

The format is the particular type of communication demanded by the situation.

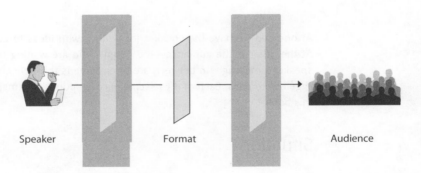

Speaker   Format   Audience

In Section A, *Communicating in everyday life*, we look at the most important formats in which people may have to communicate:

2 **Business letters**
3 **E-writing**

Language

None of this is any use, of course, unless we have a good control over the medium of communication: the English language.

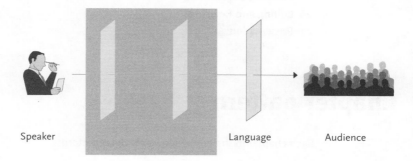

Speaker   Language   Audience

Section C, *Communication Tools*, provides guidance on:

15 **Talking about English**
   The different ways in which it is possible to describe the language.
16 **Introduction to grammar**
   The basics of English sentence structure.
17 **More about grammar**
   The structure of complex sentences.
18 **Vocabulary**
19 **Spelling**
20 **Punctuation**
21 **Speech**
   The technicalities of effective spoken communication.

Process

Situation, format, and language provide us with a lot to consider before communicating. Indeed, if we tried to think about all of them at the same time, we should probably give up the whole business. We need a strategy to tackle these things in a logical and structured way.

Speaker   Process   Audience

Section D, *The process of writing*, covers the main stages of writing:

22 **Getting ready to write**

23 **Making notes and summaries**

24 **Research**

25 **Planning and drafting**

26 **Editing and Revising**

27 **Presentation**

Chapter pattern

Each chapter in the book follows a similar pattern:

Summary of the main points ————————▶

Body of the chapter ————————————▶

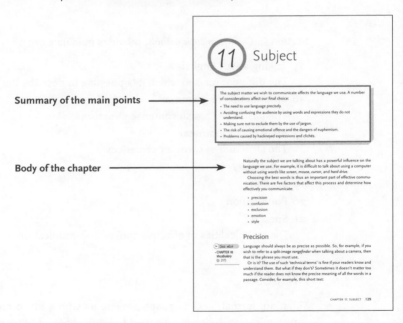

You try boxes
Many chapters contain these. They give you an opportunity to check your understanding of the points covered.

You try

The writer of this report probably did not think he was using jargon. What do you think? If it is jargon, how could it be made more 'reader-friendly'?

These principles underpinning effective performance appraisal have wider relevance than simply improvements in individual performance. They are also concerned with the development of a participative organizational culture by contributing to the broader goals of creating satisfying, effective jobs, encouraging the involvement of people in the organization, and the development of people.
  Failure to view the performance appraisal strategically as an important element in an involved organizational culture committed to the development of its individual members has resulted in problems. The early emphasis on the feedback principle, i.e. letting people know how they are performing, neglecting the involvement of the individual in the process, cast appraisers in the uncomfortable role of judge and often resulted in damage to individual development and involvement and commitment to the organization.

See page 374 for comments.

Emotion

There are situations in which we may not wish to use the most technically accurate language because it could hurt or offend our audience. For example, when breaking the news of a death to a close friend or member of the family, many people avoid blunt words such as *died* and prefer expressions such as *passed away*. This use of language is referred to as **euphemism**.
  Euphemistic language is commonly used by people when talking about death, certain kinds of illness (e.g. cancer), sex, and other bodily functions such as excretion. It even affects the language used to describe certain parts of the body. For example, that part which is most accurately referred to as the *belly* is much more frequently called the *stomach* (inaccurate) or *tummy* (euphemistic).
  We should, however, be wary of excessive use of simple or childish language. Doctors are sometimes accused of underestimating the linguistic maturity of their patients and of using unnecessarily euphemistic language. ('Any problems with the waterworks, Mrs Green?') This can not only be insulting, but may simply lead to further confusion, as in the famous story of the doctor who was explaining to a patient how to use a suppository and told him to 'place it in the back passage'. 'I did as he said,' the patient told a friend, 'and put it just outside the back door, but I might as well have stuck it up my arse for all the good it did.'

Cross references
Where a topic is mentioned that is also covered elsewhere in the book, you will find a See also box beside the main text.

See also
CHAPTER 18
Vocabulary
(p. 217)

Guidelines
The main practical points of the chapter are set out as a series of numbered guidelines, for quick reference.

Guidelines

Language skills and education

1 Think carefully about the audience's language skills, especially when writing or speaking:
 • for children
 • for speakers of English as a second or foreign language
 • for a general audience who may include a wide range of readers
 • about subjects where it is vital that every word is clearly understood—for example in matters of public safety

2 Make written text more readable by keeping sentence length down. 15–20 words per sentence is often considered to be a good average to aim for.

3 Difficult and 'long' words (three syllables or more) contribute to the difficulty of a text. When aiming for simplicity, either use shorter words or make sure that difficult words are explained or set in a context which helps the reader.

Knowledge and understanding

4 Make a careful assessment of:
 • how much your audience is likely to know about the subject
 • what background information you need to provide

5 In speech, check that you have got the knowledge level right by monitoring the reactions of your audience. In writing, consider the possibility of providing additional background information in a 'skippable' introduction or an appendix to which readers can refer.

Relationship with the audience

6 Decide how well you and your audience know each other and how close or distant you wish to be when you address them. This will determine how formal or informal your tone should be.

7 Make sure that your
 • vocabulary
 • use of long or contracted forms (e.g. *is not/ isn't*)
 • choice of pronouns (e.g. *I or one*)
 • standard or non-standard grammar
 support the decision you have made about tone.

Communicating in everyday life

2 Business letters

The structure and presentation of formal and informal business letters. How to make sure that you control the all-important element of tone in your letters.

3 E-writing

How to make the best use of email by thinking about purpose, context, format, and structure. Using attachments. How to develop a conscious email strategy. How to write for intranets and the web, taking account of the differences between web documents and more traditional formats. The importance of incorporating clear navigation features.

4 Job applications

How to research and construct a CV that is designed to meet the requirements of a particular job application. How to write a letter of application to accompany it. The importance of proper preparation for a job interview. How to analyse your strengths and weaknesses as a candidate and prepare for awkward questions.

5 Organizing a meeting

The aims, competences, and constitution of formal meetings. How to prepare an agenda, chair a meeting, and control the proposing and seconding of motions and the votes on them. How minutes should be prepared and ratified. How to run an informal meeting.

6 Presentations

Preparing a successful presentation: thinking about your audience; organizing the structure; making effective use of visual and other aids. Delivering the presentation, using prompts, making sure that you address your audience directly, and dealing effectively with questions and interruptions.

7 Reports

Brainstorming, researching, and planning a business report. The structure of a report: executive summary, introduction, body of the report, conclusions, recommendations, appendices, and bibliography. Other organizational devices. Addressing your readership.

8 Essays, papers, and dissertations

Preparing an extended piece of writing for college or university: generating ideas, doing research, ordering your material. Writing style and the use of quotations and references. The particular requirements of the undergraduate research project and the post-graduate dissertation. The importance of controlling structure and mastering academic register.

9 The media

Writing a press release: studying how newspaper reports work; organizing your material in the right order and format to ensure maximum effect. How to prepare for and undertake an interview with press, radio, and TV interviewers.

② Business letters

Structuring the letter

The key to writing an effective business letter is to have a clear definition of your purpose in writing. This should then be reflected in the structure of your letter. This normally contains three parts:

1 An **introduction** which sets out briefly the subject matter and purpose of the letter.

2 The **body of the letter** in which you develop and explain your purpose. This is normally divided into a number of paragraphs, ordered so that each covers a different aspect of your subject and each follows on logically from the one before.

3 The **conclusion** in which you re-emphasize your purpose, possibly spelling out what you would like to be done about it.

Getting the tone right

It is important to consider carefully the person who will read your letter—even if they are unknown to you—and write in a suitable **tone.** This should be neither casual nor too formal. In particular it is important to avoid pomposity and jargon.

Letter layout

Letter layouts vary considerably, but all have the same key features.

Greeting and ending

For most business letters there is a limited choice of greeting and ending, according to the degree of formality you wish to present.

It may seem strange to place business letters ahead of the more common forms of 'written' communication: email, text, and tweet. However, this has been done for a number of good reasons:

- Although printed letters are much less used than they once were, their structure, layout, and conventions still form a foundation for formal business communications. Many formal emails are, in effect, just business letters transmitted electronically.

- The very fact that in a wide range of situations printed formal letters have been replaced by electronic communications makes them even harder for many people to write. People become attuned to the more informal, conversational approach that emails and texts tend to encourage, and as a result often find that they flounder when faced by the challenge of this unusual form.

Letters have an importance and permanence that are comforting and reassuring. Even when we transact business by phone, we like to 'have something in writing' to confirm what we have agreed: a business letter. Employers still often lay great stress on the letters written by those applying for jobs.

The result of this 'special' status of letters is that they can prove quite difficult to write. Some writers, faced with having to write a job application, freeze up and cannot even think of a first sentence. So much seems to hang on what we write—our whole personality, career, life so far will be judged when the letter is opened and read!

Yet there is nothing inherently 'special' about letters. They are just another technology of communication, outdated, expensive, and rather time-consuming. The general rules we apply when using any other form of communication still hold. We still have to consider:

➤ See also

• CHAPTER 10
  Audience
  (p. 117)
• CHAPTER 12
  Time and place
  (p. 137)
• CHAPTER 13
  Purpose
  (p. 143)

• our purpose in writing
• our audience
• the conventions which govern the ways in which letters are usually set out (and which our audience will expect)

The conventions of letter-writing are placed last in this list because they are often given undue importance; it would be mistaken to believe that once you have mastered them, you know how to write a good letter. Knowing how to structure the body of the letter and being sure that you have adopted the right tone are far more important.

In this chapter the focus is on what are often called 'business' letters, letters we write to people we do not know or to those whom we know but with whom we have a business relationship rather than a personal one. They are usually letters written 'to get something done'.

Structuring the letter

If you find a particular letter difficult to write, it may well be because you have not worked out clearly in your mind what its purpose is.

Begin by asking yourself these questions:

1 Why am I writing this letter—what has led up to it?
2 What do I hope to get out of it (my maximum aims)?
3 What do I expect to get out of it (my realistic aims)?
4 What is the best way to achieve this?
   – What information do I need to provide?
   – What arguments do I need to use?

Leaving aside for a moment the precise way in which the letter should begin, most business letters have a clear three-part structure:

1 An introduction in which you outline what the letter is about.
2 The body of the letter in which you explain step by step the detail of your 'argument', or 'story'.
3 A conclusion in which you set out what you want to achieve.

Introduction

The introduction to a letter has to fulfil these requirements:

- **It must state clearly what the letter is about.**

  This enables the recipient to make an initial decision about what to do with it: deal with it now? put it in a heap of mail to be dealt with at an appointed time? pass it on to someone else? One way of doing this is to give the letter a heading immediately after the salutation:

  > Dear Mr and Mrs Green,
  >   Account No: 12345678: Confirmation of Personal Overdraft

- **It should indicate why the writer is writing it.**

  A heading such as the one quoted above only gives a general idea of the subject matter. The introduction should go on to spell out the writer's purpose:

  > I am pleased to confirm the renewal of your Personal Overdraft of £1000.

  These two functions can be expressed in a simple sentence or two. In fact in the example given, the heading is not strictly necessary because the following sentence repeats most of the information it contains. It could be rephrased to read:

  > I am pleased to confirm the renewal of your personal Overdraft of £1000 on account number 12345678.

Essentially, that is all the introduction has to do. When you have read it, you should have a clear idea of what the letter is going to be about and enough information to be able to decide how to tackle the rest of it.

Body

The letter now has to move steadily and convincingly towards the conclusion (in which you will explain what you want done, or reinforce the significance of the information you have set out). The more clearly information is expressed, and the more tellingly different items are linked, the better the letter. To see how this can work, we will look at a sequence of letters about the same subject. First, here is the body of the letter we have already quoted:

> You can overdraw up to your limit whenever you want, but you should not be permanently overdrawn by the whole amount. Please remember that personal overdrafts are repayable on demand. Details of interest and charges that apply to this overdraft are enclosed.
>
> Personal Overdraft Protection has been arranged for Mr Green, and a monthly insurance premium of £8.00 will be collected from your account on the first working day of each month. Your protection certificate, which includes details of cover, is also enclosed.

Each of these paragraphs has a clear topic. The first is about using the overdraft facility and the second concerns overdraft protection, an insurance protecting the user against being unable to repay the overdraft in the event of illness or unemployment.

Unfortunately Mr and Mrs Green hadn't requested this insurance and didn't want it. Their letter of reply followed a similar pattern:

> Dear Mr Bates,
> Account number 12345678: Confirmation of Personal Overdraft
>
> Thank you for your letter of 1st October, in which you say that Personal Overdraft Protection has been arranged at a rate of £8 per month.
>
> We don't recall asking for this protection. If we did, it was by an oversight and we do not wish to have it. We shall be grateful if you will arrange to stop it and make sure that no deductions are made for it.
>
> If this protection is a condition of the overdraft facility, then we do not wish to have the overdraft facility. It certainly isn't worth £96 p.a. before use. We only ever use it by accident when we forget to transfer money from our Deposit Account. It would be much more satisfactory if you offered the service of automatically topping up one account from another when it gets below a certain level.

Here the heading and first paragraph introduce the subject matter and link it to Mrs White's previous letter. The second paragraph deals with the subject of the unrequested insurance. The third moves the discussion on to a related but different topic. It introduces what is clearly the writer's main complaint.

Of course, such letters can have considerably more material in the body than is the case here. But the approach should be similar. Each paragraph is about a separate topic, or aspect of the main topic, and leads logically on to the next.

You will find more about paragraphing in Chapter 25: Planning and drafting, and more about presenting an argument in Chapter 14: Different ways of communicating.

Conclusion

The main point of the conclusion is to underline the purpose of the letter and, sometimes, to spell out the action the writer would like taken. In the bank's letter, the final paragraph read:

> If you require further information regarding your Personal Overdraft, please contact me and I will be happy to answer any queries you may have.

This isn't necessarily asking for any further action, but it is intended to leave the reader feeling positive towards the writer, which is always a useful aim. The Greens, however, had other uses for the conclusion to their letter:

> We look forward to receiving your confirmation that the Overdraft Protection has been cancelled.

No doubt about that!

Some time later in the negotiations between Mr and Mrs Green and the bank, an assistant manager wrote them a letter apologizing for what had happened:

> Dear Mr & Mrs Green,
>
> Your letter of 13th October has been referred to me.
>
> I take this opportunity to apologize, unreservedly, for our error in this connection.
>
> Upon examination it would appear that our letter of 1st October, referring to insurance cover on your overdraft, was sent in error.
>
> I can assure you that at no time have insurance premia been debited to your account.
>
> I believe a colleague has now sent an amended renewal letter to you, confirming your facility has been marked forward at its existing level.

> You mention that you would like to explore the possibility of our setting up an automatic transfer between your Current Account and your Deposit Account.
>
> I can confirm that such a facility is, occasionally, extended to our customers.
>
> This facility would need to be agreed by a member of the Bank's management and should you wish to pursue this option I would suggest that you contact a member of our Customer Facing Staff.
>
> I again apologize for any inconvenience caused to you following the issue of our letter of the 1st October and look forward to hearing from you if I may be of any further assistance in this or any other matter.
>
> Yours sincerely,
>
> James Bates
>
> Assistant Personal Accounts Manager

This letter differs from the two quoted so far. It is not divided into paragraphs; instead each sentence is separated out as if it were a paragraph in its own right.

- Does this make it easier or harder to follow?
- If you wanted to organize it into three or four paragraphs, how would you do so?

You will find a sample answer on page 373.

Getting the tone right

> See also

· CHAPTER 10
Audience
(p. 125)

So far the writing of letters has been treated as if business letters were directed to, and received by, anonymous 'recipients'. Of course they are not; they are received and read by individual human beings with thoughts and feelings. What makes such letters difficult to write at times is that although one is aware of this obvious fact, one has no idea of who will actually read the letter.

> See also

· CHAPTER 18
Vocabulary
(p.233)

This is why business letters sometimes fall back on jargon, over-formality, and even pomposity. There is a touch of this in the bank's second letter, quoted above. Here are some of the expressions it uses, with 'translations' alongside:

Expression	'Translation'
our error in this connection	The mistake we made
your facility has been marked forward at its existing level	your overdraft arrangement has been renewed
This facility would need to be agreed by a member of the Bank's management and should you wish to pursue this option I would suggest that you contact a member of our Customer Facing Staff.	You would need to arrange this with one of our Managers. If you would like to do this, please ask one of our staff.

Some writers are afraid of becoming too informal and offending the reader. But this should not be a real risk. The gap between writing and speaking is not so large. Imagine that instead of writing the letter, you are communicating the same subject matter face to face, speaking to a complete stranger. It is unlikely that you would offend by being too informal. You would adopt a neutral tone, and take care to explain clearly and simply what you had to say. A letter should do exactly the same thing. If you wouldn't normally say to a customer, 'should you wish to pursue this option I would suggest that you contact a member of our Customer Facing Staff', then don't write it either!

To avoid excessive formality and pomposity:

- **Avoid using the passive.**

  (e.g. 'Our letter was sent in error.') Use a personal pronoun and the active form instead. ('We sent you that letter by mistake.')

- **Avoid jargon whenever possible.**

  Terms like 'Customer Facing Staff' and 'your facility has been marked forward at its existing level' may mean something to the writer, but they are likely to alienate the reader.

- **Use shorter sentences rather than longer ones.**

  (It is difficult to be pompous in short sentences!)

To avoid unsuitable informality:

- **Don't let your own feelings get the better of you.**

  It is easy—especially when you are making a complaint and/or feel that you are in the right—to cause offence. You may wish to do so, but if you do, you are less likely to get satisfaction.

- **Don't try to be too clever.**

  Some writers get carried away with their own sentences and don't know when to stop. It is very easy for them to cause offence just because they like to 'hear the sound of their own voice'. For example, they start sounding off about how the recipient's organization ought to be managed. Such gratuitous 'advice' is likely to cause offence and very unlikely to further your cause.

- **Be clear and to the point, but don't be too blunt.**

Letter layout

There is a considerable choice of how to set out a formal letter. Different organizations have different styles governing:

- the positioning of the recipient's address
- the punctuation of the address
- the spacing and alignment of paragraphs
- the spacing and alignment of the ending ('Yours sincerely/Yours faithfully' and signature)

The examples given on pages 17 and 18 are only two of many different possible styles, therefore, and are presented as illustrations. The numbers in them refer to the list below.

1 Your address
2 The name, title, and address of the recipient
3 The date
4 Reference(s)
5 The greeting
6 The first paragraph
7 Other paragraphs
8 The ending

Greeting and ending

In British English there is a fairly simple choice of greeting and ending for business letters. Presented in descending order of formality it is:

Greeting	Ending
Dear Sir,	Yours faithfully,
Dear Madam,	A. B. Capstick
Dear Sir or Madam,	

Greeting	Ending
Dear Mr Green,	Yours sincerely,
Dear Mrs Green,	or Kind regards,
Dear Miss Green,	Alan Capstick
Dear Ms Green,	(or Alan)
Dear Alan,	Yours sincerely, Moira (or, commonly: With best wishes, Yours sincerely, Moira, or Regards, Moira, or Best wishes, Moira)

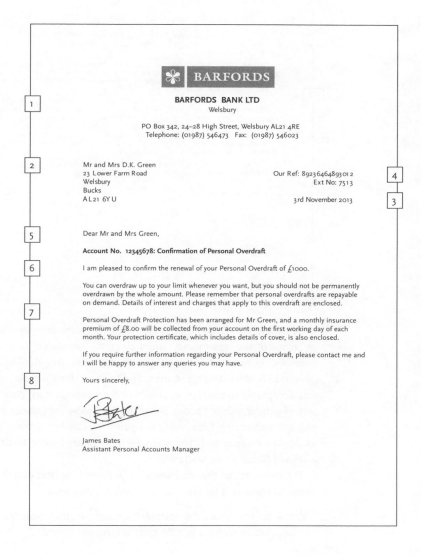

1

❈ BARFORDS

BARFORDS BANK LTD
Welsbury

PO Box 342, 24–28 High Street, Welsbury AL21 4RE
Telephone: (01987) 546473   Fax: (01987) 546023

2

Mr and Mrs D.K. Green
23 Lower Farm Road
Welsbury
Bucks
AL21 6YU

Our Ref: 8923646489301 2   **4**
Ext No: 7513

3rd November 2013   **3**

5

Dear Mr and Mrs Green,

Account No. 12345678: Confirmation of Personal Overdraft

6

I am pleased to confirm the renewal of your Personal Overdraft of £1000.

You can overdraw up to your limit whenever you want, but you should not be permanently overdrawn by the whole amount. Please remember that personal overdrafts are repayable on demand. Details of interest and charges that apply to this overdraft are enclosed.

7

Personal Overdraft Protection has been arranged for Mr Green, and a monthly insurance premium of £8.00 will be collected from your account on the first working day of each month. Your protection certificate, which includes details of cover, is also enclosed.

If you require further information regarding your Personal Overdraft, please contact me and I will be happy to answer any queries you may have.

8

Yours sincerely,

James Bates
Assistant Personal Accounts Manager

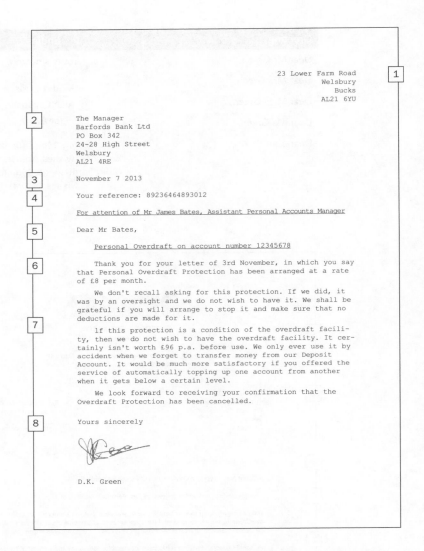

1

```
                                          23 Lower Farm Road
                                                    Welsbury
                                                       Bucks
                                                    AL21 6YU
```

2

```
The Manager
Barfords Bank Ltd
PO Box 342
24-28 High Street
Welsbury
AL21 4RE
```

3

```
November 7 2013
```

4

```
Your reference: 89236464893012

For attention of Mr James Bates, Assistant Personal Accounts Manager
```

5

```
Dear Mr Bates,

       Personal Overdraft on account number 12345678
```

6

```
      Thank you for your letter of 3rd November, in which you say
that Personal Overdraft Protection has been arranged at a rate
of £8 per month.
      We don't recall asking for this protection. If we did, it
was by an oversight and we do not wish to have it. We shall be
grateful if you will arrange to stop it and make sure that no
deductions are made for it.
```

7

```
      If this protection is a condition of the overdraft facili-
ty, then we do not wish to have the overdraft facility. It cer-
tainly isn't worth £96 p.a. before use. We only ever use it by
accident when we forget to transfer money from our Deposit
Account. It would be much more satisfactory if you offered the
service of automatically topping up one account from another
when it gets below a certain level.
      We look forward to receiving your confirmation that the
Overdraft Protection has been cancelled.
```

8

```
Yours sincerely




D.K. Green
```

Increasingly the 'Dear Sir ... Yours faithfully,' formula is being abandoned in favour of the less formal 'Yours sincerely,' versions. 'Dear Sir ... Yours faithfully,' is retained for very formal occasions: threatening letters from government departments, banks, and lawyers, for example. In the past it was acceptable to address an unknown correspondent as 'Dear Sir', regardless of gender, but not today. So unless you know the gender of the person you are addressing (in which case you probably know them well enough to use their name and 'Yours sincerely') you are forced to use the rather awkward 'Dear Sir or Madam'.

The drawback of the 'Yours sincerely' formula is that you have to have a name to address it to. Here three problems can arise:

1 You do not know the recipient's name. In this case, you are forced back on to using a job description, real or invented: 'Dear Personnel

Manager', 'Dear Fellow-sufferer', or whatever. If you are happy with that, all well and good. Otherwise you have to resort to 'Dear Sir or Madam ... Yours faithfully'.

2 You have a surname but no first name, only initials. So you do not know whether you are addressing a man or a woman. Unless you are happy with 'Dear A. B. Capstick ...', you have to use a job description, or use 'Dear Sir or Madam ...', as above.

3 You know that the recipient is a woman but do not know how she likes to be addressed. (Not, incidentally, the same as knowing her marital status—some married women prefer to be addressed as 'Ms'.) Here it is best to play safe and use 'Ms'.

The other awkwardness that can arise is whether to address the recipient as 'Dear Mrs Green', or as 'Dear Lynda'. If you have met or spoken to them, then generally there is no problem: use a first name. For many people, however, this is not acceptable if they have never met or spoken to the person concerned, although for others, especially younger writers, this is not a problem. If, when addressing a person you do not know at all, you feel that a first name is too informal and a title plus surname is too formal, you can try the intermediate position of 'Dear Lynda Green', although for some that is a rather artificial compromise.

Guidelines

1 Before you begin writing a business letter, define clearly your purpose in writing. Make sure that you have a clear idea of:

- the events that have led to your writing the letter
- your maximum aims (the most you can hope to achieve)
- your realistic aims (what you expect to achieve)
- the information you need to explain in the letter
- the arguments you need to deploy

2 The **first paragraph** of the letter should introduce the subject matter and either state or imply your purpose in writing.

3 The **body** of the letter should consist of one or more paragraphs. It should develop clearly and logically the argument and facts of the case. If there is more than one paragraph, each paragraph should focus on a separate aspect of the subject matter and there should be clear links between the paragraphs.

4 The **final paragraph** should leave the reader in no doubt about your attitude towards the subject of the letter. It may, for example, spell out what you would like to see happen. It should be positive and unambiguous.

5 Although the reader of your letter may be unknown to you, it is important to achieve a suitable **tone** in your writing. So, as far as possible, **avoid:**

- jargon
- too many long sentences
- using the passive
- letting your feelings get the better of you
- trying to be too clever
- being too blunt

6 Adopt a letter layout that is clear and consistent.

7 If you are writing to someone whose name and title you do not know, use the greeting *Dear Sir or Madam,* and the ending *Yours faithfully,* signing yourself with your initials and surname.

8 If you are writing to a named person, address them as *Dear Mr/Mrs/Miss/Ms—,* and end *Yours sincerely,* followed by your first name and surname.

9 If you have met them or spoken to them by phone, or otherwise feel that you have some acquaintance with them, address them by their first name and sign yourself *Yours sincerely,* using your first name.

③ E-writing

Increasingly we write to be read on screen rather than on paper. This chapter looks at the ways in which this affects *what* we write and *how* we write it.

Email

Email is a medium which has revolutionized the way in which we communicate with each other. It is relatively new and very popular. It is frequently influenced, and sometimes replaced, by social media and texting. Partly as a result of this, it can be used without sufficient thought. In particular it is important to consider:

1 Why you are using email.

2 The ways in which emails differ from letters and telephone conversations.

These affect:

- how the email is 'topped and tailed'
- the structure of the email
- how attachments are used
- how the email is formatted

3 How to use emails as effectively as possible. This involves:

- perspective
- reflection
- response
- organization

4 Email etiquette:

- formality
- formatting
- emotion
- initialisms
- context

Writing for intranets and the web

Increasingly organizations and individuals are replacing paper documents with information and ideas published on intranets and the web. It is important to recognize that the two media are different and require different approaches to writing.

When writing for the web, we need to be aware of:

1 How the different format affects the way in which people read:
   - the importance of line length
   - the impact of different textual and graphic elements on reading
2 Web users' expectations: the difference between 'grazing' books and 'browsing' websites.
3 The implications of this for the writer:
   - writing shorter more self-contained sections
   - the need for variety
   - adopting a pyramid structure
4 The importance of structure and navigation:
   - the positioning and use of menus
   - the effective use of hyperlinks
   - achieving easy navigation routes

E-writing? What's that?

The computer has changed writing irrevocably. This chapter focuses on forms of writing which exist almost wholly on computers:

- Email
- Writing for organizational intranets
- Writing for the web: websites and blogging

There is no widely accepted term covering these forms, so I have chosen 'e-writing'.

Email

Email has revolutionized business and personal communication, making it possible to communicate cheaply and almost instantly with people anywhere in the world. You can send any type of message, from a single word to a book-length document complete with pictures and sound files. The recipient can respond at once, or think carefully before replying. You can communicate just with one person or with a large group, every member of which can participate as much or as little as they wish.

Emails inhabit a space somewhere between personal meetings, telephones, and letters. They share advantages with each of these means of communication. Like face-to-face meetings they are instant and direct and allow a number of people to participate. Like telephone calls they are quick and inexpensive. Like letters they allow those involved to keep a permanent record of messages sent and received. But they also have disadvantages. Like letters they rely on written language. When you send them you cannot monitor the recipient's reaction to your message and then modify your message; when you receive them you may misjudge the sender's tone, because you only have words on the screen to go by. One of the great advantages of emails is that they are quick to send. On the other hand, as in a face-to-face or telephone conversation, it is easy to say something that we soon regret. By contrast, letters take longer to compose and seem to allow more time for reflection before sending. And because emails are a fairly new technology, the 'rules' governing them are less well established—different people have different ideas about the conventions and etiquette of the medium.

The situation is further complicated by the popularity of social media such as Facebook and Twitter. Many people now use Facebook rather than email to communicate with 'friends'. And for short messages (up to 140 characters) you can rapidly tweet your thoughts to your 'followers'. Mobile phone texting, too, is frequently used instead of email for short, instant messages. All these media have two important features: they are very rapid and they are generally very informal.

It is easy to carry social media habits over into more formal uses of email. While it is, of course, possible to be very informal in email, you should remember that email is also used for more formal communications between people who do not know each other. Similarly it is too easy to hit the 'Send' button on an email that is ill-considered and even rude, and which you may well later regret. Your use of email needs to be calibrated with these things in mind.

What are you using email for?

Emails are used for a wide range of different purposes. Imagine that you weren't able to send a particular email. What would you do instead? The answer is usually one of these three:

- Make a telephone call, or
- Write a letter, or
- Send a fax.

The answer you choose tells you something about *why* you want to send an email:

- **Telephone call**

  If you want an immediate response (and if you would like to be able to judge a person's reactions to what you have to say) you are likely to use the phone. On the other hand, if you don't want to interrupt someone who is busy, or if they aren't answering the phone, for whatever reason, then you will probably use email.

- **Letter**

  As we saw in the previous chapter, letters have a particular place in communications between organizations and individuals: they are permanent, often formal, and 'important'.

- **Fax**

  In the past, if you wanted a speedy response, but the message (and possibly the response) needed to be in visual form, you used a fax. To a large extent this has been replaced by email, with or without attachments. However, in some organizations a fax can still be a useful way of 'jumping the queue' of emails waiting to be answered.

So here there are three variables: time, permanence, and visual elements. But other factors also affect how you use an email.

1 **Is the email a one-off, or part of an extended exchange of messages?**
  In the first case, you have to make it clear at the beginning of the message what it is about. The 'Subject' line will help with this, but usually the first sentence or two also need to offer some kind of explanation. On the other hand if the email is part of a sequence, then this is unnecessary. For example:

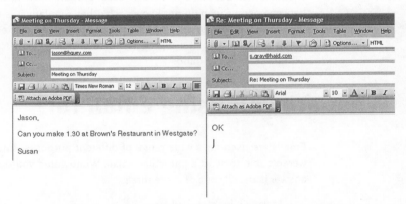

2 **Is this exchange of messages just between two people, or is it part of a group communication?**
  In the exchange illustrated above, there were only two people involved, but email is also used to communicate with groups of people. Suppose Sandra was trying to set up a meeting involving a group of people working for different organizations. She might email them like this:

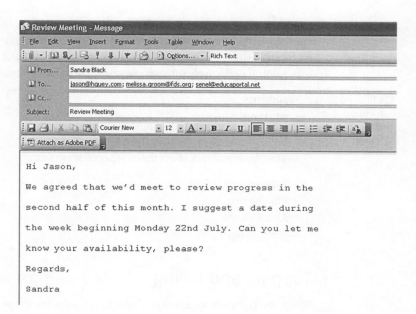

```
Review Meeting - Message

File   Edit   View   Insert   Format   Tools   Table   Window   Help

                                         Options...  ▼  Rich Text   ▼

From...    Sandra Black
To...      jason@hquey.com; melissa.groom@fds.org; senel@educaportal.net
Cc...
Subject:   Review Meeting

Courier New      ▼ 12 ▼  A ▼  B  I  U
Attach as Adobe PDF
```

```
Hi Jason,

We agreed that we'd meet to review progress in the

second half of this month. I suggest a date during

the week beginning Monday 22nd July. Can you let me

know your availability, please?

Regards,

Sandra
```

▶ There is more about the question of 'Reply to all' later in this chapter (see 'Your message in its context', p. 33).

There are more people to consider here, so Sandra can't just suggest a time; she has to ask people when they are free to meet. The others have a choice about how they reply to her message: they can either hit the 'Reply' button, or they can choose to 'Reply to all'.

3 Is this a business message, or a personal one?

As with other forms of communication, the relationship between the sender and recipient of a message affects its content, form, and tone. Here there are similarities between letters and emails. Once a letter or email has been sent the writer has no control over who will read it. Emails are even more likely than letters to be read by people other than the intended recipient. Some organizations routinely monitor emails going to employees. Errors occur and an email can end up in the inbox of someone completely unknown to the sender. This is why many people prefer to use the telephone—or even arrange a face-to-face meeting—if they have anything confidential to discuss.

What difference does it make?

Some people contend that it doesn't make any difference who you are emailing, or why, or what the circumstances are. Email is a new medium of communication, they argue, and it has its own rules; if you use email you don't have to concern yourself with the conventions that apply to other forms of communication. Spelling, punctuation, and conventional grammar are all old hat.

It is true that email is a relatively new and much more relaxed form of communication. Nevertheless it remains a way in which one person communicates with another. And people are still people. So if you wish to communicate effectively with people you still need to be aware of:

⟩ These are dealt with at length in Section B: 'Getting the message across' (p. 115).

- audience
- situation
- purpose

These considerations affect these aspects of emails:

- Topping and tailing
- Structure
- Attachments
- Formatting

Topping and tailing

When you compose an email you have to consider the frame within which your message is set. This consists of a number of elements illustrated in the following document.

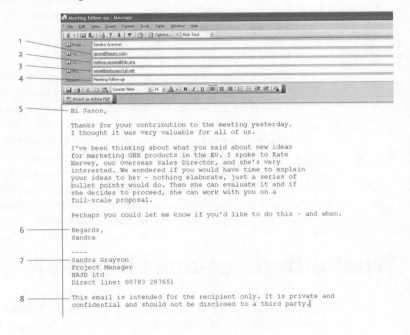

1 To
The person you are addressing.

2 Cc
Anyone you want to receive a copy. Jason will see that Melissa has been sent a copy.

3 Bcc

Blind copy. Senel will receive a copy, but Jason and Melissa won't know. (And Senel will know that they don't know.) Blind copying can be useful, but you need to be aware of its implications and the implied message that you are sending to the person receiving the blind copy.

4 Subject

A brief description of what the email is about – for ease of reference.

5 The greeting

There is a much bigger range of possibilities in an email than in a letter. You can treat an email just like an electronic letter, using 'Dear Jason'. On the other hand, because an email is a cross between a written letter and a conversation, this can seem quite formal: a bit like saying 'Good morning' to a close friend. So many people choose to open with the kind of greeting they would use in speech: 'Hello', or 'Hi'.

6 The closing salutation

Much the same applies here. 'Regards', 'Kind regards', and variations on them are frequently used.

7 Signature

Email applications allow you to use a signature block, which can contain whatever you care to include. It is commonly used for business titles, phone numbers, and publicity material.

8 Warning

Many organizations add a legal warning, in case the email falls into the wrong hands.

Structure

As we've seen, an email can vary in length from one word to thousands. Short emails are often relaxed, informal, and unstructured. But longer messages usually need a clear structure. As with letters, the structure often consists of three main parts:

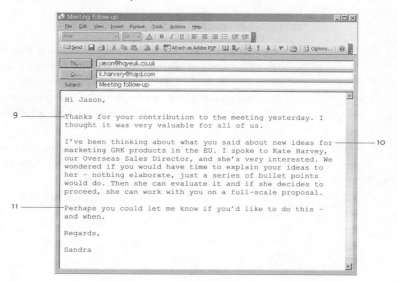

9 Introduction

You explain briefly what the message is about. This can be done purely in the 'Subject' line, but sometimes this may make the message appear somewhat abrupt. A short introduction is a good way of beginning your interaction with the recipient.

10 Body

The main part of the message.

11 Conclusion

This spells out whatever action you would like the email to lead to. It also rounds off your interaction with the person you are emailing.

Attachments

If your message is rather longer than this, you may prefer to write it as a separate document and attach it to a covering email. Attaching separate documents has a number of advantages:

1 You can send documents that already exist in digital form, or you can compose a document specially for the purpose. Either way the document itself is separate from the email and can be distributed separately from it.

2 If you are composing the document specially for the purpose you can take advantage of the formatting that is available in your word processing software—different fonts and sizes, different font formats (bold, italic, and so on), spacing, and visuals. Some of this is possible in an email but can cause problems—see Formatting, below.

3 If you are working with others on a document, you can each add your own alterations, suggestions, and comments to an original document but using a word processing feature such as Microsoft™ Word 'Track changes'.

There are, however, a few disadvantages:

• Large files can take a long time to upload and download. This can delay the receipt of other messages and waste space on the receiver's computer system. Indeed, many organizations' IT systems will not allow the downloading of a large file and simply bounce it back. This can be avoided, to some extent at least, by compressing files before sending.

• There can be problems when you transfer files from one platform to another (for example from Windows to Apple), although this is much easier than it used to be.

• Attachments can carry computer viruses, so care is needed when opening them.

Formatting emails

By default, emails usually work in plain text mode. This means that you cannot use formatting features such as bold and italic text, or different fonts and font sizes. With most email clients it is also possible to use HTML (Hypertext Markup Language) which does allow you to format in the same way that a web page is formatted.This allows you to construct messages that are better set out and clearer to read, and which can be colourful and elaborate. But there are also disadvantages. The most important are:

- HTML messages make bigger files and so take longer to download;
- the recipients may not have suitable fonts on their systems and so the message may not display properly;
- not all recipients have an email client that can read HTML messages.

So when in doubt it is better to stick to 'penny plain' text emails.

Getting the most out of email

Email is quick, effective, and convenient. But it does have some drawbacks. It is so direct and immediate that it is all too easy to read and respond to important messages without proper thought. We have all pressed the 'Send' button only to regret the action seconds later. But once a message has been sent it cannot be recalled.

An email strategy

If you adopt a conscious strategy for handling emails, you stand a much better chance of avoiding any problems. A sensible strategy has four main elements:

Perspective

 See also
- CHAPTER 10
Audience
(p. 117)

However unusual or special any particular email may appear, it always exists in a context. It was either sent by someone you know and have corresponded with before or it came from a stranger. If it is from someone you know, then the context is a personal or professional relationship (or, sometimes, a mixture of the two). There may well be a particular issue or group of issues that help define that context further. All this should help you define your audience and purpose fairly clearly, and these are the key elements that determine how you should compose your message.

If the sender is unknown to you, this in itself is a significant part of the context. The subject matter will help define things further, but the key point in interpreting the situation is that you do not know this person or how they think or express themselves. You need to bear this in mind when reading and responding to the message.

Reflection

It is easy to respond to emails emotionally rather than rationally. If you feel under pressure, or your relationship with the sender has some rough edges, it is very tempting to blast off a response to an irritating email without proper thought about how this will affect the person(s) at the other end, or your relationship with them.

As the poet Horace said, *Semel emissum volat irrevocabile verbum.* Once a word has escaped it cannot be recalled. It is far better in such situations to wait until later and then compose a more considered reply. Alternatively, compose a message that expresses how you feel, but then save it in the Drafts folder. After you have had time to cool down, return to your draft and consider whether this wording is really what you want your correspondent to receive.

Response

When you do respond, bear in mind that, like you, the other person probably leads a busy life. Keep your message as short as is feasible, and structure it so that it is easy to read and understand. When you have finished the message, read it through for sense and errors. If your email application includes a spell checker, keep it switched on, so that you can spot careless mistakes. (There is a strange theory that in emails spelling, punctuation, and grammar don't matter. They do. The fact is that many people will judge you by these external signs, just as they do in letters or speech, so there is no reason to be slack just because it's an email, although, of course, what you do in a personal email is a matter of personal style.) When you are happy that the message represents clearly what you want to say—and represents you as a person—then hit 'Send'.

Organization

One of the drawbacks of the growth of email is the sheer number of messages we receive every day. Many of them are junk, or only of brief importance, and can be discarded. Others need to be kept while a particular subject or project is relevant. These need to be stored for a period and can then be thrown away. A third group have long-term importance and will need to be stored more or less indefinitely, for example for legal reasons.

So it is important to have a system for organizing your emails. Most email applications offer a folder system so that you can store messages about the same subject, or from the same person in a named file. Many also offer a filtering system so that messages will automatically be placed in the relevant folder as soon as they arrive. These are useful features. Even so it is necessary to check through folders of messages periodically to identify those which can now safely be thrown away, and those which need to be archived.

Email etiquette

Email does encourage a more relaxed way of writing than other more traditional forms of communication. Nevertheless a number of conventions have been established, which are often referred to as email etiquette.

The message itself

1 Salutation and formality

Some email users are unsure about how to address the person to whom they are sending their message. Should they treat the email like an electronic letter with a formal salutation and farewell? Or is it more like a note you leave on someone's desk, with their first name at the top, underlined, followed by a short message, and ending with your first name?

As was suggested earlier, the answer depends on the way you see your relationship with the other person. If it is someone you don't know and do not wish to offend or irritate, it is best to play safe and use a fairly formal tone, opening with 'Dear Mr X ...' and ending with 'Yours sincerely ...' With someone you do know and have fairly frequent contact with, you can adopt a much more informal tone, opening with just their first name and ending with yours. There are many variations of formality and informality in between.

2 Formatting

As pointed out earlier, you can compose an email in HTML. This is useful if you wish to include any of the following:

a) Emphasis (using bold or italic text)

b) Bulleted lists

c) Numbered lists

One further point to remember about formatting is that it is safer not to write dates in a purely numerical format: the date '5/7/05' means different things to different people. To a reader in the US it is 7th May, while to someone in Britain it is 5th July.

3 Emotion

As we have already seen, it is easy to respond over-emotionally to an email. This phenomenon is sometimes referred to as 'flaming'. It can be avoided in the ways already suggested: taking time to reflect, not sending messages off straightaway, and so on. You should also do everything you can to avoid your message being at all ambiguous. Jokes and irony can be very tricky when composing an email message. Some writers try to get round this by putting brief explanations in brackets:

'and if I don't hear from you by the end of the week I shall get on to your father (only joking)... .'

Some emailers use what many people refer to as acronyms (or 'text-speak'), but which are in fact initialisms. These can please or irritate depending on your age and experience. On the whole these are a form of jargon that is best avoided, especially in more formal emails.

Initialism	Meaning
AAMOF	As a matter of fact
AFAIK	As far as I know

Initialism	Meaning
ASL	Age, sex, location
ATB	All the best
B	Be
B2B	Business to business
B4	Before
BFN	Bye for now
BTW	By the way
C	See
CUL8R	See you later
FAQ	Frequently asked questions
F2F	Face to face
F2T	Free to talk
FWIW	For what it's worth
FYI	For your information
GAL	Get a life
GR8	Great
HAND	Have a nice day
H8	Hate
HSIK	How should I know?
HTH	Hope this helps
IMO/IMCO/IMHO	In my opinion/in my considered opinion/in my humble opinion
IOW	In other words
JIC	Just in case
JK	Just kidding
KISS	Keep it simple, stupid!
KIT	Keep in touch
L8R	Later
LOL	Laugh out loud
MOB	Mobile
MSG	Message
MYOB	Mind your own business
NE	Any
NE1	Anyone

Initialism	Meaning
NO1	No one
OTOH	On the other hand
PCM	Please call me
PLS	Please
PPL	People
R	Are
ROTF(L)	Rolling on the floor (laughing)
RTFM	Read the flaming (*or worse*) manual
SOM1	Someone
SPK	Speak
TTYL	Talk to you later
TX	Thanks
U	You
WAN2	Want to
W/	With
WKND	Weekend
WYSIWYG	What you see is what you get
XLNT	Excellent
XOXOX	Hugs and kisses
YR	Your
2	To, too
2DAY	Today
2MORO	Tomorrow
2NITE	Tonight
4	For

4 Your message in its context

As said earlier, your message has to be seen its context. This means thinking about the other person(s) you are communicating with. There are a number of rules it is worth following:

a Don't break the thread

When replying to a message do so by using 'Reply' rather than creating a new message; this means that the thread of messages on a single subject can be kept together by those involved.

b Reply to whom?

In general it is better not to 'Reply to all' unless there is a good reason for doing so. Overuse of this feature contributes to the mass of useless emails that flow into your Inbox. Work groups often set up their own rules on this.

c Reply when?

Emails are a rapid form of communication, but they can go astray, and the sender is never entirely sure if they have arrived. For all these reasons it is helpful to reply promptly, even if only with a one-liner acknowledging receipt, and promising to answer more fully later.

d Quoting in the reply

Another thing that bulks out emails unnecessarily is the habit of copying the whole of the message you have received in your reply. Some email clients do this by default, but it is usually possible to organize things so that the program copies only those parts that you want it to. Doing this can be very useful, especially if you have been asked a number of questions—you can follow each copied question with your answer.

e Cc or Bcc?

If you are sending the email to more than one person, think for a moment about how you are going to do this. The person in the 'To' box is regarded as more important than anyone in the 'Cc' box, so if you are addressing two people of equal status, put them both in the 'To' box. If you are sending to a large number of people, you have to choose between the 'Cc' and 'Bcc' boxes. Many people don't like their email addresses being known by strangers, so it is better to address the email to yourself, and then put all the recipients in the 'Bcc' box. That way the recipients don't have to share their contact details with all and sundry.

f Forwarding

You may wish to forward a message you have received to someone else to whom it was not originally sent. There are a couple of things to remember here. The sender may not have wished anyone else but you to see the message at this stage, so it is only courteous to ask permission before forwarding it. Strictly speaking all messages are the copyright of the person who sent them (or of their employer, if the email is written as part of their work), so copying them without permission is a breach of the copyright law. In fact forwarding emails is normal practice within organizations or amongst other groups where there is a clear common goal, and forwarding is expected by those concerned.

5 Paper Trail

Although they may seem insubstantial, emails never really disappear. They are retained on other people's servers more or less indefinitely. If you work for an organization, or are dealing with one, your emails become part of that organization's email archive. In the event of any kind of legal dispute, the organization can call up the relevant exchange of emails as part of a chain of evidence. When you write an email in any organizational context, you should remember this. Your email may be dredged up many years later and examined by readers with little knowledge of the original context beyond what appears in the chain of emails.

Writing for intranets and the web

Just as letters are increasingly replaced by emails, many of the paper documents produced within and for organizations are moving to intranets and the web. Reports, training materials, and other written documents are placed on a company's intranet rather than being circulated in printed form. Paper catalogues, brochures, and flyers about new products are still distributed to customers by mail, but people also expect to find them online, or receive them as email newsletters.

Within many companies and other organizations, this is still a straight translation: written documents appear online in the same form as they do on paper. However, this is to ignore the major differences that exist between reading on the printed page and on screen. It also fails to take advantage of the many benefits that electronic presentation affords.

Differences of format

Books are most commonly in portrait format: the height is greater than the width. By contrast, computer screens are in landscape format. Sometimes there is a choice, as with tablets such as Apple's iPad, where you can rotate the screen and the presentation automatically adjusts from landscape to portrait and vice versa. However, websites are generally designed for viewing in landscape mode.

A typical book consisting mainly of text carries that text across the full width of the page. It is generally considered that a full line of text should contain an average of between 50 and 75 characters, or 10–15 words. There is some evidence to suggest that on screen, lines of up to 95 characters (19 words) can be read more rapidly, but that once the length exceeds about 100 characters reading speed drops off. (This is not to say that readers *prefer* lines as long as 95 characters.)

A typical web page has far more space available than will be taken up by a single column of text even 100 characters wide—unless those characters are very large. So very often web pages consist of a number of different elements, both text and graphics. While the same is true of an illustrated book, web pages frequently contain a greater number and variety of these different elements. As a result readers have to make more choices of where to look to find the information they are looking for. In addition, research suggests that some readers, at least, read more slowly on screen, and retain less of what they read than on the printed page.

All of which suggests that simply transferring printed material—or the habits of thought that produce it—from book to screen is unlikely to be the best strategy. Instead e-writers need to spend time re-working (or 're-purposing', as some prefer to call it) their material for this new medium.

Differences of expectation

The application we use to view websites and intranets is commonly called a 'browser'. The name is significant. It describes the way people approach websites and the expectations they have. Wild animals that feed by browsing typically move from tree to tree, nibbling one tasty morsel here and another there. By contrast, animals that *graze* move more slowly, focusing on one small area of pasture, only moving when the food in that section has been exhausted. It is not too fanciful to argue that reading a book is grazing, while interacting with a website is browsing.

Implications for the writer

The implication of this is that writing for intranets and the web requires a radically different kind of writing:

- Individual items of information need to be shorter and more easily digested.
- Items need to be as self-contained as possible, so that if readers leave after reading only one item in a group, they still take away a complete idea or piece of information.
- The writer needs to incorporate more variety to hold the reader's interest, using not only different kinds of text, but incorporating visuals, headings, and lists.
- Since readers may move on at any time, it is best to adopt the journalist's pyramid structure, placing the gist of the story in the opening paragraphs, then expanding into more detailed information.
- On longer web pages, where the reader may have to scroll downwards, it is important to place the most important information in the top section ('above the fold' in newspaper terms). Many readers become impatient of long screens and, instead of scrolling down, move on to another page.

Structure and navigation

Just as longer printed documents have their conventions about structure and navigation, so do websites, and sections within them. While this is not the place for an extended treatment of designing websites, one or two general points are worth making.

- Increasingly there is a standardized basic navigation on a website, with the main menu along the top of the screen and subsidiary menus placed in a side column. This is where users will look first for navigation.
- The second, but equally important, means of navigating is by hyperlinks inserted in the text. While these are usually marked by colour and style, the supporting text should also make it clear where these links will take the reader.
- A subsidiary way in which the purpose of hyperlinks can be indicated is by giving the hyperlink a title when setting it up. This will then show up when the user allows the mouse pointer to hover over it. A well-chosen title provides useful feedback for the reader.
- When planning a series of web pages, it is important to think carefully about how easy or difficult it is for the reader to find any individual piece of information: how many mouse clicks does it take to get there? In order to avoid frustrating users you may need to rearrange pages and the relationships between them.

Writing for e-books

Just as emails have increasingly replaced traditional letters, e-books are doing something very similar to printed books. Especially in the field of fiction, readers expect new books to be published on Kindle and EPUB as well as in physical book form. While this development is, of course, commercially driven, particularly by Amazon, there is something very attractive about being able to 'carry' dozens of books in a slim, lightweight e-reader.

In a conventional printed book the relationship between the different elements—headings, body text, and illustrations—is fixed. The 'traditional' way of digitizing print is to use the Portable Document Format (PDF), which keeps this fixed relationship exactly as it is. In a PDF the fonts, pictures, and layout all appear exactly as the designer intended. If you reduce the size of the PDF page, all the elements are scaled down proportionately, until you reach a point where the text is too small to read—as anyone who has tried to read a PDF on a smartphone will know. The only alternative is to choose to view part of the page at a readable size and scroll through it bit by bit, but this is laborious and time-consuming.

E-readers, on the other hand, are formatted in variations of Hypertext Markup Language (HTML). As a result, they are more like portable websites than rigidly formatted books. This means that their content flows to fill the space available to them in the window in which they are being viewed. The viewer can determine the size of type (and sometimes the actual font) in which the text appears, and headings are shown relative to the chosen size. Images are not fixed, but flow with the text. The implications for the book designer are profound, but those for the writer are less obvious.

If the text is illustrated with pictures or diagrams, then the way the words relate to the images must be considered, along with the fact that some e-readers have very small screens. This means that large and complex images will not work very well and will probably have to be broken down into smaller units. Navigation, too, is very different in an e-book. By their nature, e-books cannot have fixed page numbering, so it is impossible to insert cross-references such as 'There is more about this on page 58'. Instead the writer has to insert a hyperlink with suitable wording: 'There is more about this here.' By tapping or clicking on the word 'here' the reader can navigate to the cross reference. Alternatively a clickable footnote or endnote can be inserted with the same effect. Internal hyperlinks can also be used to construct lists of chapter or section contents, and external hyperlinks can take the reader to relevant websites.

By comparison with print, e-books have both advantages and disadvantages. As ever, the best training for the writer is to become a practised reader of the medium.

Guidelines

Emails

1 Bear in mind why you are using email rather than a letter or a telephone call. Sometimes the formality and permanence of a letter may be preferable. At other times a telephone call may be more private (or conveniently impermanent!).

2 Although emails are relatively new, they share key features with other means of communication. You still need to have in mind:

- your purpose in communicating
- the audience you are addressing
- the situation in which the email occurs (business, personal ...)

3 Make proper use of email format:

- always give the message a subject
- distinguish properly between open and blind copies
- use a signature, and a warning, if appropriate

4 In extended business emails, structure your message so that readers can grasp the essentials quickly and without risk of misunderstanding.

5 When responding to other people's emails, think about the effect your reply will have; don't hit the 'send' button and then regret it immediately

you have done so. If in doubt, save your reply in the 'Drafts' folder and return to it later in the day.

6 In replies avoid breaking the thread of a sequence of messages.

7 Don't automatically 'Reply to all', unless it is expected or useful.

8 In replies only quote as much as is necessary to place your message in its context (often the subject line will do this).

9 Think before forwarding someone else's message; if in doubt ask their permission.

10 Set up a proper system for filing emails and weed out unwanted messages regularly.

11 When composing a message be aware of the context within which you are communicating; make a judgement about how informal you can afford to be.

12 Avoid excessive use of capital letters and don't use HTML formatting unless its special features are really necessary.

13 Be aware of the dangers of flaming.

14 Only use initialisms in messages to people who are likely to appreciate them.

Intranets and the web

15 Don't assume that a printed document can be transferred to the web without re-working.

16 When you write, see your text as part of a whole web page and be aware of how the different elements on it interact.

17 Remember that web readers are more likely to 'browse' than 'graze', and write accordingly.

18 Aim to write short, self-contained sections.

19 Produce sufficient variety to hold the reader's interest.

20 Use a pyramid structure, placing the gist of the text at the beginning.

21 Be aware of the need for clear, simple navigation.

E-books

22 Remember that e-books are formatted, and therefore read, in a different way from print books.

23 Think carefully about the way in which your text relates to illustrations.

24 Plan the navigation of your text with the medium in mind: use hyperlinks and clickable footnotes for cross-referencing.

25 Remember that e-books make it possible for the reader to move seamlessly from the book to the web and back again.

> **Further reading**

Email

David Shipley and Will Schwalbe, *Send: Why People Email So Badly and How to Do It Better* (Vintage, 2007), ISBN 9780307275998.

Web writing

Janice Redish, *Letting Go of the Words: Writing Web Content that Works* (2nd edn, Morgan Kaufman, 2012), ISBN 9780123859303.

E-books

John Seely, *ePublish! From Manuscript to Finished E-book in 10 Easy Stages* (Oxpecker, 2012), ISBN 9781908948021 (print and e-book versions).

$\widehat{4}$ Job applications

Preparation

It is essential to prepare carefully for a job application. You need to think about:

- Your own experience, interests, skills, and personal qualities;
- The job and the organization advertising it.

The CV

You can adopt a chronological approach or a functional one. Each has its own advantages and each has a different layout.

The letter of application

The accompanying letter is an important selling tool and needs careful thought.

The interview

- Careful preparation is again important.
- The interview has four main stages:
  1 Introductions and explanations
  2 Questions asked of you
  3 Questions you ask
  4 Conclusion

Preparation

The key to effective job applications is thorough preparation. You need to think and research:

- yourself
- the job

Researching yourself

Begin by thinking about these four areas:

- experience
- interests
- skills
- personal qualities

There are various ways in which you can do this. What follows is only one possibility. Whichever approach you choose, however, make sure that you make detailed notes of your ideas, even if you think they may not be relevant. Also, keep all your lists and sheets of notes 'open': go back to them from time to time and make sure that you haven't missed anything out. This preparation stage is essentially one of brainstorming. Selection and ordering come later.

Experience

Many people find it easiest to start with this, because it is the most concrete. Begin by thinking of your life as divided into a number of stages.

What these are depends on you: the divisions between the stages may be marked by changes of job, moves from one place to another, or by key events in your life, for example, marrying, having children, buying a house, and so on. Your notes on your experience should certainly include:

- education
- any professional training
- periods of employment (include part-time jobs and those which didn't last very long, as well as 'proper' jobs)
- other extended periods in which your life focused on a particular activity (for example, periods of foreign travel)
- any voluntary work you have done

Interests

You might question why you should consider your personal interests when preparing a job application. After all, these are the things you do in your spare time when you are not working. Interests are relevant for a number of reasons:

- They are one of the ways in which your personality can be defined; and your personality is very relevant indeed to a job application.
- They frequently indicate skills you have which are not currently used at work. (See 'Skills' below.)
- They often have a bearing on why you are interested in particular types of employment.
- They may point the way to other kinds of employment that you had not previously thought of.

Skills

Your notes on your experience should provide you with useful prompts when it comes to listing your skills. Look at each of the different stages of your life and ask yourself:

- Which skills did I use here that I already had?
- Which skills did I improve on or consolidate?
- What new skills did I learn?

In addition, think about your leisure time interests: perhaps these also entail useful skills which may be relevant to a job application.

Make sure that you include not only skills related to your trade or profession, but also personal skills, for example:

organizing events	training staff	interviewing
giving advice	chairing meetings	making presesentations
supervising	trouble-shooting	meeting the public

Don't be too concerned at this stage about whether the skills you list are relevant. That can come later. For now write them all down.

When you have finished, look back through the list and consider whether each item is one separate skill, or, in fact, a bundle of skills that should be separated out. For example, you may have written 'communicating', when it might be preferable to list:

- simplifying technical subject matter
- writing simple technical manuals
- training non-specialist workers

Personal qualities

This is the area that many people find most difficult; they are unhappy talking about themselves and their qualities because they feel it is big-headed or 'pushy'. They may also find it quite difficult to step back and look at themselves objectively. On the other hand, if you don't tell a potential employer about your personal qualities, who will?

It is sometimes difficult to begin such a list, so here are some qualities to start you off. Write down any which you think apply to you, and then add others of your own. For each one you choose, make sure that you can think of incidents in your own life and work experience that bear them out.

accurate	adaptable	astute
can work under pressure	careful	committed
	cooperative	courteous
competent	dedicated	energetic
decisive	flexible	friendly
extrovert	good communicator	good sense of humour
get on well with other people	hardworking	imaginative
	lively	logical
good time-keeper	methodical	meticulous
independent worker	organized	positive
loyal	receptive	relaxed
orderly	self-confident	self-motivated

practical	thorough	thoughtful
reliable	works well with others	
sensitive		
vigilant		

Researching the job

There are three sources of information for any job you are applying for.

The advertisement

Job adverts, even quite brief ones, can provide you with valuable clues about the job and the organization that is offering it. For example:

- **Where is the advertisement placed?**

  It may be in exactly the kind of publication and section you might expect. On the other hand it may have appeared in a slightly unexpected place. For example an advertisement for an administrator for a community theatre might appear amongst 'Creative and Media' adverts, or it might be found in the 'Social Services and Local Government' section. This can give useful information about how the advertiser sees the post.

- **What is the tone of the advert?**

  Some job adverts are dry and factual, while others are more casual or dynamic. The organization that begins its advert, 'Outstanding sales jobs up for grabs' is sending out a different message from the one that heads an advert, 'Key account managers'. Such differences of tone can provide useful clues about how to approach your application.

- **What is the sub-text?**

  Look carefully at the exact wording of the advert: every word will have been chosen with care. Can you read anything between the lines? If, for example, the advert lists a number of qualities expected in the successful applicant, is this list exactly what you would have expected, or are there surprising omissions or inclusions? This again can provide helpful clues.

Information offered to applicants

Many advertisements invite applicants to apply for further information. It should go without saying that you should do so. The information offered may include any or all of the following:

- more detailed information about the job
- a description of the organization and its activities
- an annual report
- a copy of an in-house newsletter or similar publication

These provide a valuable insight on how the company likes to regard itself—although, of course, it is again possible to read between the lines.

Your own research

For any middle-ranking or senior position you will be expected to have done some homework on the organization to which you are applying. This could include:

➤ *See also*

• CHAPTER 24
  Research
  (p. 313)

• **Web-based research**

  Organizations of any size normally have a web site, and this is a useful starting point for research. Keying the name of the organization into a search engine like Google will also throw up a variety of sources of information. If the organization is of any size, some of this may be critical, or worse: valuable if you are to gain a rounded picture of a prospective employer!

• **Library-based research**

  Public libraries often contain directories that will help you, particularly when researching non-commercial organizations.

The CV

The online *Oxford Dictionaries Pro* defines a curriculum vitae, or CV, as: *a brief account of a person's education, qualifications, and previous occupations, typically sent with a job application.*

Basics

Begin by making a list of the basic information required for your CV:

1 Full name
2 Address and telephone number
3 Age, date, and place of birth
4 Nationality
5 Marital status
6 Number of children
7 Dates and places of primary, secondary, and tertiary education
8 Educational qualifications (public examinations taken and grades/ degrees achieved)
9 Chronological record of your life since leaving school, college, or university, to include:
   • details of each period of employment
     ◦ company/organization
     ◦ position held
     ◦ dates
   • periods of unpaid work
     ◦ internships

- ○ other work experience placements
- ○ voluntary work
- periods of unemployment

10 More detailed information about current position held, including salary

11 Interests

12 Names of at least two people who will provide references. This should include one character reference and one professional/work reference.

Name:	James Michael Brown	
Address:	76, Lower Green Road, Newbury, Berks, AB1 2CD	
Telephone:	04321 987654	
Born:	23rd February 1981, Liverpool, England	
Age:	32	
Nationality:	British	
Marital status:	Divorced	
Children:	None	
Education:	1986–1992	St Francis' Primary School, Huyton
	1992–1997	Gondersfield High School
	1997–1999	Huyton Sixth Form College
	1999–2002	East Midlands University
Qualifications:	1997	GCSE English (A), Maths (B), Geography (B), Chemistry (A), Physics (B), Biology (A), French (C)
	1999	GCE 'A' level Maths (C), Physics (D), Chemistry (B)
	2002	BA Honours Class 2/2 Chemical Engineering
Employment:	2002–2006	Graduate trainee with Myersons-Chemco Ltd, Nottingham
	2006–2009	Assistant Sales Manager, Alders & Green, Leicester
Current Position:	from 2009	Sales Manager, Brown-Petlow, Solihull Responsible for department of 12 and sales team of 24 representatives
Current salary:		£39,500
Interests:	Golf, swimming, scuba diving	
	Member Solihull Round Table	
	Member St James, Edenlow, Parochial Church Council	
Referees:	Mrs Mary Hayling Mr	Peter Smithson
	23 Orchard Close	The Meadows
	Graystoke	Peterlee
	Essex	Reading
	EF4 5GH	JK6 7LM
	(Telephone: 01234 567890)	(Telephone: 04321 098765)

In the past, such a list was considered to constitute a satisfactory CV. However, things have changed. It is true that most, if not all, of this information is of importance to a potential employer. But the layout and ordering are not particularly helpful, and the document does little to 'sell' the person concerned. Traditionally this was done in the accompanying letter, in which the applicant explained what was attractive about the job and why he or she was suitable for it.

There were, however, disadvantages to this approach. The accompanying letter had to be quite substantial, since it had to do all the work of promoting the applicant's case. It could only do this in conventional prose, so the employer was faced with the task of reading a considerable amount in order to determine whether this was the right person for the job, or at least worth calling to interview. The CV didn't really help here, since it was a bald recital of facts with little guidance as to which were the important ones.

The solution to this is to make the CV a 'selling document', a prospectus in which the applicant's virtues are set out, together with supporting details. The letter then becomes a reinforcement of the CV (and a proof that the applicant can write satisfactory English).

You should by now have a full set of rough notes. (It doesn't matter how rough they are, provided they are as detailed as possible.) The next stage is to decide how you want to order your CV. This can be done in one of two ways:

- chronologically
- functionally

A chronological CV

In the chronological approach, you present your education and work experience either in the order in which they happened, or in reverse order, with your most recent experience first. Since recent experience is probably of most interest to an employer, this latter method is now generally used. The advantages of a chronological CV are that it emphasizes the companies or organizations you have worked for (and the periods of time involved) and your continuity of employment. The disadvantage is that if your career has had ups and downs, especially if it includes periods of unemployment, these show up very clearly. The employer who is looking for a steady and reliable employee will probably favour this approach.

A functional CV

A functional CV is organized by skills and qualities. If, for example, your experience is in motor-parts sales, both as a representative and in head office, the functions you could use as headings might be:

- presenting the product range
- customer care
- information technology

Under each one you can provide further details of specific experience. The advantage of this approach is that you can focus on your strengths without having to spell out relative inexperience or periods of unemployment. The disadvantage is that it may not make clear important periods of employment with impressive employers. The employer who is looking for applicants with particular skills and capabilities will find the functional CV more helpful than the chronological.

Chronological CV

Mary J. Morris

'The Larches'
Spottonham Road
Larswick
Lincs
SP12 5MS

tel: 01234 567890
email: mjmorris@larswick.net

Experience

2008–present

Education and Publications Officer, Boston Museum. Responsible for organizing annual programme of school visits, lectures, and holiday courses. In charge of liaison with primary and secondary schools. Preparing and publishing a range of leaflets and 'mini-guides' to the Museum's collections. Managing an annual budget of £300,000.

2003–2008

Head of Humanities, Larswick Middle School. Responsible for department of four teaching history, geography, religious education. Preparing and administering departmental policy documents. Member of School's Senior Management Team. Pastoral care tutor to 35 pupils. Responsible for school magazine.

1999–2003

Teacher of History at St Wulfstan's High School, Scunthorpe. Teaching pupils across full ability and age range (11-18). Preparing classes for GCSE examinations, GCE 'A' levels and university entrance. House tutor.

Qualifications and training

1997–1998: Postgraduate Certificate in Education, University of Hull
1994–1997: BA Honours 2nd class, History and Economics, York University
1994: 'A' level English, History, French
1992: GCSE English, English Literature, Maths, French, History, Geography, Biology

Interests

Mountain walking and rock climbing
Foreign travel
Voluntary social work with local women's refuge

Referees

Dr P. J. Cleary
Director, Boston Museum
Boston
Lincs
AA1 2BB

Mrs S. P. Greenwick
34, High Street
Brentham
Surrey
CC3 4DD

Functional CV

Katherine Hardwick

22 Redden Road
Hartwell
North Yorkshire
YO7 4PQ

Tel/Fax: 09876 543210
Email: k.hardwick@mailmall.co.uk

Profile

Enthusiastic, responsible graduate with a Post-graduate Printing and Publishing Diploma and good organizational skills. Able to work independently using initiative and as part of a team to tight deadlines. With editing, desktop publishing, and keyboarding skills.

Training

Has recently completed the Post-graduate Diploma in Printing and Publishing at the Birmingham Institute of Design and Publishing.

Skills gained

- Design
- Desktop Publishing
- Costing & Estimating
- Letter Assembly
- Graphic Reproduction
- Screen Printing
- Printing Processes
- Data Processing & Information Systems
- Publishing Administration
- Print Finishing & Bookbinding
- Technology of Printing Materials
- Technology of Colour Reproduction

Experience

2009–present

Assistant editor, Quantum publishing, a company specializing in business and IT publications. Work includes:

- Word processing, using MS Word™
- Onscreen editing in Adobe InDesign™
- Research
- General office administration

2008

6 months' internship, Eduform Online Publishing
3 months' work experience, Elivira Professional Publishing

Education

Post-graduate	Diploma in Printing and Publishing, Birmingham Institute of Design and Publishing (2007)
Degree	BA (Hons) with major in English (2.2), East Midlands University (2003–2006)
A levels	English Literature
	French
	Art & Design
GCSEs	Eight Grade C or above, including English and Maths

Interests

Music: playing the saxophone
Riding a mountain bike
Cinema and theatre-going

Referees

Dr J. M. Barker, B.Sc., PhD
Birmingham Institute of Design and Publishing
Castle Street
Birmingham
B12 3CD

Mrs J. W. Pawsey
29, Lower Redhill Lane
Downham
EF4 5GH

So far, the CV has been considered in a vacuum. In fact, when you are applying for a job, it should be adjusted to suit the particular post you are applying for. Once you have written the original CV, this is not difficult, assuming that you have word-processed it and stored it as a computer file. A word of caution, however: make sure that you check, and if necessary update it, before sending it off. Print out a file copy of the particular version you use for each application.

The letter of application

Your CV should be accompanied by a letter of application, and these two items form a package. The letter has a number of purposes:

➤ See also

• CHAPTER 2
  Business Letters
  (p. 9)

- It allows you to sell yourself by pointing out key features of your CV: how your skills and experience fit you for this particular position.
- It gives you the opportunity to include material that is not in the CV, especially personal qualities that you listed when making your preparations.
- It shows a prospective employer that you know how to write a letter. While this may be of decreasing importance in an electronic age, many employers still value it highly, both as a skill in its own right and as a test of your ability to communicate clearly and effectively.

The letter of application should follow the general guidelines for all business letters. It should have an introduction, a body, and a conclusion.

In the introduction you should detail the job you are applying for, and, if relevant, the circumstances that have led to this (for example an advertisement, or the recommendation of an agency).

The body of the letter provides you with an opportunity to present yourself to the employer:

- Tell the reader about your present job and why you are looking to move on.
- Explain why you are suitable for this job.
- Emphasize the skills you have which make you particularly suitable for the job.
- List briefly the personal qualities you would bring to it.
- Answer any specific questions posed by the advert or job details.

It is important not to write too much, however. Two, or at most three, short punchy paragraphs are much more effective than two sides of rambling prose.

The conclusion should round the letter off, leaving the reader with a positive image. It should sum up briefly the selling points made in the body of the letter, mention any items (including the CV) you are enclosing, and express willingness to provide any further information that the reader may want.

JAYNE SAUNDERS
143 Farndon Street, Blackstock, Essex JK6 7LM
TEL/FAX (01234) 987654

Ms Cath Harries
Human Resources Manager
Harpen Books Ltd
9–11 Clapton Street
Poole
Dorset
NP8 9QR

29th August 2013

Dear Ms Harries,

Editor

I wish to apply for the above post, advertised in *The Bookseller*.

Currently I am working in a new small publishing company, *Notions,* that specializes in highly designed, high-quality non-fiction books. Since I started here I have been the only full-time employee working on all editorial aspects of the books. Answering directly to the Publishing Director and the Editorial Director, I have a very wide range of responsibilities including: editing on screen in InDesign and Microsoft Word, liaising with the designers and freelance editors, checking manuscripts at the film stage, managing the stationery budget, Americanizing text, as well as signing off books, having checked the proofs.

I have been at *Notions* for over a year, and have learnt a great deal, but there is no longer the scope to use all my knowledge and experience. I am seeking a position that offers responsibility for the full range of publishing and editorial skills, as well as the opportunity to meet and work with a range of people. I like to think that I bring enthusiasm and adaptability to my work.

I would welcome the opportunity to discuss this letter and my enclosed curriculum vitae. The telephone number I have given is my home one and all calls are answered.

I look forward to hearing from you.

Yours sincerely,

Jayne Saunders

The interview

It is very rare for a job to be offered without some kind of interview. Often there is more than one interview stage. There may be a preliminary telephone interview followed by one or more face-to-face interviews. These may be with a single interviewer or with a group. Face-to-face interviews may take place in a formal atmosphere in a meeting room, or they may involve both such an encounter and a tour of the organization's premises.

Preparation

Whatever the format, it is important to be well-prepared. However apprehensive or nervous you may feel about the interview itself, if you have prepared thoroughly you will gain considerably in confidence and will give a good interview.

The job and the company

Look again at the job advert and the information you have collected about the company. Examine them from every angle: what are the hidden snags and unanswered questions? You know what is desirable and attractive about the job: that is why you have applied for it. What are the less attractive features of it? Is there likely to be anything about it that might make you regret having taken it on? Make a list of questions you need to ask about the job, phrasing them in a positive or, at least, neutral way.

Now imagine that you have been successful and it is your first day with the company. What do you see yourself doing and what questions do you need to ask? Write them down on a sheet of paper. Use them as a starting point for a list of questions that you want to put about the job and the organization. Use these questions as a stimulus to further questions. Then organize your questions by theme: questions about the company's structure, questions about your own responsibilities, and so on.

There will be a section of the interview during which you are told more about the company and the job and are invited to ask questions. This is when you should use your list of questions. It shows that you have made a thoughtful preparation for the interview and are serious about the job.

Your application

For the next stage of preparation, you need:

- your letter of application
- your CV
- a copy of your application form, if you had to complete one
- any job description you have been given

For the company, the purpose of the interview is to find out how suitable you really are for their purposes. They have summarized these purposes in the job description you have in front of you. When they read the information you have sent them they will want to ask two types of question:

- those which seek further information, giving you an opportunity to enhance your attractiveness as a candidate
- those which probe the gaps and weaknesses in the information you have given and which may detract from your attractiveness as a candidate.

You can prepare for the first group of questions using your CV as a memory-jogger. The second group contains questions that are harder to answer and to prepare for.

Good interviewers ask difficult questions not out of some inborn sadism, but because they have to establish the weaknesses as well as the strengths of each candidate. This is the best way for them to work out who is the strongest candidate overall.

Begin by placing yourself in the interviewer's shoes. Look again carefully at your CV. Make a list of gaps, weaknesses, and other 'problem areas' in it. Make a list of questions that you as an interviewer would want to ask this candidate. Take each question in turn and work out the best way of answering it:

- **Be positive**

  There are usually two ways of answering difficult questions: positive and negative. For example, you might have left a job after only a short time in it and then had a period of unemployment before finding another post. If asked, 'Why did you leave that job after such a short time?' you could answer, 'Because I had a row with my boss.' That is the negative response. Another reply might be: 'There was an unfortunate conflict of personalities between me and a senior manager and we agreed that it was better if I left the company.' That is really a longer way of saying the same thing, but it has the advantage of putting the two people concerned on an equal footing—it was as much the manager's fault as yours. A better answer might be, 'My boss would not accept my professional judgement on a key issue so I was forced to resign', but only if it's true, because you will certainly be asked what the issue was.

- **Make sure you answer the question**

  Don't try to sidetrack or to put up a smokescreen, because a skilled interviewer will not be impressed. In many jobs you have to face hard questions and the way in which you answer such questions in an interview is thus a useful indication of how you will answer them in the job.

- **Be honest**

  Similarly, there is little point in lying. Even if the moral considerations do not bother you, the legal ones should. If you lie in a job application and are subsequently appointed, you are liable to instant dismissal when the lie is discovered. In any case, there is a positive merit in frankly admitting that you made a mistake. Everyone makes mistakes from time to time, and admitting this and accepting that you have learned from it is often to your credit in an interview, rather than the reverse.

If you have someone who can help you in your preparation for the interview you may find it useful to get them to role-play the interview with you. Give them the list of hard questions and let them put them to you, together with any others they may think of themselves. Ask afterwards how they thought you tackled the questions. This not only gives you practice, but it also helps to fix some of the key ideas in your mind.

The preparation listed earlier should be completed in plenty of time and not left until the night before. Better to have a relaxed evening and a good night's sleep than to go to bed late with all the possible questions and problems buzzing around inside your head.

Practical matters

In any conversation we receive messages not only from the words a person speaks, but also from their appearance and body language. It is unfortunately true that we begin to make judgements about a person even before we hear them speak; their face, build, posture, and clothing all contribute to that first impression. Candidates at interview are judged in just these ways, and it is important to think about the impression you want to create and to present yourself accordingly. Generally it is better to err on the side of dressing too formally rather than not formally enough.

Take with you to the interview the papers you have been using in your preparation. Place the list of the questions you would like to ask about the company and the job in a clean file together with some writing paper so that you can make notes during the interview if necessary. Take this folder into the interview with you so that you can refer to the papers as necessary.

Check the information you have been supplied: are there any particular things you have been asked to take with you or be prepared for?

Check the route to the interview. Give yourself plenty of time to get to the place where you are being interviewed, but avoid arriving too early, since it will mean that you have a long wait, which only serves to build up the tension.

The interview itself

Most interviews consist of four parts:

1 Introductions and explanations

You will probably be collected for interview from the room in which you have been waiting, and escorted by a member of staff, who may well be one of the interviewers. So as soon as you are called, the interview has begun.

As you enter the room, look round and make eye contact with the people there. Smile and greet them when introduced. Shake hands if that is expected, and sit when invited to do so. If you find that the chair you are offered is placed so that it is difficult for you to see the people interviewing you comfortably without having to keep moving around, then by all means alter its position.

The early questions will probably be 'ice-breakers', about the sort of journey you had and so on. Answer them politely but not at too great length. Use this period to settle yourself and take stock of the situation.

A common strategy is for the interviewer(s) to move on to explain about the company and the job. Some of this information may already be known to you and some will answer questions on your list. Pay careful attention to this, because at some point in the interview—either now or, more commonly, at the end—you will be asked if you have any questions you wish to put. This is where you can make use of your prepared questions.

2 Questions asked of you

The interview will probably then move on to your experience and skills. Assuming you have prepared carefully, much of this stage of the interview should progress fairly smoothly—until you reach the stage of difficult questions.

The thing to remember here is that the interviewer has a set of questions he or she wishes to ask and you have answers you want to give. These may not match perfectly. Part of the art of being interviewed is to say what you want to say while appearing to be answering the question or at least not to be seeming to evade it.

Even when you are dealing with a gap or a problem in your CV, your aim should be to turn this to your advantage. Answer the question, deal briefly with the negative aspects, and move on to a detailed account of the positive aspects of the situation. Compare these two dialogues:

A	INTERVIEWER:	You only worked at Parker-Brown for two years and then you left. Why was that?
	CANDIDATE:	Unfortunately the company was going through a difficult patch and I was made redundant.
	INTERVIEWER:	Why?
	CANDIDATE:	I've just explained. The company—
	INTERVIEWER:	No, why you? Why you and not someone else?
B	INTERVIEWER:	You only worked at Parker-Brown for two years and then you left. Why was that?
	CANDIDATE:	Unfortunately the company was going through a difficult patch and I was made redundant. That was how I was able to do a refresher course on spreadsheet construction which I found invaluable in my next job.
	INTERVIEWER:	At Myersons?
	CANDIDATE:	Yes.
	INTERVIEWER:	Tell us about that.

In Dialogue A the candidate is forced onto the back foot, having to explain why she was the one made redundant, and not someone else. In Dialogue B she is able to turn the question so that she can tell the interviewer that she has additional skills in spreadsheet construction.

When you are being interviewed, you are under a certain amount of stress. Things can go wrong. The commonest is that you suddenly just dry up. Your mind goes blank and you don't know what to say. The temptation in such situations is just to talk, to say anything to cover the silence and to hide your confusion. This is a mistake, because you will probably find yourself talking nonsense. It is much better to pause for a moment and try to relax. Then either ask the interviewer to repeat the question, or—if you have dried up because you cannot answer a difficult question—admit that you don't know.

From time to time you may encounter an interviewer who is aggressive, or who irritates or annoys you for some other reason. Be polite, but not cringing. If you believe in what you are saying, stick to your guns. But don't answer rudeness or aggression with similar behaviour, unless you have already decided that you don't want the job, in which case it possibly doesn't matter. (Although even then it may be unwise—especially if you have gained the interview through an agency.)

3 Questions you ask

Normally you will be asked whether you have any questions you would like to put to the interviewer. Use your list of questions and draw from it any questions which have not already been answered and to which you really need to have an answer. Don't ask too many questions. This is the section of the interview in which you are most obviously in control and if you bore the interviewer, or hold up the day's timetable, you will not be popular. On the other hand it is important that you satisfy yourself that you really do have a clear idea about both the job and the company.

4 Conclusion

As the interviewer brings the interview to a close, rise, say your thanks, shake hands, if this is expected, and turn to leave. At the door, turn and smile, thank the interviewer again and say goodbye. Remember that last impressions are nearly as important as first ones.

Later, when you have had time to relax, go through the interview in your mind and analyse how it went. There will have been good features and bad. Analyse the bad to see how they can be avoided in future—and, of course, remember the good.

Guidelines

1 Begin by mapping what you are bringing to the job application: chart the stages of your life (education, jobs, other extended periods devoted to a particular experience or activity).

2 List your interests and consider how these may be relevant.

3 Make a list of your skills, technical and professional.

4 Analyse and list important personal qualities. You can begin this process by looking at the 'Personal qualities' list on pages 43–4.

5 Research the job. Begin by analysing the advertisement.

6 Read through all the information sent to applicants.

7 Research the company or organization on the internet and in relevant reference books.

8 Decide whether you wish to construct your CV on a chronological or functional basis.

Advantages of chronological	Disadvantages of chronological
shows continuity	does not easily highlight skills
emphasizes key periods of employment	shows up inexperience and periods of unemployment
Advantages of functional	**Disadvantages of functional**
highlights skills	does not easily highlight key periods of employment
helps to conceal inexperience and periods of unemployment	does not highlight continuity of employment and reliability

9 Word-process your CV so that it is clear and uncluttered and the eye is led to the key features.

10 Try to keep it to one side of A4. Certainly make sure that all the important information is on the first side. Never go beyond two sides of A4.

11 Use the letter of application to emphasize your selling points and to include key personal qualities that do not appear in the CV.

12 Begin with a brief explanation of what you are applying for and why.

13 Use the body of the letter to highlight exactly why the job attracts you and why you think you are very suitable for it.

14 Write a brief conclusion designed to leave the reader with the best possible impression.

15 Both documents should be word-processed and printed on a good printer, using high-quality paper. Layout and typefaces should be chosen with care.

16 Prepare for your interview carefully. Begin by looking again at the notes you made about the company or organization.

17 Look at your CV and letter of application. Make a list of 'straight' questions you expect to be asked. Make sure that you can answer them fluently.

18 Look again and think of the 'awkward' questions you could be asked. Make sure that you can answer them positively.

19 If possible, get a friend to interview you, using your lists of questions plus any others that come up during this rehearsal.

20 Enter confidently and greet the interviewer(s) politely.

21 Use the introductory questions to settle yourself and take stock of the interviewer(s).

22 When asked difficult questions, try to turn them so that your answer ends positively.

23 If you are thrown by a question, don't waffle. If you don't know the answer, say so. If you are confused, gain valuable time for thinking by asking the interviewer to repeat the question (but don't do this too often!).

24 When invited to ask questions, select one or two from your prepared list, but don't go on too long.

25 Leave the interview confidently and pleasantly, remembering that this last impression is very important.

26 Later, take stock of how the interview went and make a note of lessons you have learned from it.

➤ Further reading

Max Eggert, *Perfect CV*
(Random House, 2007), ISBN 9781905211739 (print and e-book versions).

Ros Jay, *Brilliant Interview*
(Prentice Hall, 2010), ISBN 9780273743934.

Patricia Scudamore and Hilton Catt, *Successful Job Applications in a Week*
(Hodder Education, 2012), ISBN 9781444158892.

⑤ Organizing a meeting

Formal meetings

When preparing a formal meeting you need to consider:

- Your **aims:** what you hope the meeting will achieve.
- The **competence** of the meeting: what it can practically and legally achieve.
- The **agenda:** the list of items to be considered.

When running the meeting:

- The role of the **chair** is very important.
- The organization of **motions and voting** should be clearly defined.
- Accurate **minutes** should be kept (and ratified at the subsequent meeting).

Informal meetings

Many meetings, especially in the workplace, do not need such a formal organization, but there is still a need for sensible **planning** and **organization**.

Most people at some time in their lives have to attend meetings of one kind or another: from community organizations to board meetings. Such organizations all have their own special rules and customs, but they also have many things in common. In this chapter we look primarily at what are loosely called 'formal meetings'. By this is meant any meeting which is big enough or 'official' enough to require a chair, an agenda, and minutes.

At the end of the chapter there is a short section on informal meetings. This deals with those ad hoc meetings which are set up, often at short notice, to discuss specific points and decide upon a course of action: in the workplace, or as part of the work of a social grouping of some kind.

Preparing for a formal meeting

One of the secrets of successful meetings is careful preparation. Obviously this is particularly important for the person chairing the meeting, but good preparation is important for other participants as well. If participants are not well prepared, perhaps because they don't have the time or don't think it is necessary, the result is a meeting that takes longer than it should and achieves less than it could.

Aims

It is important to define what the meeting is for. Most of us have attended meetings which seemed rambling and interminable just because those involved had no clear idea of exactly what they were trying to achieve. The person responsible for chairing the meeting should:

- Write a brief and clear definition of the purpose of the meeting.
- Distribute it to those invited to the meeting (or publish it in a suitable place if the meeting is a public one).
- Remind the meeting of that purpose at the start (or make sure that it is expressed in the agenda which is distributed to participants).
- Keep it clearly in mind as the meeting proceeds.

Competence

Meetings of committees and other constituted bodies frequently have a clearly defined competence: what they can and cannot do is set down in their constitution and/or standing orders. For example, many organizations have annual general meetings. These are open to all members or shareholders, but the rules limit what those attending can do at the meeting. So they may be able to select (or deselect) the committee, but may not be allowed to propose or vote on motions of their own.

It is essential that the chair and the participants know clearly the competence of the meeting. This may require an understanding of the constitution of the organization and a knowledge of any standing orders set down to govern meetings of its members or committees. Some participants may have only a hazy grasp of the 'small print' of these, or may, in the heat of debate, forget them, but the chair must always have them clearly in mind. In practice it often falls to the secretary to have a copy of any rules and to refer members to them if they are in danger of breaking their own rules.

The competence of a meeting defines what it can and cannot do. If there is no constitution to refer to then it is up to those organizing the meeting to define in their own minds what the competence of the meeting is. This should be made clear to those taking part and then kept to. The chair of a public meeting might begin by saying:

This meeting has been called by the Sports Field Committee to consult local people about their plans for the field. We have already made a detailed planning application, but we are aware that there is some local opposition. We should like to find out in more detail what that opposition is. Then we shall—if necessary—apply to the District Council to amend our plans accordingly. I should point out that this is only a consultation meeting. It can't decide anything and there will be no votes.

Agenda

Most meetings should have an agenda, a list of topics to be covered, presented in the order in which they should be tackled. In the case of any official meeting, the form the agenda takes may well be laid down, but this is a fairly common form of agenda:

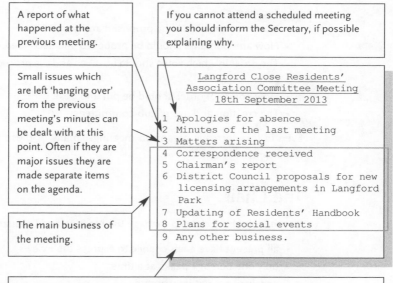

A report of what happened at the previous meeting.

If you cannot attend a scheduled meeting you should inform the Secretary, if possible explaining why.

Small issues which are left 'hanging over' from the previous meeting's minutes can be dealt with at this point. Often if they are major issues they are made separate items on the agenda.

The main business of the meeting.

Langford Close Residents'
Association Committee Meeting
18th September 2013

1 Apologies for absence
2 Minutes of the last meeting
3 Matters arising
4 Correspondence received
5 Chairman's report
6 District Council proposals for new
  licensing arrangements in Langford
  Park
7 Updating of Residents' Handbook
8 Plans for social events
9 Any other business.

Sometimes referred to as 'AOB', this allows members to raise issues not on the agenda. Some committees do not allow this item, on the grounds that it can lead to major issues being raised for which committee members are not prepared (and at a time when most people want to close the meeting and go home).

Agendas can be much longer and more detailed than this, but their form is normally similar. They are essentially a list. If it is necessary for those attending the meeting to have more details these can be supplied as separate documents to which the agenda refers.

Running a formal meeting

Constituted bodies like local government committees and those that run recognized charities have constitutions which determine their powers. They may also have standing orders which determine how their meetings should be run. These usually cover matters such as:

- Frequency and duration of meetings.
- How many members make up a quorum (the minimum number required for a meeting).
- Officials (and when and how they should be elected).
- If and how members can be co-opted.
- Which matters may and may not be included in the agenda.
- How items for the agenda of a meeting should be tabled.
- How the meeting should be chaired and the rules governing individual speakers.
- How motions should be proposed and seconded.
- How amendments should be proposed and seconded.
- The order in which votes should be taken and the procedures for doing so.
- How points of order should be put and dealt with.
- The creation and use of sub-committees.

Even in less formally organized meetings, many of these points are still important.

The Chair

It is the job of the chair to manage the meeting and to ensure that:

- all present have a fair chance to express their views
- only one person speaks at a time
- speakers are not interrupted
- the agenda is followed and items are discussed in the correct order
- if votes are to be taken, this is organized properly and everyone present knows exactly what is being voted on and in what order.

Those present should address their remarks to the Chair and not directly to each other. This may seem pedantic, but it is a useful device for maintaining order within the meeting. If two participants at a meeting start addressing each other directly, it becomes very difficult for the Chair to maintain control of what is going on, or for others to make their own voice heard.

Chairing is a skilled matter. You have to balance the ideal of fairness with an awareness of how much time is available for the meeting and what it is reasonable to expect to achieve. Some speakers have a much better grasp of the subject matter than others and can speak clearly and concisely. Some may have a far weaker grasp or a greater desire to speak at length (sometimes at great length). Others may have valuable points to make but may be reticent or unable to find a point at which to intervene. A good Chair will not only balance the demands of the subject matter and the speakers, but also try to make sure that everyone has a chance to be heard. This will be done with patience and good humour so that even when determined speakers are interrupted and asked to give way they do not feel aggrieved or irritated.

Voting

Some meetings have to have votes; others never do. It depends on the competence of the meeting. If you are an advisory body, you may well not wish to vote, but prefer to achieve consensus, or—if you cannot agree—an agreed description of the balance of views expressed:

> There was general agreement that a new locker room should be built. A clear majority of the committee felt that the existing plans should be retained, but a significant minority expressed the view that these plans should be reduced in scale and expense.

If you do have votes, it is important to make sure that everyone knows exactly what they are voting on. This may sound self-evident, but it is easy for confusion to arise, especially if there are both a motion and amendments to be voted on. The procedure usually runs along these lines:

1 There is a motion to be voted on. This may have been tabled before the meeting or at the meeting. (The word 'tabled' is commonly used in British English (Br. E.), as it is in this chapter, to mean that an item is placed 'on the table' for the consideration of the meeting. Rather confusingly it can also mean 'put aside, taken out of consideration'. This is the sense in which it is used in the USA.) Tabling a motion (Br. E.) generally requires a proposer and a seconder.

2 The Chair places the motion before the meeting for debate and then speakers—at the invitation of the chair—express their views.

3 Anyone who is not happy with the motion can propose an amendment. This takes the form of a change to part of the wording of the motion, or an addition to it. (It is important that the Chair gets a precise wording for the amendment and makes sure that, with it, the motion still makes sense.) The amendment must be seconded.

4 Other views are expressed and possibly other amendments are tabled.

5 A vote is taken on the amendments first. Those which are carried then become part of the motion.

6 A vote is then taken on the motion incorporating any amendments that have been carried.

7 If any vote is a tie, the Chair has the casting vote. The convention is that this is normally cast in favour of the status quo (i.e. no change), although this is not necessarily always done.

Minutes

➤ *See also*

• CHAPTER 23
Making notes and summaries
(p. 297) **for** advice on how to make notes.

The secretary of the committee is required to make a record of what happens at the meeting—the minutes. At a public meeting called for a specific purpose there may not be a secretary, but it is useful to appoint one to make such a record, if only to supply those who enquire—and the local press—with information.

The minutes of a meeting summarize the main points which are debated and the main views expressed. They should go into sufficient detail to make the substance of the meeting clear, but should not be too detailed, unless there is an important reason for this:

> **7. Annual Conference 2014**
>
> Possible themes and venues were discussed. It was agreed that the Conference secretary should approach UBC for more information about facilities and rates. Various possible themes were debated and it was decided that the title of the conference would be 'Marketing your own work'.
>
> **8. Dates of Meetings 2013**
>
> These were agreed as follows: 14th February, 15th May, 25th September. The AGM would take place on 27th November.
>
> **9. Any Other Business**
>
> Peter Bowman raised the question of illegal copying of members' work on the internet. After a lively discussion it was decided to set up a working group to investigate the extent of the problem. Members: Peter Bowman (convenor), Hilary Dupont, Mark Haycroft.
>
> The meeting closed at 4.45 pm.

Agreeing the minutes

Usually the minutes are distributed to members of a committee along with the agenda for the next meeting. The meeting is then asked to confirm their accuracy or to propose any amendments, before they are signed by the chair as a true record of what took place at the meeting.

Informal meetings

It is difficult to make generalizations about informal meetings—those occasions that fall somewhere between a formal meeting and a conversation between acquaintances. Some of the points that have been made about formal meetings, however, can be adapted to informal meetings.

Aims and competence

If you call a meeting, it is useful to have in your mind an idea of what you would like to cover and what you can realistically expect to achieve. The word 'realistically' is important here: it is easy to imagine that more can be achieved in the time available than is actually the case.

Agenda

While it may not be necessary to have a published agenda, it is very useful to jot down a list of the main points you want to cover—and the best possible order in which to tackle them. Not only does this mean that you don't forget important points, but also it helps you keep an eye on how you are getting on, especially if time is limited.

It is also useful to make sure that those invited to attend an informal meeting know what it will be about; if they need to prepare for the meeting, they obviously need sufficient warning.

Procedure

Again, while the informal meeting probably does not need any kind of set procedure, it is important to make sure that it is orderly and that everyone gets a fair chance to speak.

In the case of meetings that have no clear leader, it is often a good idea to begin by discussing how you will proceed and possibly electing someone to act as Chair for the duration of the meeting.

Minutes

Decisions at informal meetings are often recorded—for example, in the form of a list of action points recorded in an internal memo, or a letter to those who attended. This provides a useful record of the meeting to go on file.

If there is no pre-arranged way of doing this it is often useful to appoint an ad hoc secretary for the meeting to keep a note of what happens.

Guidelines

If you are chairing or organizing a formal meeting, these points are worth remembering:

Preparation

1 Have a clear idea of the aims of the meeting.
2 Make sure that you understand the competence of the meeting.
3 Work out a clear and logical agenda.

Chairing the meeting

4 You are in command; others present depend on you to make sure that the meeting is organized fairly and efficiently.
5 Make sure that everyone has an equal chance to express their views. (It may be necessary to suggest or even impose time limits to achieve this.)

6 Keep speakers to the point firmly but pleasantly.

7 Keep to the agenda, or—if necessary—make it clear that you are pro-posing it should be altered and why. (If necessary, put this to a vote.)

8 Try to keep the meeting good-humoured but to the point. (Don't let it descend into irrelevant chat.)

Votes

9 Make sure that any motion for debate is clearly worded and under-stood by the meeting.

10 Motions and amendments should be formally proposed and seconded.

11 The process should be as follows:

- a motion is proposed and seconded
- it is debated
- any amendments are proposed and seconded
- amendments are debated
- amendments are voted on
- any amendments that are carried are applied to the wording of the motion
- the (amended) motion is put to the vote.

> **Further reading**

Duncan Peberdy and Jane Hammersley, *Brilliant Meetings: What to Know, Say and Do to Have Fewer, Better Meetings*
(Pearson Business, 2009), ISBN 9780273721826.

⑥ Presentations

Preparation

When preparing for a presentation it is important to think about:

- **Purpose**
  Is your primary aim to inform, to persuade, to entertain, or to interact?
- **Audience**
  Consider their knowledge, education, ability to follow what you have to say; their expectations; their needs—practical, intellectual, personal.
- **Structure**
  This includes thinking about: content, priorities, ordering.
- **Communication aids**
  These include data projector, whiteboard, and flipchart.

Delivery

- Most speakers need some form of prompt to make sure that they follow their pre-planned line or argument. This needs careful management.
- A number of strategies are available to make sure that you address the audience directly and maintain their attention.
- Questions and interruptions need to be handled firmly and skilfully.

Less formal occasions

- Even when you are asked to speak at a more informal gathering, many of the principles listed above are still relevant.

Spoken presentations to an audience can come in a variety of forms. For example:

- the introduction of a new product to a company sales team
- a training session for new employees
- a student presentation to a seminar

All have these key features:

- one or more speakers presenting information and ideas
- a clearly defined purpose
- an audience

Preparation

The key to a successful presentation is careful and intelligent preparation. Without this, the presentation may be hopelessly disorganized. Even professionals can and sometimes do fail to make proper preparation, whether out of over-confidence, lack of time, or even laziness, as this real-life example demonstrates.

> The scene is a large teaching space in a college arts faculty. The occasion is a lecture on the history and theory of photography. At the time the lecture is due to begin, about forty students are assembled, waiting for something to happen. They are sitting on chairs arranged in no particular order. After a few minutes the lecturer staggers in carrying a slide projector, two slide carousels, and a pile of handouts. He looks round at the room, realizes that there is no blackout, and decides to move the lecture to an adjoining space. He spends the next ten minutes setting up projector, stand, and screen, trying to work out how the focus and remote control work, and alternating apologies for the delay with complaints about the fact that the college hasn't got proper facilities for his lecture. Eventually everything is ready and the lecture begins.
>
> If lecture it can be called. It is more a kind of rambling chat linking the slides, some of which are projected back to front or even upside down. Towards the end the lecturer passes round some handouts, but there aren't enough to go round because he left copying them until the last minute and the copying machine broke down. He promises more copies next week, but these never materialize. He finishes and shambles off, leaving the students feeling bored, possibly confused, and certainly dissatisfied.

Unfortunately such performances are not uncommon. We cannot all be brilliant, witty, or elegant public speakers, but anyone can turn in a polished and professional performance—if they want to. The key is in the organization.

Think of your purpose

➤ See also
· CHAPTER 13
  Purpose
  (p.143)

Begin by thinking about **why** you are making the presentation. It may be:

- to inform
- to persuade
- to entertain
- to meet and get on with your audience

Frequently it will be a mixture of some or all of these.

To inform

> See also

· CHAPTER 14
  *Different
  ways of
  communicating*
  (p.155)

Most presentations provide information, often considerable amounts of it. It is not uncommon for members of an audience to go away with the feeling that 'there was a lot of good stuff there, but it was far more than I could take in at one sitting'. With this in mind, it is valuable to break 'information talk' down into different kinds:

* **straight facts (data)**

  While these are undoubtedly important, they are often the most difficult to digest. A string of unrelated figures, dates, names, and events is very difficult for most of us to remember, so the speaker has to provide as much help as possible by putting such data into contexts, patterns, and pictures. Information of this kind is an obvious candidate for inclusion in a handout.

* **stories**

  People find stories much easier to remember. There are two reasons for this. First, a story has its own built-in pattern, and patterns make facts easier to remember; and secondly, stories fulfil a very primitive need in human beings—the love of a beginning, a middle, and an end, and the desire to 'know what happens next' are strong in almost everybody. 'Story' may sound rather a childish name; in the 'grown-up' world, stories are often called narratives, or 'reports'.

* **descriptions and explanations**

  Descriptions of what things or people look like are easy to remember in the same way that stories are. More often, however, it is necessary to explain the functioning of organizations, machines, or institutions. Here it is important to make sure that the description creates clear patterns to help the audience visualize what is being described, for example by using images or analogies. This type of exposition is often best conveyed through the use of carefully devised visuals.

To persuade

Many business presentations have as their chief purpose to persuade the audience to do something: buy your product, sign up to a different way of doing things, agree to a particular course of action. Even apparently factual presentations such as a college lecture may involve persuasion: for example, the lecturer may wish to persuade students to take a subject more seriously than they currently do, or to open their minds to a new and challenging way of thinking.

To entertain

Sometimes—as in the case of an after-dinner speech—the speaker's main aim may be to entertain. But even when it is not the primary aim of a presentation, it is very often an important secondary aim. If you can entertain your audience it often makes your primary aim of informing or persuading very much easier.

To meet and get on with your audience

Occasionally the primary purpose of a presentation may be to meet and get on with the members of the audience; for example, a new manager may set up such a meeting with those he or she will be working with. Any presentation to a new audience must have this as a secondary aim, especially if you are dealing with potential clients; and if your presentation is to people whom you meet on a regular basis—students or members of your company—then you need to keep in mind your continuing relationship with them.

Some of this is fairly obvious, but it is important to be aware of **all** your purposes in making a presentation and not just the primary or most obvious one.

Think of your audience

> See also
· CHAPTER 10
  Audience
  (p. 117)

The lecturer we encountered in the story at the beginning of this section would probably have argued that he **was** thinking of his audience. 'I made the slides and prepared the handout,' he would argue. 'That took me a long time.' What he had forgotten is that the audience sees the whole event as a package that begins when they arrive and ends when they leave. Everything that happens between those two times is part of the presentation as far as they are concerned. So the waiting around, the need to move to another venue, the confusion, the incompetence with the slides were all part of it. The lecturer's preparation time was not.

This may make the preparatory work required appear rather daunting, but it need not be, if it is approached step by step.

Where they are now

The starting point should be a clear idea of 'where the audience are now': what they currently know and understand about the subject matter of the presentation:

- their theoretical knowledge
- their practical knowledge
- their intelligence
- their level of education
- the terminology they are confident about handling
- how quickly they can pick up new ideas
- their likely concentration span

This information may not be easy to establish and you may have to make assumptions and deductions about it. It is also important to remember that your audience may contain a wide range of experience, education, and expectations.

Their expectations

The audience have come for a reason. They may be enthusiastic volunteers bursting to hear your words, or they may be unwilling conscripts who can think of many things they would rather be doing. More likely they will be somewhere between these two extremes. Whatever their attitude to the event, they will have a bundle of expectations and hopes about it. The students at the lecture, for example, were there because it was a compulsory part of their course. Since it took place first thing on a Monday morning, some, at least, may have been unwilling conscripts. This lack of enthusiasm will have been tempered by a willingness to learn and a belief that the lecture would be useful—if only to help them pass one of the modules on the course. Notice how the lecturer's behaviour both reinforced their negative feelings ('We've got to be here and he can't even be bothered to turn up on time.') and damaged their positive ones ('This could be really useful, but he can't even project the slides the right way round.').

If you have delivered a presentation on the same subject once or more in the past it is very tempting to churn out exactly the same material again. This can, however, lead to a dull and uninspiring performance. The subject matter may not be new to you, but this particular audience have not encountered it before, and it is important to assess the audience's needs afresh and to adapt your material accordingly.

Their practical needs

It is also important to remember the practical needs of your audience:

- In an ad hoc space, where will you place your screen and projector, if you are using them?
- In a space with specialist audio-visual provision, is everything arranged to your satisfaction?
- How you will arrange the seating so that
  - everyone can see without straining?
  - everyone can hear?
  - the participants are in the best relationship with you and with each other?
- Where will you place yourself, and do you want to be able to move around?
- What lighting (or blackout) do you need?
- Do you need a microphone and loudspeakers and, if so, how should these be placed?

All this requires thought and preparation. If you are operating on home ground, this is more straightforward, but even if you are a visiting speaker, most of these points can be organized in advance. Be sure to arrive in sufficient time to check that all the equipment is set up correctly *and is working*. This is particularly important if you have to link up your own equipment, for example a laptop or tablet computer, to a projector that belongs to the venue.

Their intellectual needs

You should already have some idea of this, having considered the list of points given earlier in this chapter under 'Where they are now'. You need a strategy for structuring your presentation to make it as effective as possible. This should include:

- **the order in which you present material**
- **the communication aids you will use:**
  - data projector

- audio or video tape or film
- verbal aids such as stories and anecdotes, images and analogies, and mnemonics
- handouts
- **the use of rhythm and variety to keep your audience interested and alert**

Their personal needs

Consider also the personal needs of your audience. If a presentation session goes on too long, without opportunities for the audience to relax physically and mentally, then it will become increasingly ineffective. In the course of a long session there should be periods for such relaxation: chances for a chat, to stretch your legs, have a coffee, and so on. These need to be carefully planned so that they do not diminish the impact of what you have to say. Once you have 'released' your audience for a coffee break it is sometimes difficult to gather them back together in a reasonable time!

Build a structure

How you structure your presentation will depend on the particular circumstances, but there are a number of general rules which apply to most situations.

Content

How much should you try to get through? This depends on three variables:

- what you want to include
- how much time you have
- how much your audience can tackle

This may seem obvious, but people often forget that these three requirements generally pull in conflicting directions. The commonest mistake that presenters make is to try to cover too much ground. As a result, their presentation takes much longer than planned or they have to rush the last part of the presentation, or they are forced to miss out important material altogether. It is always better to err on the side of caution when deciding how much material to include, and to develop a structure that is carefully timed, but has sufficient flexibility so that you can adapt as you see how the time is going.

Priorities

Be realistic. Much of what you have to say will be forgotten soon after you have said it, and frequently the things that are remembered are not necessarily the most important. (An audience may come away from a presentation remembering the jokes the speaker made, but forgetting the key points s/he was attempting to get across—just as one can say after a TV commercial, 'That was good', but not be able to remember what it was advertising.)

Select a small number of key points that you consider it is absolutely essential your listeners should take away with them at the end of the presentation. The main part of your presentation should be devoted to making sure that these key points are understood and remembered.

More detailed information that you want your audience to retain should be communicated in the presentation, preferably using whatever aids are available, but should also be distributed in a handout.

Ordering

A number of factors will help you decide on the order in which material is presented. First and most obviously

- **the logic of the subject**

  Frequently choice is limited; the subject matter will often dictate the ordering.

- **the logic of learning and understanding**

  Move from the known to the unknown, and from the easy to the difficult.

- **the need for variety**

  From time to time, break the strictly logical order in order to provide variety.

Other points to bear in mind are:

- Try to start with a 'bang'—a lively and memorable statement or question to catch the listeners' attention.
- Give yourself time to size your audience up, to develop some rapport, before launching into the main substance of your presentation. If the occasion is one which allows a to-and-fro of questions between speaker and audience, it is helpful to warm them up and find out about them by questioning them about their experience of the subject and what they hope to gain from the presentation.
- Make the structure of your presentation clear from the start. The old saying 'Tell 'em what you're going to do—do it—then tell 'em you've done it' is a good one here. An audience feels much more comfortable if they 'know where they are' throughout a presentation.
- After the detailed explanation of each key point allow time to recap not just that point but its relationship to what has gone before. This not only helps to clarify the material but also reinforces the listeners' sense of the structure of the whole presentation.
- End memorably, summing up what has been said and giving the audience something to think about and remember as they go away.

Communication aids

A brilliant speaker can communicate effectively without using aids, and a disastrous one can make a bad presentation even worse by mismanaging them. Most of us fall somewhere between 'brilliant' and 'disastrous' and need to make effective use of the best aids available.

Data projector

The commonest aid used by presenters is a laptop or desktop computer linked to a data projector.

Effectively used, a computer and data projector provide a powerful tool-kit for the presenter. But the key qualification in that statement is in the words 'effectively used'. Anyone who has sat through a few PowerPoint presentations knows how mind-numbingly tedious they can be when the equipment and software are ineffectively used.

Presentation applications

PowerPoint and similar applications such as Apple's Keynote make possible highly sophisticated visual presentations combining text, charts, images, sounds, and movie clips. Slides can fade, glide across the screen, or arrive in a variety of different ways, all with appropriate (or, some would say, inappropriate) sound effects. You can also use the software to produce handouts in several different formats. Your presentation can be stored for future use, with or without voiceover, and can be broadcast on the web as a webinar.

All this comes at a cost. The program isn't cheap and it takes time to learn how to use it proficiently. You need to be in charge of the software and hardware and not the other way round. It is all too common to see presentations which suffer from weaknesses such as these:

- the computer and the projector won't talk to each other (and the presenter walks round them hopelessly muttering, 'It was all right when I tried it out earlier').
- the presenter shows a series of screens with text on them and just reads the text out to the audience with nothing added or taken away. At the end s/he gives out a handout with exactly the same words on it.
- the presenter is so carried away with all the technological bells and whistles that the presentation is confusing and irritating to everyone else.

On the other hand, presentation applications are powerful tools and there are pressures on presenters to use them—increasing numbers of audiences won't take you seriously unless you do. So use them, but remember some important points:

- Adopt a 'belt and braces' approach—be prepared for the equipment not to work (or not to work in the way that you had planned). Even today, breakdowns can and do occur. Be ready to use a whiteboard or flipchart, in association with the handouts you have prepared.
- Remember that your audience want to see and hear *you*. Microsoft™ PowerPoint is only an assistant to you and not the other way round.
- Think carefully about the sequencing of:

  a you speaking

  b you changing what the audience can see

c the audience reading what is on the screen

- It is useful to have blank screens so that you can remove the last words or images without having to replace them with something else for the audience to look at. That way they can re-focus on you and what you are saying.
- Number your slides consecutively in your notes, and check that you know how to turn back to a slide if you wish to refer to it again.

Whiteboard

An old-fashioned whiteboard and a set of coloured markers provide a useful ancillary tool for the presenter. (And can be used as a fall-back when more sophisticated equipment fails.)

With a whiteboard, you can:

- Build up a summary of key points as you proceed with the presentation.
- Collect ideas from participants in a brainstorming session.
- Demonstrate links between ideas collected in this way.
- Quickly show the spelling of important technical terms and names.

Disadvantages include:

- Not everyone can write neatly and clearly on a whiteboard.
- The amount of space is limited, so you may have to remove important material to make way for more.
- When you write on the whiteboard you have to turn away from your audience, so talking and writing require careful management.

Flipchart

A flipchart can be used for the same purposes, but has a number of advantages:

- There is no need to erase unwanted material; you simply flip to the next sheet.
- Important material, including diagrams, can be prepared in advance.
- Even when you want the apparent spontaneity of writing up new material as you speak, it is possible to 'cheat' by writing a small pencil version of your text in one corner of the sheet beforehand, as a memory-jogger. Alternatively, the main lines of a diagram can be lightly pencilled in to guide your drawing.
- After the presentation and discussion, the pages of the flipchart can be retained to form the basis of a report or summary of what has been discussed and agreed.

Delivery

Giving a presentation can be a daunting prospect. Nervous about audience reactions, and anxious not to miss out anything important, some speakers resort to reading a prepared text. Such occasions are rarely a success. A reader finds it difficult to engage with an audience in the way that an unscripted speaker can. When you read, your eyes are, for much of the time, turned down towards your script and thus away from the audience. You do not make eye contact and cannot be properly aware of the way in which your listeners are responding to your words. For them it is like listening to the radio with a not very animated puppet miming to the words.

At the other extreme, it is very difficult to sustain a presentation of any duration without some kind of written prompt. It is too easy to lose the thread of your discourse and either flannel, or be led down some tempting but irrelevant by-road. So it is a question of what form of written preparation to make.

Prompt cards

A popular solution is to use a set of cards, about the size of postcards, on which the main points of the presentation are written. Each card is numbered and one key point to be made is written on each, plus any additional details you need to remember. It is preferable to write on only one side of each card so that after you have used it you can turn it over to remind you that it has been used.

The other advantage of this system is that if you find you are running short of time, you can quickly skip over cards carrying less important points and move on to the more important topics. It is even possible to mark on the cards the approximate time at which you plan to reach that point, so that you have a check on how things are progressing.

Using presentation applications

If you are using PowerPoint or a similar application, you have a choice:

- On-screen prompts
- Printouts

If you plan to stay close to the computer, you can use on-screen notes as you move from slide to slide. This has the advantage that you have everything there in front of you. The disadvantage is that it is difficult to look ahead to remind yourself of what is coming next.

The alternative is to print out your slides and place your notes alongside each one on the page. The advantage here is that if you want to be mobile (using a remote control to move from slide to slide), you can carry your notes with you. The disadvantages are that it is just one more thing to carry around, and if the room lights are dimmed for the projection, it may be more difficult to read your notes.

Talking to your audience

However you tackle the question of remembering what to say, it is essential to address your main attention to the audience. If your listeners do not feel that you are talking to them personally, then they might just as well have stayed at home and listened to a tape recording of your talk. What gives a live presentation its interest is just that: it is live. The audience are hearing it as it happens, and **how** it happens is affected by the way they respond, or it should be.

So speak to them directly. Look at them. Early on, try to locate one or two friendly faces in the crowd, people whose eyes—or, even better, their smiles—tell you that they are favourably disposed towards you. Remember where they are, so that from time to time you look at them and address remarks to them personally. That does **you** some good, by boosting your confidence. The rest of the time your attention should be divided fairly evenly between your other listeners. Let your eyes move over the audience as you speak, focusing briefly on individuals and addressing that part of your speech to them, before moving on again. The purpose of this is that every member of the audience should feel that your words are intended for them personally.

Dealing with interruptions and questions

Speakers sometimes invite the audience to interrupt them to ask questions or even to challenge what is being said. This can be a useful way of engaging with your listeners and providing a lively discourse. It has a number of disadvantages, however. For one thing, your audience do not know what you are planning to say later and so may ask questions that will be answered when you come to that stage of your presentation. Secondly, it can drag you away from the sequence of points you wish to make down a number of blind alleys. And it is an invitation to the bore, the crank, or the attention-seeker to monopolize your attention, to the irritation of everyone else present. A presentation is a presentation, and not primarily a discussion or a public meeting.

It is generally better to offer one or more slots for questions and discussion at moments in the presentation selected by **you**. If people interrupt without being invited to, you can then ask them, politely, to hold their fire until you reach the chosen moment. If they insist, then try to deal with the point briefly and then move on to your next point.

Question-and-answer sessions can be tricky to handle. The rest of the time you are, or should be, firmly in control; here you are to some extent at the mercy of events. Begin by allocating a set period of time—even if you are actually prepared to spend longer than the stated time on questions. That way if one person threatens to monopolize the session you can point out that others, too, have questions they wish to ask and the time is limited—and then hope that someone else **does** have a question!

Things that have to be read

Any text that your audience can see needs careful handling. If you project a text, you must allow sufficient time for it to be read—and some people are slow readers. Some speakers get round this by reading the text aloud, but audience members may find this irritating. On the other hand, if the projected text is at the limits of legibility because of the size of the room, then it is advisable to read it out.

The question of handouts is more complicated. The trouble is that if you distribute handouts before or during your talk, people tend to read them and not listen to what you are saying. So unless there is a good reason to do otherwise, only distribute them at the end of the presentation. It is also helpful to advise your audience that you will be doing this, and to tell them roughly what the handout contains, so that listeners are saved the trouble of taking unnecessary notes. (Also, during the presentation, when you refer to important details it is helpful to say, 'Those details are in the handout which you will receive at the end.')

Less formal occasions

Much of what has gone before refers to the kind of formal presentation that occurs in an institutional context: in an office, training centre, or college seminar, for example. But there are many occasions on which we are asked to 'say a few words' to a small or large gathering of people. For example you may be asked to propose a vote of thanks at the end of a talk, or speak at a wedding. It is outside the scope of a book like this to deal in detail with all the different situations in which this may occur. However, many of the general points made earlier still apply, especially those relating to your relationship with your audience. If you focus on them, and think about their identity, needs, and expectations, you will be well on the way to success. Beyond that, the most obvious points to make are that however informal the occasion, you should still prepare and, unless you are a very experienced speaker, have at least a few prompt points on a sheet of paper or on a few cards, as described earlier. And, more often than not, jokes help.

Guidelines

Preparation

Careful and thorough preparation is the key to a successful presentation.

1 Think carefully about your purpose. Is it to inform, to persuade, to entertain, to interact with your audience? Or if, as is likely, it is a mixture of these, what is the balance?

2 If you have the provision of information as a primary aim, think in detail about how you will achieve your aim. How will you combine factual information, narrative, description, and explanation?

3 Make a careful analysis of the audience you expect to address. Begin by considering how well equipped they will be to handle the information and ideas you wish to communicate. How can you make their task of understanding easier?

4 Think also about the expectations and needs they bring to the occasion. If you do not satisfy these—at least in part—they will go away feeling that their time has been wasted.

5 Analyse the content that you wish to communicate, bearing in mind that the amount you can do is limited by the time available and what the audience can take in. It is better to underestimate how much you can do than to be overambitious.

6 Set yourself priorities to make sure that the most important points are grasped **and remembered** by your audience, even if it means reducing the total amount covered.

7 Think carefully about the order in which material should be covered, bearing in mind the logic of the subject, the need to move from the known to the unknown, and the value of variety.

8 Decide which communication aids are most suitable for your purposes. (The advantages and disadvantages of each are listed on pages 73–5.) Prepare accordingly.

9 Prepare your prompt cards or other notes.

10 Prepare any handouts you intend to distribute.

Delivery

11 Aim to have every member of your audience going away with the impression that you were talking directly to them.

12 Identify one or two members of the audience who are clearly favourably disposed to you and use them as 'home bases' to return to regularly when speaking. This helps maintain and develop your sense of confidence and rapport.

13 From them let your gaze cover the rest of the audience regularly, coming to rest on individuals and staying on them for a few moments, before moving on. Try to make each person you look at feel that you are talking to them personally.

14 Allocate one or more definite slots for questions and/or discussion and try to confine audience participation to these. If people ask questions at other times, or otherwise interrupt, answer them politely but firmly and return to your line of argument as quickly as possible.

15 Remember that if you display or distribute text, people will want to read it. Build in time for your audience to read the text you display and try to delay distributing handouts until the end of the presentation.

> Further reading

Cliff Atkinson, *Beyond Bullet Points: Using Microsoft PowerPoint to Create Presentations That Inform, Motivate, and Inspire*
(Microsoft Press, 2011), ISBN 9780735627352.

Carmine Gallo, *The Presentation Secrets of Steve Jobs: How to Be Insanely Great in Front of Any Audience*
(McGraw-Hill Professional, 2009), ISBN 9780071636087.

⑦ Reports

Modern life depends on the flow of information. For managers this can seem a mixed blessing, as their in-trays overflow with the stuff: reports on Topic A vie for their attention with proposals about Project X and all clamour for a response. It seems that 'of making many reports there is no end'.

Yet management is impossible without information. Before you can make a decision you need to have at your disposal all the relevant facts, and these often come in the form of a report. It is important, therefore, that such documents are prepared and constructed in the most useful possible way.

Most documents designed to provide information leading to action can be placed on a spectrum.

The report

At one end is what might be called the 'pure' report, intended to provide accurate and unbiased information about a situation. If it deals with possible courses of action, it presents all the possibilities and their likely outcomes without favouring one above another. An example of this type of report might be described in this way:

> **The teaching of Shakespeare**
> The study was conducted to examine approaches to the teaching of Shakespeare at undergraduate level in British universities.

The proposal

At the other extreme is the proposal, which is, from the outset, openly and unashamedly biased. Its purpose is to promote a particular course of action. Like the report it provides information and judgements about that information, but it uses these to further its own ends. If other possibilities are considered, it is only to show why they are wrong and the favoured one is right. An example is the proposals that authors prepare to convince publishers that they should publish their books. These often contain considerable detail, spelling out not only what the book contains but also where in the market it is placed and how it compares (favourably, of course) with the competition.

The range

Most reports and proposals fall somewhere between these two extremes. They are designed to be read by decision-makers. They survey a range of information, make judgements about it, and come to conclusions, often in the form of recommendations. So a typical report might be described as follows:

> **Off-road cycling in the South West**
> A survey of current facilities for off-road cycling in the woodlands of South West England and an assessment of the opportunities for further developments in the region.

Here the factual element ('a survey of current facilities') is followed by recommendations ('an assessment of the opportunities'). Some reports will tend towards the objective end of the spectrum, while others will take a more committed stance, but all tend to follow similar patterns and to be prepared in similar ways—which is the subject matter of this chapter.

Preparing a report

Objective

It is impossible to write a clear and cogent report without a clear objective, or set of objectives. So it is important to formulate this as precisely—and briefly—as possible at the outset. For example:

> To audit the current provision of off-road cycling facilities in the region, estimate future demand, consider how it might be provided for, and assess the potential impact on the local economy.

Audience

It is also very important to have a clear idea of the audience for the report. The example above could be aimed at a number of different audiences:

➤ See also
· CHAPTER 10
  Audience
  (p. 117)

- The Forestry Commission
- Tourism organizations
- County and District Councils
- Landowners
- Chambers of Commerce, and other local business organizations

Each of these audiences has

- a different understanding of the subject
- different concerns

So while it is relatively easy to work out what to say and how to say it to one of these audiences, addressing your report to all five is much more difficult.

Planning your research

Doing the necessary research for a report is much easier if you begin by making two lists:

➤ See also
· CHAPTER 24
  Research
  (p. 311)

- questions you need to ask
- people and places where you hope to find the answers

The second list may well not be as complete as the first. It may be necessary to do preliminary research in order to complete it. In the example we are following, you might ask this question:

> What do off-road cyclists do at present?

and then, on reflection you might decide to break it into two:

1 What do cyclists say they do?
2 What do they actually do?

It is fairly easy to find answers to question 1, but question 2 is much more tricky. If time does not allow for detailed surveys of current facilities and cyclist behaviour, you must look for secondary sources of information, research data and other publications. But where? In this situation Forestry Commission Rangers would clearly be a logical starting point. The person who can answer questions directly is an important resource, but so is the person who can direct you to where you can find out answers to the questions that are left.

Sources of information

Given the very diverse nature of all the reports that people are asked to write, it is impossible to provide a useful detailed list of sources of information. The following list is intended to cover the general areas that need to be considered:

- **Direct observation**

  possibly the most dependable, but also the most time-consuming, source of information

- **People**

  using personal contacts (via email, telephone, fax), questionnaires, meetings, focus groups

- **Publications**

  books, journals, government publications including legislation

- **Research findings**

  a wide range of commercial, government, academic, and other independent organizations sponsor and carry out research and publish their findings

- **The internet**

  large numbers of informative documents are readily available from government and other official and semi-official web sites

- **Documents and data within your own organization**

Scheduling research

Your list of questions and sources of information can be used to generate a list of things to do. Some of these may be easy and informal, like asking a colleague for an opinion or a piece of information. Others will be more complex and time-consuming, such as contacting a provider of commercial information, acquiring a list of publications, discovering which are relevant, acquiring and reading them, finding relevant information, and making notes on it.

So it is important to make a research plan:

1 Group similar activities together, especially those which involve contacting the same people.

2 Identify those topics which are going to take a long time and so need to be started as early as possible.

3 Work out whether any aspects are interdependent and decide the order in which they must be tackled.

4 Calculate approximately how long each part of the research is likely to take.

5 Order the actions logically, using all this information.

Writing the report

Structure

The structure of a report is determined by its content and the needs of its readers. While the following structure is not the only one, it is a popular one and contains all the features that would be expected in a fairly lengthy report.

1 **Contents list**
2 **Executive Summary**
3 **Introduction**
4 **Body of the report**
5 **Conclusions**
6 **Recommendations**
7 **Appendices**
8 **Bibliography**

If the report is any more than a few pages long it needs a contents list detailing the main sections and the pages on which they appear.

Contents list

Contents

Executive summary

Executive Summary

The readers of a report are usually busy people. They haven't got time to wade through page after page of text just to find out which parts of a report may be of value to them—if any. The purpose of the executive summary is to set out the substance of the report briefly and in such a way that busy readers can see at a glance whether the report is relevant to them and, if so, which aspects of it are of most interest. Ideally it should not exceed one side of a page. Executive summaries that run to several pages can be self-defeating.

Executive summary

The Study

Roger Tym & Partners and Total Marketing Solutions were commissioned in 2006 by the Forestry Commission, Woodland Renaissance, South West Tourism, and South West Protected Landscapes Forum to study the opportunities for off-road cycling in South West woodlands. IMBA-UK and the CTC helped guide the study.

The study estimates the current demand for woodland cycling in the region, the economic impact and the potential demand for woodland off-road cycling. It includes an audit of woodland cycling locations, a survey of 800 woodland cyclists, and discussion with cycling clubs, landowners, and stakeholders.

The study considers the different types of off-road cycling facilities that might be developed in woodland and sets out a framework to assess these development options against environmental, economic, and community impacts. It also reviews commercial opportunities from woodland off-road cycling.

This study is a response to issues facing traditional forestry, with falling timber prices, less employment, reduced maintenance, and lower harvesting rates.

The Key Findings

Demand

There is considerable demand for woodland cycling across the South West...

Introduction

This should contain the following information:

- **The origins of the report**

  The background and events leading to the need for the report.

- **Its terms of reference**

  The scope (and limitations) of the report and its purpose.

- **How it was conducted and by whom**

  This can also include acknowledgements of help received.

- **Other introductory information**

  It is important to think of the readers of the report and to include at this point any other background information they will need in order to understand the material in the body of the report.

1 Introduction

1.1 Roger Tym & Partners and Total Marketing Solutions were commissioned by the Forestry Commission, Woodland Renaissance, South West Protected Landscapes Forum and South West Tourism to undertake this study of off-road cycling in woodlands in the South West.

1.2 The objectives of the study were to:

- **Assess existing supply**
  - Audit of current provision
  - Assessment of current carrying capacity and potential for increasing capacity, including non-financial barriers

- **Analyse current and potential demand**
  - Assess current and potential future demand for off-road cycling in the woodlands of the SW
  - Calculate current levels of income the activity generates
  - Identify potential opportunities for increasing income to woodland owners and the wider rural economy
  - Assess need for dedicated off-road cycling sites within Mendip Hills, Quantock Hills, Tamar Valley, Exmoor, Dartmoor, and Blackdown Hills, Forest of Dean, New Forest, Forest of Avon & Great Western Community Forests, and South West Forest

- **Provide recommendations for product development**
  - Analyse the strategic location of current provision in relation to demand

1.3 The study considers the variety of markets for off-road cycling in woodlands, from expert mountain bikers seeking technical and challenging experiences to families seeking high quality countryside environments for traffic-free recreation.

Study Process

1.4 The study used a variety of published and unpublished information sources to identify woodland cycling locations in South West England. This information was supplemented through interviews with stakeholders, including the Forestry Commission, AONB officers, land owners, and cycling clubs.

1.5 Once the main locations had been identified, further detail was collected and collated for the main woodland cycling hubs...

Body of the report

The main part of the report contains:

- a detailed account of what your research discovered
- the conclusions that you draw from it
- references to sources that you have quoted. The sources should be listed in the bibliography, and the references should follow a standard pattern (see 'References' below).

A report of any length will be divided into a number of main sections, each on a separate topic or theme. These in turn will probably be subdivided into subsections. All sections and subsections will need headings and, to avoid confusion, it is very desirable to use a numbering system. A commonly used one is decimal: the first main section is numbered 1; subsections are then numbered 1.1, 1.2, etc., and their subsections become 1.1.1, 1.1.2, and so on.

The body of the report will consist of the details of the research—often in the form of tables, charts, and figures, with relevant quotations:

> 5.20 Spend associated with cycling will be spread across a range of different sectors. The two pie charts below illustrate the spending pattern in Devon for general tourist and day visitors.

Day visitors

Staying visitors

5.21 Overall the largest sector for expenditure is food and drink (28%) followed closely by accommodation (26%). Day visitors predominantly spend on food and drink and shopping whereas staying visitors will spend money on accommodation (36%). While cycle visitors may have some different expenditure patterns, it is likely that they will broadly replicate the general spending pattern.

The argument may be presented in continuous prose, and/or as a series of bullet or numbered points:

5.18 The impacts at Haldon are likely to grow in the future as the total volume of use and the proportion of staying visitors grow. The 7stanes project in Scotland had just over 170,000 users per year after Phase One, with 25% staying visitors. The day and staying visitor expenditure supported over 70 FTE jobs at a regional level. 6.5 of these jobs were on site and the rest were in the wider economy. Since Phase One, growth has continued to around 350,000 to 400,000 visits per year.

5.19 This illustrates that:

i. Woodland cycling has benefits to the wider economy
ii. The woodland managers receive little of the overall wealth generated
iii. The more staying visitors attracted, the more value to the local economy

If the material you are handling is detailed, there is a danger that the main thrust of your argument will become obscured by details. In such situations it is better to place highly detailed material in appendices and to refer to it in the body of the report in numbered notes. While the reference number appears at the relevant point in the text, the note itself can either be placed at the foot of the page or at the end of the section or chapter. If there are not too many notes, it is better to put them at the bottom of the page, since it is irritating for the reader to have to keep turning pages to find the relevant note. If there are a lot of notes, however, they are better placed at the end of the chapter, since to place them at the foot of the page will make the pages look messy and unbalanced.

Conclusions

Each section of the report should lead to a number of conclusions. At the end of the section these are spelled out and the reasoning behind them explained. If there is a separate *Conclusions* section these conclusions are pulled out and presented as an ordered sequence. Sometimes a report that is divided into major sections will have a short Summary at the end of each section:

Summary

3.76 In terms of estimating the current level of demand for cycling in the region's woodlands, the true figure lies somewhere between 4 million trips per year, as estimated using GBDVS data and 8 million trips per year, as estimated using the IMBA approach. Using either method, the current demand level appears to be significant.

3.77 The latent potential demand from within both the local population and the tourist population also appears to be considerable...

Recommendations

Not all reports present recommendations; some are merely required to present a set of information based on research. Where there are recommendations, these may be presented as part of the report's conclusions, or in a separate section which may be placed towards the end of the report, after the conclusions, or immediately after the executive summary. Indeed, some writers prefer to make their recommendations part of the executive summary, since they are an important part of what the busy reader wants to know first.

Appendices

The value of placing certain lengthy detailed information in a series of appendices (sometimes called *annexes*) has already been mentioned. The type of information that may go in appendices includes:

- a detailed description of the research method, including the questionnaire(s) used and how the sample was selected
- the research brief and the members of the team producing the report
- detailed research data
- case studies

Bibliography

It is essential that when published or unpublished textual sources are referred to, they are clearly identified so that readers can, if they wish, check the original. In the case of books, the following information should be given:

- the name(s) of the author(s)
- the full title
- the name of the publisher and place of publication
- the year of first publication or, if it is a subsequent edition, the number of the edition and the date of its publication

A common style for doing this is:

Seely, John. *The Oxford A-Z of Grammar and Punctuation*. 3rd edn. Oxford: Oxford University Press, 2013.

This information should appear in the bibliography at the end of the report. References to the book in the text should simply use the author's name and date followed by the page(s) referred to:

Seely (2004), 34–5

References to periodicals and journals should appear in the bibliography in this style:

> Haywood, Kevin. 'Teaching algebra to 11-year-olds', *Modern Maths Quarterly* 4/2. 68-73. 2003.

Addressing your readership

We have already seen that you need to think carefully about your readers when considering the content and structure of the report. It is equally important to remember your readers when drafting the report itself.

Normally a report should be written in a fairly impersonal and formal style. Reports are formal documents and, even if you have a very good idea of who will read what you write and know them all quite well, you cannot know for certain who will read it at some later date. Reports are usually stored for later reference and may be passed to anyone with a legitimate interest in the subject, so it is unwise to write them in too relaxed or informal a style. On the other hand, this is not to suggest that you should imagine that you are a nineteenth-century bureaucrat. In particular, try to avoid writing sentences that are too long or involved.

Guidelines

Preparation

1 Begin by defining clearly your objective(s) and your readership.
2 Plan your research. Begin by making two lists:
  * questions you want to ask
  * the people and places where you can expect to find an answer (or where you can get advice on relevant sources of information)
3 Use your lists to help you schedule your research.

Writing the report

The main items a report can contain are:

4 **A table of contents**
5 **An executive summary.** Use this to state clearly and concisely what the report is about and what it discovered. You may also wish to include your principal recommendations here. (But see 9, below.)
6 **An introduction.** Use this to explain the history of the commissioning of the report, its terms of reference, how it was conducted, and any other important background information.
7 **The body of the report.** Here you should set out the main information which your research uncovered and the conclusions that you draw from

it. If the material is dense and/or detailed, you may prefer to place the detail in one or more appendices and refer to it through footnotes.

8 **The conclusions.** It is often a good idea to repeat the conclusions you reached again in a separate section, referring back to relevant sections of the report as necessary.

9 **The recommendations.** You can list these separately after the *conclusions*, or place them in or after the *executive summary*.

10 **Appendices.** Use these for material such as detailed research data, a description of the research methodology, and case studies.

11 **Bibliography.** This should contain details of all published and unpublished texts quoted or referred to, following one of the conventional styles.

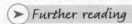 Further reading

John Bowden, *Writing a Report*
(How To Books, 2011), ISBN 9781845284701 (print and e-book versions).

8 Essays, papers, and dissertations

Preparation

- The differences between academic writing and other kinds of writing
- Defining the subject and analysing questions
- Generating ideas
- Research
- Ordering your material

Writing

- Structure
- Register
- Using quotations and references

Projects and dissertations

- Structure
- Writing approach
- Shaping
- Other considerations

What the report is to the business world, the essay, paper, and dissertation are to the academic community. From the sixth-form essay to the Ph.D. thesis, the writing of an extended piece of prose is used to demonstrate and measure the writer's grasp of a given subject.

There is, however, a major difference between these two types of writing. A manager normally reads a report in order to learn new information about a topic—the writer knows more about the subject than the reader. A university lecturer reads a paper or dissertation in order to judge how well the writer has understood the subject; here the reader probably knows more about the subject than the writer. (Although that is not to say that it is impossible for the writer to surprise the reader with a new and challenging interpretation.)

This is one of the reasons why some students have writing problems. It seems artificial to be telling the reader something that he or she probably already knows. In addition, the dissertation is almost certainly by far the longest piece of writing the student has ever undertaken; the task seems daunting. It seems impossible to prepare, initiate, and then control such an extended piece of prose, even leaving aside the additional difficulties caused by one's uncertainty about the purpose and audience of such a text.

Such a view is not uncommon, and can be crippling, but there is a positive side to each of the negatives it contains. The fact that the reader already has a good knowledge of the subject means that there is no need to provide a lot of low-level explanation at the outset. The academic context means that there are well-established conventions for structuring and composing this type of writing—and readily available research material. The situation in which it is written means that plenty of time is allowed for writing it (or should be). Most important of all, this type of extended writing allows the writer really to get to grips with a substantial subject and come to understand it fully.

This chapter goes through the process of writing an essay, paper, or dissertation step by step. For convenience it refers to an 'essay' throughout, but most of what is said applies to the whole range of writing of this type. The main differences between an essay and a dissertation are that the dissertation is much longer and has a more elaborate formal structure. It is also normally written in rather different circumstances, as we shall see. There is a separate section on writing dissertations at the end of the chapter.

In this chapter the various stages of writing are covered fairly briefly. Readers who wish to study the process of writing in more depth should turn to Section D of this book, *The process of writing*, where six chapters are devoted to it.

Preparation

It is difficult to write at any length without some form of preparation. Nevertheless it is surprising how many writers do just launch themselves into writing straightaway, only to find that after a page or two they come to a halt, uncertain as to how to proceed. Planning may be a lengthy process, but it need not be. How much you do depends on the subject, how well you know it, and how much research you need to do.

That said, different writers will prefer different approaches (and the same writer may tackle different assignments in different ways). Some prefer to make a detailed plan at the outset and then stick to it fairly rigidly as they write. Others prefer to plan as they write, using the process of drafting and re-drafting to help them clarify and crystallize their thoughts. Such an approach may ultimately take longer, but sometimes it is the only way for the writer to proceed: 'How do I know what I think until I see what I say?' as E. M. Forster put it.

Defining the subject

Some of the problems a writer may face arise because the subject of the essay has not been clearly defined or understood. Sometimes teachers set topics that are imprecise or vaguely worded. But if students just go along with this and write the essay without trying to define the subject more precisely, then they only have themselves to blame. It is better either to tackle the person who set the subject and ask them to clarify it, or, failing that, to redefine it yourself. (If you do this, you should, of course, make it clear that you have done so.)

Some question-setters, of course, are deliberately vague or imprecise, in order to challenge the student writer. Others like to set little traps in the way a question is worded. They may, for example, imply or assume something in the question which is not necessarily the case. A question might ask, for example, 'In what ways does Shakespeare lead us to sympathise with the character of Cordelia in *King Lear*?' The obvious assumption is that we *do* sympathise with Cordelia, but we may not. We may find her a cold and undutiful daughter at the beginning of the play. The question also assumes that Shakespeare did in fact set out with this intention, which may not have been the case. More radically, there is a school of thought which questions the whole idea of 'character' in Shakespeare's plays. So there is plenty in the wording of this question for the writer to challenge.

'Not answering the question' *may* be the fault of the questioner, or the result of a trap that he or she has set. More often, however, it is the fault of the writer, who has not thought carefully enough about what the question means. A good starting point is to ask yourself, 'What is the question asking me to *do*?' Essay questions often provide helpful clues to what is expected. For example:

1. What has been the impact of e-commerce on EU business in the period from 1995 to the present?
2. What is meant by 'factoring'?
3. In *King Lear*, Gloucester and Lear both learn through suffering. In what other ways are they similar and how might their circumstances be said to be different?
4. 'Global food shortages are the main factor driving social and political unrest in the Middle East'. Discuss.
5. What were the main events leading up to the American Civil War?

Each of these questions asks the writer to perform a different task:

- **Analyse**

  Question 1 asks the writer to examine a particular phenomenon and analyse its likely effects. Analytical questions ask the writer to tease out the significant features of a situation, to describe them, and to explain why they are significant.

- **Define**

 See also

• CHAPTER 14
*Different ways of
communicating*
(p. 155)

  Question 2 asks for a definition of an economic term. The writer is required to list its defining features and to support this definition by reference to good examples from the real world.

- **Compare and contrast**

  Question 3 refers to two characters from a play who have similarities and differences and asks the writer to set these out. The question does not ask the writer to describe one character, describe the other, and then compare them. Instead the writer has to find key features of similarity and difference and build the essay up around these.

- **Argue a case**

  Question 4 puts a challenging interpretation of a piece of recent history and asks the writer to examine the two sides of the argument and evaluate them.

- **Narrate**

  In Question 5 the writer is being asked to tell a story. The danger of narrative is that writing it seems easy: anyone can tell a story and many people enjoy doing so. As a result writers often fall back on narrative, when they should be analysing, defining, or arguing.

Each of these types of question has its own distinctive structures and approaches. Sometimes questions are 'pure' examples of one type, as in the examples quoted. Often they are hybrids, combining two or more types in one question.

Generating ideas

 See also

• CHAPTER 23
*Making notes
and summaries*
(p. 297)

Once you have analysed the wording of the question and decided what kind of question it is, you can begin to develop your ideas.

It is a good idea to 'think on paper'. In its simplest form this just involves jotting down a **list** of ideas as they occur to you:

> Impact of e-commerce since 1995
> – initially slow take-up
> – patchy interest + suspicion among older managers
> – effect of bursting of dot com bubble
> – successes of businesses growing organically into internet sales

Some questions lend themselves to putting ideas into two or more columns:

Lear/Gloucester similarities	Differences
both 'blind' about children	At start of play Lear has absolute power, Gloucester doesn't
both deceived and then humiliated by favoured child(ren)	

An alternative is the 'web' or 'spider' diagram:

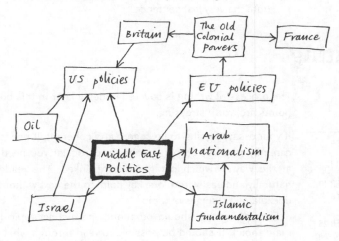

Research

> See also

- CHAPTER 24
Research
(p. 311), where
this subject is
covered in much
more detail.

Three key points to remember about effective research are:

- Make effective notes. (Although taking notes is more laborious than making photocopies, notes are often more useful because they force you to focus on the text and determine its key points.)
- Keep a careful record of the source of all material, including full bibliographical details.
- Distinguish carefully between information and ideas that you have abstracted from a source and direct quotations. Otherwise you risk using someone else's words as if they were your own (plagiarizing).

Ordering your material

> See also

- CHAPTER 25
Planning and
drafting
(p. 321)

Once your ideas and material have been developed, you can begin to order them into a logical sequence. How you do this will be determined by the demands of the question and how you have decided to respond to it.

1 You need to decide first how many main sections there should be, apart from an introduction and a conclusion. There should be enough to encompass all the ideas you have generated, but few enough for the pattern of the essay to be clear to the reader.

2 You should decide how best to order these sections so that your material can be presented in a logical and interesting way.

3 You can then arrange your material, fitting all your ideas into the relevant sections.

4 Now decide how you will introduce your essay and conclude it. The introduction needs to indicate the approach you propose to take, but should avoid giving the game away right at the start. If you tell the reader everything that you are going to say in the course of the first paragraph, there is little incentive to read on. Similarly the conclusion should refer to the main points you have made without being repetitive; but if possible you should save up a telling, interesting, or

amusing point for the conclusion, so that the reader's interest is held until the very last sentence.

Writing

The process of writing is covered in detail later in this book. Here two key points are worth stressing.

Structure

➤ See also
- CHAPTER 10
  Audience
  (p. 117)
- CHAPTER 25
  Planning and
  drafting
  (p. 321)

If your essay is going to be cogent and coherent, it needs to be built up of carefully constructed paragraphs. In particular you need to look carefully at the way in which paragraphs are linked. The reader should be led naturally and easily from one key point to the next without sudden leaps or unexplained changes of topic.

Each paragraph should be about one distinct topic (or aspect of the main topic). It should be possible to read through what you have written and sum up the content of each paragraph in a short phrase:

- If it requires more than a short phrase—for example, a long phrase or an extended sentence—then you should consider whether the paragraph should be split into two.
- If two adjacent paragraphs can only be summed up with the same phrase, then you should consider either combining them into one paragraph, or re-writing them so that their content is more obviously different.

The ending of one paragraph should lead naturally into the beginning of the next. There should be a 'hook' linking the two together. Here, for example, is one complete paragraph of an essay about Shakespeare's *King Lear* with the opening sentence of the next:

> In the first scene Cordelia is the focus of two love contests: the one that Lear has set up, to find an answer to the question, 'Which of you shall we say doth love us most?', and the competition between France and Burgundy for her hand in marriage. Lear orders the two suitors to be summoned, but they do not appear until later, presumably because he wishes to settle family business first. It would make sense to determine the size of Cordelia's dowry before her suitors convened to discuss any possible marriage settlement.
>
> This provides the background to Cordelia's dilemma—for Shakespeare makes it clear that it **is** a dilemma.

The final sentence of the first paragraph sums up the situation at this point in the play. The second paragraph begins with the word 'this', referring back to the previous sentence. In this way the two paragraphs are hooked together: the writer makes it clear that he is picking up this part of the argument and proposes to develop it.

When reviewing your writing, you should examine your paragraphs from this point of view. Ask yourself the questions, 'Does each paragraph lead logically to the next?' 'Are these logical links made clear by the words I have used?' 'Are there ways in which I can signal these links more transparently to the reader?' It is almost always possible to improve a first draft very considerably by attending to the links between paragraphs.

Register

Academic essays and dissertations should be written in the style expected for such writing. Features of this include:

- **Impersonal tone**

  The writing avoids referring to 'me' and 'you'. Instead it generally uses third person constructions. So, for example, instead of saying, 'I cannot imagine what led him to this curious idea.,', it will say, 'It is difficult to imagine what led him to this curious idea.'

- **No contractions**

  In less formal writing we often make use of contractions, such as 'won't' and 'couldn't' instead of 'will not' and 'could not'. In academic writing this is best avoided.

- **Avoidance of slang and excessive colloquialisms**

  While academic writing doesn't have to appear too stiff and starchy, it generally avoids being overly colloquial, chatty, or slangy.

- **Unemotional, evidence-driven argument**

  The underlying assumption of academic discourse is that it is logical and based on evidence. It is not the place for appeals to emotion, whether explicit or implicit.

Quotations and references

Make sure that it is clear when you are quoting directly from another person. Short quotations can go into the body of your text, marked off by quotation marks. Longer quotations should be separated and indented.

All quotations must be properly attributed. This is normally done in a separate bibliography at the end of the essay. This can include not only printed and digital material, but also audio, video, and other sources of information. As well as the sources of textual quotations, it should list works that have been consulted or referred to in the preparation and writing of the essay—although this should not be used as an excuse to list all the books on a given topic, regardless of whether you have consulted them or not. You will soon get found out and marked down if you do that.

Different institutions have different requirements about:

- how information in the bibliography should be presented;
- how this information should be referred to in the body of the essay, including the use of footnotes.

You may well be referred to one of a number of style guides, of which the best known for the humanities is probably that provided by the Modern Language Association (usually abbreviated to MLA). Such guides not only provide guidance on how to list every type of reference material in a bibli-ography, but also how to refer to it in the body of the writing. Guidance is also provided on topics such as:

- spelling and usage
- names
- abbreviations
- punctuation

To get a feel of how such guides work, you can download a free copy of the MHRA Style Guide, prepared by the Modern Humanities Research Association, at http://www.mhra.org.uk/Publications/Books/StyleGuide/download.shtml.

Projects and dissertations

At first degree level, students are often required to produce a piece of writing of greater length than the normal essay. Such extended writing may be called a 'research project' or 'dissertation'. Those working for a Master's degree will certainly be expected to write a dissertation. For the purposes of this section, I shall refer to both types of writing as a dissertation.

The most obvious distinguishing feature of dissertations is their length. But to think of a dissertation as simply a long essay is misleading. Once a piece of writing reaches a certain length a number of problems arise—mainly because the reader finds it increasingly difficult to keep a grasp of what is going on. The writer, therefore, needs to keep checking that the reader is still following the argument. This is partly a question of structure and partly one of writing approach. The circumstances of writing a disser-tation are usually different from those of writing an essay. While the essay writer is frequently left to his or her own devices, when it comes to a dis-sertation, the writing is often supported by supervision.

Structure

Readers need as many structural devices as possible to help them keep track of the argument. These can include:

- **A table of contents**
- **An introduction** explaining the nature of the subject, the treatment, and the reasons for choosing this approach.
- **Division of the text into sections or chapters.** Each should be treated as an essay in its own right with:
  - an introduction which introduces the subject matter and explains its link to what has gone before
  - a conclusion which sums up the main points and leads on to the next section.
- **A conclusion** which sums up the entire argument, referring back, where necessary, to specific sections of the main text.

- **A bibliography** and list of other sources used.
- In some circumstances it may also be necessary to include one or more **appendices**. For example, in a dissertation based on film, you might need to include the text of an unpublished screenplay so that you can refer to it in the dissertation.

It is worth pointing out, however, that different universities and other institutions have their own 'rules' about how a text should be structured. Some, for example, say that sub-headings are unacceptable, and others ban bullet points.

Writing approach

How you approach the writing of your dissertation is, partly at least, a matter of negotiation between you and your supervisor. That said, the responsibility for the project ultimately rests with the writer, so you need to be comfortable with the agreed approach. A typical timetable might be:

1 Writer and supervisor discuss the writer's ideas about subject matter.
2 The writer then prepares a detailed **proposal** setting out the content and structure of the dissertation. (This may well change fairly radically as the writing proceeds, but the writer needs to demonstrate at this stage in some detail what the content is going to be and how the material can be shaped.)
3 The writer then goes away and produces a first draft of part at least of the dissertation.
4 This is submitted to the supervisor, who then discusses it with the writer (depending on circumstances this may be face-to-face, by telephone, or by email).
5 This process then proceeds over the arranged number of supervisions.

During this process you may expect the content and structure of your writing to change, sometimes very radically. What seemed at the beginning of the process to be a clear and straightforward approach may turn out to be anything but. The experience of writing can reveal flaws in an argument, and the process of research may well throw up important evidence that leads you to question your assumptions and re-think. And, of course, you can expect your ideas and their expression to be questioned at every stage by your supervisor. Writing a dissertation may seem daunting, but it should be a challenging, exciting, and rewarding experience.

Shaping

➤ See also
- CHAPTER 25 Planning and drafting (p. 321), where this subject is covered in much greater detail.

As you write, you should try to carry in your mind the structure of the whole dissertation, being aware of how what you are writing at this particular moment relates to what has gone before and what is yet to come. When you are working on a first draft this is difficult to achieve, but it is certainly something you should remember when you come to redraft a section. As you read the first draft through, keep checking how the parts relate to each other and asking yourself whether you are providing sufficient signposts for your readers as they travel with you from the beginning to the end.

Above all, make use of whatever help other people can give you. All writers, however skilful and experienced, depend on constructive criticism from people whose judgement they trust.

Other considerations

As was noted above, many institutions provide detailed guidelines on how to prepare a dissertation, which must, of course, be followed. These will almost certainly include the question of presentation. Any set of dissertations submitted for assessment will almost certainly divide into three categories:

- those which fail to observe the presentation guidelines given to students
- those which do the minimum required
- those whose writers have used the guidelines and have done everything in their power to make their work as clear and reader-friendly as possible

Given the pressures of time and workload under which the assessors have to work, there are no prizes for guessing which dissertations will receive the most favourable treatment.

Guidelines

Note

There is more detailed guidance on the processes of writing in Section D:

Chapter 22: Getting ready to write (p. 289)
Chapter 23: Making notes and summaries (p. 297)
Chapter 24: Research (p. 311)
Chapter 25: Planning and drafting (p. 321)
Chapter 26: Editing and revising (p. 335)
Chapter 27: Presentation (p. 345)

1 It is important to realize that academic writing is different from other kinds of writing: it has its own conventions that you are expected to follow. If you do not, you may find it difficult to get a proper hearing.

2 Begin by analysing the question to make sure that you understand not only the **content** of your writing, but also the **approach** and **type of writing** that are required.

3 Generate ideas on paper, using lists, columns, or web diagrams.

4 Do your research, making sure that:
- you make detailed notes
- you distinguish carefully between quotations and your own words
- you keep a detailed record of books and articles you refer to

5 Produce a written plan ordering your material into a small number of main sections, giving the essay an introduction and a conclusion.

6 Make sure that your paragraphs are carefully constructed, with 'hooks' linking them to the paragraphs which precede and follow them.

7 Use an impersonal and fairly formal style, avoiding contractions, slang, and excessive colloquialism.

8 Mark off short quotations with quotation marks, and longer ones by starting a new line and indenting the whole quotation. Make sure that all quoted material is correctly attributed, using a bibliography at the end of the essay and a brief textual reference at the point of quotation.

Projects and dissertations

9 Use structural devices such as a table of contents, separate sections, an introduction, and a conclusion to make your text as 'transparent' as possible to the reader. You may also need to add one or more appendices.

10 Make full use of the opportunities offered by the supervision process as you develop your ideas and draft and re-draft your text.

11 Present the final draft in as polished and reader-friendly a way as possible.

12 Make sure that you have followed the rules and guidelines laid down by your college or university in your final draft.

➤ *Further reading*

Jonathan Weyers and Kathleen McMillan, *How to Write Dissertations & Project Reports* (Prentice Hall, 2011), ISBN 9780273743835.

Jonathan Weyers and Kathleen McMillan, *How to Write Essays & Assignments* (Prentice Hall, 2011), ISBN 9780273743811.

Chris Mounsey, *How to Write: Successful Essays, Dissertations, and Exams* (Oxford University Press, 2013), ISBN: 9780199670741.

⑨ The media

There are two common ways in which one may expect to encounter the media in everyday life and work:

- the press release
- the interview

These are the subject matter of this chapter.

Writing a press release

If you have something you wish to publicize, then you should aim to have it reported in local, regional, or national press, radio, or TV. It is always possible, of course, to buy advertising space and put your message across in that way. But getting a report in the press or on the air has the distinct advantage of being free. Reports are also—sometimes at least—given more attention and credence.

You might wonder why a newspaper or local radio station should be interested in the news you wish to promote. They may well not be particularly interested, but they almost certainly need it. The media have a voracious appetite for material; the radio or television station has so many hours of airtime to fill, and the newspaper so many column inches to occupy. Their resources for collecting material are limited, so ready-made news is a godsend—provided that it is interesting to their audience (or can be made so) and is in a form that is easy to use.

The commonest way of contacting the media with a story that you would like them to publish is to issue a press release. In the past this would have been done at a press conference to which reporters were invited. It is much more common now to use email and to distribute your press release directly to known media contacts, and/or to use the services of a press release distribution service (free or, more likely, paid).

Before constructing a press release, it is worth studying how news reports are put together. If you can pattern your text on actual report style you will make the journalist's job a lot easier and so increase the chances of getting the story published. The report that follows is taken from a regional newspaper and could well have originated in a press release. The main features of the story's structure are shown alongside.

> See also

· CHAPTER 7
Reports (p. 81), where the other common type of report is described—very different, of course, from the press report.

Heading	**LEE'S A HIGH FLIER**
Subhead	**His career is taking off and now at 20 he's teaching others to be pilots**
Lead paragraph	PILOT Lee Bayliss is reaching new heights of expertise in his soaraway career.
Main story	He has become Britain's youngest flying instructor at the age of 20. Lee had his first flying lesson for his 13th birthday, earned his pilot's licence at 17 and got a commercial licence a year later.
	Now Lee, from Twyning, near Tewkesbury, whose ambition is to become an airline pilot, has become an instructor at the South Warwickshire flying school at Stratford upon Avon.
	'I decided I wanted to fly when I was four', he said. 'My mother worries about me. She stopped my father flying because she thought it was too dangerous, but I wouldn't stop'.
Interesting details	Lee worked in a flour factory and took other temporary jobs to raise the £18,000 needed to finance his high-flying career.
	He caught the flying bug while jetting off with his parents Tony and Heather on family holidays.
Background information	Mr Bayliss, aged 47, works as a civil engineer while Lee's brother, also called Tony, 22, runs the family's smallholding.
	'My husband never took his pilot's licence because I was unhappy about him flying', said Mrs Bayliss.
	'I went up with him in a light-aircraft once and didn't like it one bit'.
Comments by people involved	'I tried to talk Lee out of it but he was determined that it was something he wanted to do'.
	'I still worry about him and I make sure that he always rings me after going up to put my mind at rest'.

> Flying-school principal Rodney Galiffe said Lee flew through his exams and got first-time passes in all of them.
>
> 'We've checked it out and he definitely is the youngest instructor, he said.
>
> 'He did everything as quickly as possible and qualified as an instructor in the shortest possible time'.

At first sight the ordering of information in a news story like this seems rather wayward. It appears to jump around in time so that a lot of events that happened at the beginning of the real story (like Lee working to earn money for his lessons) come nowhere near the beginning of the news report. There is a good reason for this, however. Most people do not read a newspaper like a novel, beginning on page 1 and working steadily through until they reach the end. They dot around, scanning a page until something interesting catches their eye. Then they may read just part of the report before moving on again.

The structure of the story about Lee Bayliss is based on this habit of reading. It begins with a **heading** and **sub-heading** designed to catch the eye. The **lead paragraph** continues this approach before the succeeding two or three paragraphs tell the **main story** briefly and clearly. At this point some readers will opt out, but others will be more interested and will have the patience to read on. So the remainder of the report offers more **interesting details** about the main story, **background information** and, if available, **comments by people involved.** This has the added advantage of extending the human interest of the story.

Constructing a press release

When you construct a press release, you should bear all this in mind:

1 Begin with the **name of the organization** issuing the press release and to whom it is directed.

2 State **when** the information can be used. It may be for immediate use, or it may be embargoed until a particular time and date.

3 Give it a **heading** designed to inform readers what the story is about but which also catches their interest.

4 If appropriate add a **lead paragraph** which develops interest and leads into the main story.

5 Tell the **main story** in two or three *short* paragraphs.

6 Follow this with one or two paragraphs containing **interesting details** and another two or three which provide **background information**.

7 If you have any useful **quotations or comments**, use these to round the story off.

At the end of the story should be stated the name of the person who can be contacted for further information and their contact details.

MIKRON LIMITED
MEDIA RELEASE

FOR IMMEDIATE USE

MIKRON SALES REACH NEW RECORD

Mikron Sales Director Andrew Bruce found himself face to face with an elephant on a lonely Tanzanian road while promoting sales of the company's revolutionary new knapsack crop sprayer.

The two-month journey to Kenya, Uganda, and Tanzania was part of Mikron's 1997 drive to top 2 million sales overseas by the end of the year. Andrew Bruce travelled over 5000 miles on dusty tropical roads, visiting regional agricultural advisers, government officials, and leading farmers.

His tour was a triumphant success and the company now has full order books for the rest of the year. It is planning to take on 10 new fulltime staff at its Wolverhampton factory.

But the trip had its worrying moments, as the Mikron Sales Director found when his Landrover broke down in central Tanzania. He was just figuring out what to do, when he turned round and saw he was being approached at some speed by an inquisitive elephant.

'Fortunately he saw that I wasn't a threat and made off,' said the 33-year-old Birmingham man. 'But I have to admit I was a bit worried at the time.'

Mikron Crop Sprayers opened on the Langford Road Industrial Estate in 1991 with a workforce of just three. The last six years have seen the company grow until it now has a turnover of £10 million and employs 23 staff.

Its main products are knapsack-style sprayers with a simple battery-operated pump, which are robust, easy to use and repair, and have an average lifetime of five years. These are particularly effective against the many insect pests that threaten crops of coffee, tea, and cotton in tropical Africa.
'We have a very healthy pattern of investment and technical development,' said Managing Director George Green. 'There is no reason why 1998 should not see even further rapid growth.'

---15TH JANUARY 1998--ENDS------------------------

For further information, please contact:

Jennie Haswell, Press Officer
Mikron Crop Sprayers Ltd
Phone: 01873 467590
Fax: 01873 467591

Whenever possible, give the story a human-interest angle. For example your press release may be about the company's success in doubling its overseas sales of portable crop sprayers; but if your sales director has just returned from an interesting and unusual trip to remote parts of East Africa, use this as a key feature of the story to attract interest.

Links and attachments

An important function of your press release should be to lead readers to the related web page giving further information about its subject matter. So remember to provide clickable links as well as other useful e-data: your email address, Facebook page(s), Twitter handle, and so on. It is also possible to add attachments containing background information and picture files, but this should not be overdone.

The media interview

The interview with press, radio, or TV may come about as a result of a press release, it may be deliberately set up by the organization of which you are a member, or it may come out of the blue.

As remarked earlier, the media have a hunger for new material. This does not mean, however, that if you agree to an interview they will necessarily give you an easy time. You may well find that your agenda and that of the person interviewing you are radically different. In fact, as likely as not you will. This is not surprising. Journalists are entertainers; if they fail to keep the interest of their audience, they fail totally. This means that every interview involves a search for the unusual, the entertaining, the controversial...anything that keeps the reader reading, the listener listening, and the viewer watching.

So you may find that the interview you agreed to give on the economics of farming in North Herefordshire suddenly turns into a heated debate about the ethics of factory farming, or the measured discussion of the merits of secondary-school selection develops into a harangue about falling standards in our schools.

The answer is to be prepared. This may sound paradoxical in the case of the unexpected interview, but it isn't really.

As far as possible it is important to keep control of the terms of the interview. Unless you are desperate to be interviewed and the interviewer is less than enthusiastic, you can normally achieve quite a lot simply because you have got something that the interviewer wants: a slice of your time. So you can make demands and bargain. In particular you should give thought to the advice that follows.

Where and when the interview takes place

Journalists like to keep control of when and where an interview takes place. A press reporter or a radio journalist will often prefer to do the interview by phone; it is easier and saves time. Telephone interviews are also frequently used by TV. If you are happy about that, fine; otherwise insist on a face-to-face meeting at your convenience. Sometimes, particularly for print media, journalists may prefer to conduct an informal interview by email. This allows the interviewee as much time as required to respond to questions.

Telephone interviews have the advantage that you can do them at home or in the office, and so have any necessary notes and other documents to hand. They have the disadvantage—especially in the case of radio and TV—that ultimate control tends to rest with the interviewer, who can always switch you off with ease and poise, whereas unless you are very experienced you will probably just sound petulant if you put the phone down.

If you are confronted by a reporter—in the street, or by telephone—refuse to give an interview unless you are sure you want to. Find out what the interviewer wants and arrange a meeting so that you have time to prepare yourself.

For a face-to-face interview, try to ensure that it is arranged at a time and place to suit you, so that you are relaxed, in familiar surroundings, and not under pressure of time.

The terms of the interview

As noted earlier, your agenda and that of the interviewer may well be different. Ask the interviewer to explain the kind of questions that will be asked. Think carefully about what you are and are not prepared to discuss in public. Explain the guidelines you wish to be observed and make it clear that you mean business. If the journalist goes outside these—and you can be sure that if this happens it won't be accidental—point this out and, if necessary, terminate the interview.

Preparing for the interview

However well you lay down your own guidelines, the interview may well develop into a battle for the agenda. You therefore need to have a clear idea of:

- the topics you want to talk about
- any topics that are off limits
- topics the interviewer may want to raise which you think are less important, or wish to avoid

Suppose, for example, you are the representative of a group promoting traffic-calming measures in your locality. The dangers caused by the pressure and speed of traffic in the area, and the advantages of different traffic-calming schemes are the topics you wish to discuss. Recently, however, the chair of your group resigned after an acrimonious row, news of which soon became public. This is human interest that a journalist might wish to question you about but which you, reasonably, do not wish to discuss, so it is something you should place off limits. On the other hand the questioner may also want to ask you about your career as a rally driver—more human interest. This is an irrelevance as far as you are concerned, but you can expect questions about it and should look to turn them back to your chosen topics. You could point out, for example, that rally drivers are highly trained and drive on roads that are closed to the general public but that many drivers have a fantasy that they are rally drivers when they are driving along the B4224, which is what causes the danger to pedestrians.

If you need to quote facts and figures in the interview, it is a good idea to prepare notes to which you can refer while it is in progress. For a press or radio interview on home ground there is no problem about referring to these, as long as you don't make it too obvious and—in the case of radio—make too much noise rustling paper. In other situations, such as the live TV interview, you will have to use them to refresh your memory before the interview and hope to keep the information clear in your mind that way.

It is a good idea to practise giving answers that are pithy, striking, but above all *short*. This is the age of the sound-bite and there are two good reasons for accepting this situation and working within it. First, your interview may well be heavily edited and you will help that process considerably if you provide plenty of 'quotable quotes'. Secondly, even if the whole interview is broadcast, many listeners will find it much easier to grasp if you concentrate the information and ideas you are giving into neat and digestible 10–15 second 'bites'.

The interview itself

Interviews can be stressful occasions. You probably only do interviews very occasionally, while the interviewer is experienced and practised. However carefully you have prepared, it is difficult to control what happens. The interviewer is the professional and has immediate control of the interview as well as, in many cases, ultimate control of how it will be edited and used. (If you are seriously concerned about being misrepresented, it is a useful idea to make your own recording of the original interview as a check on the way in which it is edited.)

Even if you are feeling stressed about the situation, it is important to appear as relaxed and confident as possible. Don't be rushed into the interview; sometimes radio journalists interviewing by phone launch into their questions after the briefest of introductions. Slow them down by greeting them; take your time.

As the interview progresses, you will probably find that your confidence increases. This should be good for the authority with which you respond to questions, but avoid the dangers of overconfidence. It is easy to say something which you later regret. If in doubt, shut up.

Many interviewers on radio or TV make use of silence as a way of getting their subjects to say more than they originally intended:

> Silence is a wonderful prompter. People—if you don't say anything when they've finished—think, 'Oh, I'd better go on.' So they say something else and very often the thing that they say after that silence is the very thing that you wanted them to say all the time. That's the way to get the last thing out.
>
> **Jenni Mills, broadcaster and writer**

It is difficult to let a silence just hang in the air without feeling you have to break it, but if you have said everything you want to, that is what it is best to do.

During the interview, remember that the interviewer has an agenda and will be constantly guiding the interview so that that agenda is covered. You too have an agenda; if it is not being covered, seek out opportunities to redirect the conversation towards it. (If you want to see how this is done, listen to interviews with politicians; they are experts in this field.)

Above all, don't lose your temper. If you feel that the line of questioning is becoming too personal or is, in some other way, impertinent, remain polite and simply decline to answer.

Assessing the result

Finally, when the interview is over, it is useful to weigh up how it went and seek to learn from what you did. Read the newspaper report based on a press interview; watch or listen to the recording of the broadcast interview. Look out for points where you could have expressed yourself more clearly, and occasions where you could have steered the conversation on to more useful ground. Don't, however, be too self-critical if you don't think you have completely succeeded. Many interviews are compromises. The journalist gets some of the answers he or she wants, while you make some but not all of the points on your list. An interview that you are dissatisfied with is much more likely to be an honourable draw than an out-and-out defeat.

Guidelines

Press release

1 Bear in mind the needs of the journalist when writing your press release.
2 Give it a heading designed to inform readers what the story is about but which also catches their interest.
3 If appropriate, add a sub-heading and/or a lead paragraph which develops interest and leads into the main story.
4 Tell the main story in two or three short paragraphs.
5 Follow this with one or two paragraphs containing interesting details and another two or three which provide background information.
6 If you have any useful quotations or comments, use these to round the story off.
7 At the head of the first page state when the story can be used.
8 At the end give the name and contact details of a person who can provide further information.

Media interview

1 Remember that normally the interviewer needs the interview as much as or more than you.

2 Try to organize the time and place of the interview so that they suit you. At least make sure that you are not interviewed at a time and place that you find difficult or inhibiting.

3 Discuss the terms of the interview and make clear any topics that are off limits.

4 Make sure that you have clear in your mind the points that you want to make.

5 Think about topics that the interviewer may wish to pursue and how you can use them to your advantage.

6 Make notes of any facts, figures, or quotations that you wish to use. If possible have these available during the interview.

7 During the interview, relax as much as possible and try to impose your own pace on it, rather than being hurried.

8 Remember the dangers of overconfidence and don't be led to say things that you will later regret.

9 Don't be pressured by silence into saying more than you intended.

10 Keep your temper and, if necessary, refuse to answer improper questions or deflect them back on to the interviewer.

11 Afterwards assess your performance and note points to remember for future interviews.

> ## Further reading

Judith Byrne, *Face the Media*
(How To Books, 2002), ISBN 9781857037975.

Steven Lewis, *How to Write Perfect Press Releases*
(Taleist 2012), ISBN 9780980855968 (print and e-book versions).

B Getting the message across

10 Audience

We need to be aware of the needs of our audience when writing and speaking. We need to consider their language skills, education, and level of comprehension; their knowledge and understanding of the subject matter; and the relationship we have with them. These three factors will help us choose the best vocabulary, sentence structures, and general style for our purpose.

11 Subject

The subject matter we are writing or speaking about has important effects on the language we use. We need to be precise, and to use the correct terminology required by the subject. On the other hand, we have to try not to use language that is too difficult for our audience; to confuse or irritate them with jargon; or to offend them by being too blunt or too coy. We also need to avoid excessive use of clichés.

12 Time and place

Time and place affect the language we use and the messages we give to each other. We need to be aware of this—especially of how particular situations and institutions tend to determine what we feel we can and cannot say and write.

13 Purpose

All communication takes place for a purpose. Is it to inform, to enquire, to interact, to influence, to regulate, to entertain, to record, or some combination of these? Being aware of our purpose can help us decide our overall approach and select the most suitable vocabulary, sentence structures, and style.

14 Different ways of communicating

Traditionally people have considered that there were four ways of writing and speaking: narrative (story-telling), description, exposition (explanation), and argument. This fourfold approach is still a useful way of looking at the process of communication, especially when we are required to write at any length.

Audience

When we communicate we should be aware of our audience.

Language skills and intelligence

This involves considering:

- age
- education
- intelligence

Assessing the readability of a text includes a consideration of:

- sentence length
- vocabulary

Knowledge and understanding

It is important to:

- be aware of how much the audience is likely to know about the subject
- check their understanding, or give them opportunities to plug gaps in their knowledge as necessary

The relationship between speaker/writer and audience

We need to consider:

- how well we know them
- how formal we wish to be

This affects:

- vocabulary
- sentence grammar

Communication takes place in social situations. When you speak or write you need to think about your audience. You need to consider:

- their language skills
- their knowledge of the subject
- your relationship with them

Language skills and intelligence

You should begin by assessing how skilfully the reader or listener can use the language. For example, it would be unwise to assume that a five-year-old will be able to cope with lengthy and complicated sentences containing many long and unusual words. On the other hand highly educated adults will not take kindly to being addressed as if they had the understanding of five-year-olds.

The three factors we need to bear in mind are:

- age
- education
- intelligence

Writing for children

You can see the importance of readability very clearly if you look at writing for young children. Experienced writers in this field know that they must use:

- a controlled vocabulary
- a limited range of sentence structures

This is illustrated by these two extracts from information books describing how the human eye works:

A   In the middle of each eye there is a small black hole covered by clear skin. It is called your pupil.

Your pupils are like windows. They let in the light rays from everything you look at.

If it is quite dark your pupils get bigger to collect more light. If it is very bright, your pupils get smaller to let less light in.

B   An image of what you are looking at is focused on the retina, which contains about 126 million light-sensitive cells. These cells are divided into two types—rod cells and cone cells. They get their names from their shapes. The brain gets a constant stream of messages from the rods and cones. These messages are transmitted to the brain along the optic nerve.

Rod cells only make a black and white image, so they send black and white messages to the brain. The good thing about rods is that they need only a little light to work. Because there is so much light during the day, the rods are permanently activated. When you first enter a darkened room, you have difficulty seeing things. This is because it takes the rods a few minutes to become dark-adapted.

The child for whom 'A' is suitable will struggle with 'B'. It contains difficult words such as *focused, retina, light-sensitive* and the sentences are longer and more complicated. Conversely, the child for whom 'B' is suitable will find 'A' boring and childish. Both writers have worked hard to make their texts suitable for their intended audience. We can see this by comparing them with a text on the same subject written for adults:

C   The amount of light entering the eye is restricted by the aperture in the iris, the pupil.

   When a person is in a dark room, his pupil is large, perhaps eight millimetres (0.3 inch) in diameter, or more. When the room is lighted there is an immediate constriction of the pupil, the light reflex; this is bilateral, so that even if only one eye is exposed to the light both pupils contract to nearly the same extent. After a time the pupils expand even though the bright light is maintained, but the expansion is not large. The final state is determined by the actual degree of illumination; if this is high, then the final state may be a diameter of only about three to four millimetres (about 0.15 inch); if it is not so high, then the initial constriction may be nearly the same, but the final state may be with a pupil of four to five millimetres (about 0.18 inch).

Here there are far more difficult words, but what really makes the text harder to read is the length and complexity of the sentences. Many adults would struggle to follow this text at a first reading.

Writing for adults

A very common mistake made by those who write for adults is that they underestimate the problems their audience may have in reading their text. Journalists, whose livelihood depends on effective written communication, are very aware of their audience. Newspapers provide a good example of how writers approach different audiences. Compare these two reports of the same news story:

D   Facebook today announced it has topped one billion users each month—about one in seven of the world's population.

   Founder Mark Zuckerberg, 28, said on his Facebook status: 'Helping a billion people connect is amazing, humbling and by far the thing I am most proud of in my life.'

   But he said in a US TV interview that the past few months had not been easy since the firm's lacklustre float on the stock market in May.

   Valued at £62 billion when it went public, Facebook is now worth nearly half that.

   He told NBC: 'We're in a tough cycle and that doesn't help morale but people are focused on what they're building.'

   Some on Wall Street have questioned whether he has the ability to lead a large public company.

But Zuckerberg stressed he was the right person for Facebook, which began life in 2004.

He said: 'I take this responsibility very seriously.'

The firm is facing lawsuits from shareholders and there are concerns about its revenue potential.

The share price has fallen from £23.50 when stocks were first offered in May to Wednesday's closing price of £13.50.

E   Facebook, which has added 100 million active members since April, is now growing fastest in new markets, having reached saturation point in the countries where it first became popular, such as the United States and Britain.

Since its Wall Street flotation in May, Facebook stock has tumbled to little over half its initial value, however, amid doubts it can convert its massive membership and stores of personal data into revenue and profit.

Facebook has admitted it faces a particular challenge from the boom in mobile internet usage and apps, as its advertising business is almost entirely based on its traditional website. Today it said that more than 600 million members now access their account via a mobile device at least once per month, up from 552 million in June.

The firm has introduced a host of new initiatives to try to address the threat and open new revenue streams recently, including gambling, the ability to order gifts for friends via Facebook, and new forms of advertising such as promoted events. It has also overhauled its mobile apps and embarked on a recruitment drive for mobile developers.

Readability

'D' is from a tabloid, while 'E' comes from a broadsheet. Analysing why 'D' is easier to read than 'E' will help to highlight some of the issues involved in readability.

Sentence length

Both texts are the same length, yet 'D' has 10 sentences while 'E' only has 6. So the sentences in 'E' are over one and a half times as long as those in 'D'. Compare:

> See also

- CHAPTER 16
  Introduction to
  grammar
  (p. 187)

- CHAPTER 17
  More about
  grammar
  (p. 203)

D   But he said in a US TV interview that the past few months had not been easy since the firm's lacklustre float on the stock market in May.

Valued at £62billion when it went public, Facebook is now worth nearly half that.

(2 sentences, one of 28 words and one of 15 words)

E   Since its Wall Street flotation in May, Facebook stock has tumbled to little over half its initial value, however, amid doubts it can convert its massive membership and stores of personal data into revenue and profit.

(1 sentence of 36 words)

Advocates of 'Plain English' usually recommend that average sentence length in a text should not exceed 15–20 words. In 'D' the average is 19, while in 'E' it is 31.

Another thing that can cause problems for the reader is the use of too many long words.

What is a 'long' word?

Any word of three or more syllables, but excluding:

- personal names and place names
- verbs which are over two syllables because they have had *-ing*, *-ed*, or *-es* added
- plural nouns which are over two syllables because they have had *-es* added

Using this definition 'D' contains 9 unique long words, while 'E' has 18.

The Gunning fog index

A simple mathematical way of assessing readability is the fog Index. It was devised by the American Robert Gunning, who considered that the more a writer uses long sentences and long words, the more the clarity of the text is 'fogged'. It is calculated like this:

1 Take a sample of about 100 words, ending with the end of a sentence.
2 Count the number of sentences and divide the number of words by the number of sentences to produce the average sentence length (ASL).
3 Count the number of long words (NLW).
4 Perform this calculation:
   Gunning fog index = (ASL + NLW) × 0.4

Using this formula a figure is produced on a scale of readability:

5	easy
10	more difficult
15	difficult
20	very difficult

A commonly used guideline is that the average 15-year-old can cope with texts with an index of 10 while the average level for university students is 14–16.

Extract 'D' has a Gunning fog Index of 8.4, while that of 'E' is 18.

Length is not everything

While calculations like the Gunning fog index are a handy short way of looking at a text (and certainly direct our attention to important features of readability) they do not give the full picture. Shorter sentences are not always easier to read. Compare these two:

1 What figure of us think you he will bear? (9 words)
2 How well do you think he will do when he acts as my representative? (15 words)

Also, not all long words are difficult to read, any more than all short ones are easy. Anyone who has helped a small child learn to read will know that it is not just the length of a word that causes problems. Children can sometimes read quite long words at a very early age. If a word is part of a child's spoken vocabulary and has a distinctive shape—like *elephant*, for example—then it may be recognized quite easily.

Similar considerations apply to adult readers. Extract 'D' contains few difficult long words. Most of the three-syllable words are in common use—like *population* and *billion*. While 'E' has its share of such words, it also includes more demanding vocabulary like *saturation* and *initiatives*. Clearly the more common a long word is, the fewer problems it will cause the average reader.

The frequency with which words occur in normal use is another guide to difficulty; the less common a word, the more likely it is to cause problems. As long ago as 1932 C. K. Ogden created the *Basic English Word List* containing the 850 commonest and most useful words in the English language. (It can be found online at <http://ogden.basic-english.org/words.html>.) Ogden extended his list to 2,000 words, by adding a number of slightly more specialist lists. He considered that a mastery of this 2,000-word list constituted a mastery of standard English vocabulary. More information is available at <http://ogden.basic-english.org/word2000.html>. Modern linguists would qualify this, of course, but the assessment of word frequency and familiarity is still an important feature of the creation of texts that are easy to read.

You try

These three extracts are all about the same subject, but are at different levels of difficulty. What kind of audience do you think each would be suitable for, and why?

A Mummies are the first things most people think about at the mention of Ancient Egypt, but what exactly are they and how and why were they made? Although the term 'mummy' is associated with Ancient Egypt, it is also applied to preserved bodies from many other cultures. The word itself comes from the Arabic name for 'bitumen', and was used to describe these bodies because their black appearance suggested that they had been coated in pitch. Most of the bandaged mummies that have survived date from the New Kingdom or the later half of Egyptian history. By this time, the embalming process, which had previously been reserved for royalty, became available to all who could afford it.

→

B The Ancient Egyptians were firm believers in life after death. But first you had to make sure your soul survived in the next world. This wouldn't happen if your body was left to rot away. And so you were mummified to make you last!

C Traditionally, the royal body was first washed and anointed, after which mortuary priests removed the viscera by way of a small incision in the left side of the abdomen. By the 18th dynasty, the removal of the brain was also common—usually through the nostrils, but occasionally in other ways (the cranial tissue of King Amosis was removed through an incision at the back of the neck). The liver, lungs, stomach and intestines were extracted, treated and stored in canopic containers and the body packed with absorbent materials which hastened the process of desiccation. The body was then placed on a slanted bed and covered with powdered natron. After 40 days the body would have lost some 75 per cent of its weight through the dehydrative action of this salt-like compound and it was then rewashed, dried, bandaged and adorned with protective amulets—each stage of the process being carried out with the recitation of appropriate spells and incantations.

See page 373 to find out where these texts came from.

Knowledge and understanding

Some audiences are self-defining. If you are preparing copy for an automotive parts catalogue, for example, it is reasonable to assume that your reader knows quite a lot about cars and how they work. On the other hand, the writer of 'The reluctant car mechanic' could not make such an assumption, but could safely expect that his readers were interested in the subject and willing to make the effort to understand what he was telling them.

These two texts about growing roses clearly assume very different audiences:

A **Roses**
Preparation and Planting
All types of rose do best in a sunny well-drained area, but they are tough and will survive fairly unfavourable conditions. As always, make sure the ground is well prepared with animal manure, especially on light sandy soils, and the bottom of the planting hole broken up to ensure good drainage. The roots should be well spaced. Standards and half standards will need staking.

B Culture of Dwarf Roses: Soil, deep, rich loam well enriched with decayed manure. Add clay and cow dung to light soils, road grit, leaf-mould, burnt refuse, horse dung and lime to heavy soils. Do not mix lime with manure but apply to surface after manure has been well dug in. Position, sunny beds or borders. Plant, Nov.; or Feb. to March, average distance apart 18 in. to 2 ft. Depth of soil over roots should be 4 to 6 in. on heavy and 7 to 8 in. on light soils. Prune end of March or early in April. Hybrid Perpetuals should have damaged and weak shoots removed and others shortened to dormant bud to 18 in. from base according to strength...

Other situations are not so simple. Any writing done for 'a general audience' can be much more problematic. It is safest to assume little or no prior knowledge of your subject, unless you have good reason to believe otherwise. Far more people have been put off reading a text because they could not understand it than because they were offended at being treated like idiots. The latter can, in any case, be avoided by allowing for different levels of knowledge and making the structure of your text clear: 'The first part of this text is introductory and can be skipped by those who have some knowledge of the subject...'.

Checking the channel

In conversations, we can check that the assumptions we have made about another person's knowledge are correct. I can tell from my audience's facial expressions and other non-verbal signals (gestures, nods, grunts, and so on) whether my subject matter is one which is familiar and whether I am tackling it at the right level. In a written text this is more difficult, although sometimes it may be done quite explicitly. A letter may say, 'Please contact me for further details.' An instruction book can suggest, 'If you are not sure how to..., turn to page...'.

You try

These two texts both come from the introductions to instruction booklets for computer users. What level of knowledge do you think each assumes in its readers?

A Moving the monitor
Handle the monitor with care. Carry the monitor with its screen facing you (most of its weight is near the screen). If you have to bend to lift it, bend at your knees, not your waist. Leave a few inches behind the monitor clear when you position it so you can tilt and swivel it freely on its base.

B The preparation of a drive or cartridge for use by Macintosh is done at three levels. The low level format writes over the entire disk, erasing all data. The partition operation divides the space on the drive into separate areas, or partitions, including one (or more) areas to hold your files. It also sets aside an area for a table of partitions, and an area for the software which operates the drive. Partitioning or re-partitioning your drive effectively erases any data held on it. The third layer...

Comments on these two texts will be found on page 374.

What is the relationship?

Our relationship with our audience affects the way in which we frame even the most casual message. The better you know people, the more relaxed you can be about the way in which you express yourself to them. This works at many different levels. With a person you know very well, for example, you can use words that carry a special meaning which only they will understand. Some people have a complete private language reserved for a particular relationship. At the other end of the scale, we have to be much more careful when addressing people we do not know at all.

The choices speakers and writers make are often subtle and complicated and usually take place without conscious thought. But it is useful to set out some of the more obvious features of them.

One way of looking at the effects of relationship on language is to ask two simple questions:

- How well do we know each other?
- How close or distant do I want to be?

We can represent this on a simple diagram:

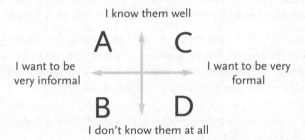

It might seem strange to think of communicating very formally with someone whom you know very well, but such situations can occur: for example, a letter about the distribution of family property from a husband to his wife following an acrimonious divorce.

Effects on language

How we view the relationship can affect:

- choice of vocabulary
- use of short forms in writing
- choice of pronouns
- choice of standard or non-standard grammar

Vocabulary

➤ See also
- CHAPTER 18
  Vocabulary
  (p. 217)

Some words are considered by many people to be informal, colloquial, slang, or even obscene. Dictionaries often indicate this by abbreviations, for example:

colloq.	colloquial
inf.	informal
sl.	slang

Such definitions can be misleading, however. It is very difficult to draw a clear line between what is 'formal' and what is 'informal' language. Language is constantly developing as society changes; words come and go, and yesterday's slang is often acceptable today. For example, in Shakespeare's day, if you called someone *naughty* it was a serious accusation of moral depravity. Today it is normally reserved as a term of mild reproof for children and if applied to adults is used ironically or archly. By contrast, Chaucer did not consider the word *shit* unsuitable for a poem to be read aloud in mixed upper-class society, whereas it would still not be acceptable in some social settings today.

Use of contractions in writing

With people we know and can relax with, it is quite acceptable to use contractions like *can't* and *shouldn't* in writing. In more formal settings this is still frowned on, although here usage is clearly on the move.

Choice of pronouns in writing

In this book I have made use of *I* and *you*, when referring to the writer and the reader. This is considered by some people to be rather informal; they would prefer that the writer remained anonymous and the reader was referred to in the third person. Instead of writing:

> If you are consulting this book, it probably means that you have a particular problem in mind.

they would prefer:

> Most people who consult a book like this do so because they have a particular problem in mind.

Dialects often use grammatical forms that are different from those of Standard English. Here, for example, is an account of how the speaker used to leave dough to rise and then bake it to make bread:

> Well, I leaves it in yewn for about twenty minutes and then I has a look at it to see how it's ganning on. And if it, oven isn't hot enough, I pokes fire up. And if it is over hot, I shoves damper in. Then I, when it's had another twenty minutes, I has another look at it and see how it's ganning on. And then I leaves it another twenty minutes, then it should be ready.

This dialect, from East Yorkshire, contains different vocabulary from standard English: 'yewn' for 'oven', and 'ganning on' for 'getting on'. The grammar is different, too. She says 'I leaves' instead of 'I leave'.

Standard or non-standard grammar

Many people, including children, commonly switch between dialect and a more standard form of English according to their audience. For children, standard English is more suitable when talking to schoolteachers, for example. On the other hand their peers might laugh at them if they used it in the playground. Similar shifting is done by many adults as they move from one social setting to another.

There are certain situations in which many people find it difficult to address their audience using the right tone. One of these is when writing letters to newspapers. The following letter was sent to a local newspaper shortly after the announcement that the local cathedral had accepted a donation from a company that processes battery-farmed chickens. What is wrong with it?

Cathedral support for Sun Valley?

How ennobling of Hereford Cathedral to broiler breeders as the presumed epicentre for our community's future new spiritual and ethic values, to be seen through your columns (intentionally or otherwise) as seeming to confer recent 'blessing' upon those involved in the trade's intensive factory-farming methods by accepting local charity from the profits of same to restore a part of its permanently crumbling edifice.

Nowadays, the 'established Church' desires to be perceived as 'Being-All-Things-To-All-Men', a self-delusion by which she considers it 'Good-for-God's Business' and often AN Other's too!, the latter view relating to our cathedral's acceptance of charity from Hereford's (reported) 'largest employer'. That company will now doubtless be 'over-the-moon' as a result of the report of October 17.

Somewhat ironically, the very nature of that article could not avoid affording the donor great satisfaction in being given publicity (always eagerly sought) when involved in its chosen philanthropy.

At present, the company basks in its warm relationship with the Hereford Cathedral authorities.

This seems tantamount to it believing that our cathedral condones, even if it does not perhaps tacitly support, the ethics of intensive factory-farming, which Sun Valley Foods cannot deny that it is directly involved in.

I therefore call on the Dean and Chapter of Hereford to now publicly clarify and confirm, through the columns of The Hereford Times if possible, their stance on this highly emotive subject. Caring people are utterly disgusted by these factory farming practices. The church, by reason of locally associating itself with Sun Valley Foods, now has an urgent duty to explain its attitude.

See page 374 for comments.

Guidelines

Language skills and education

1 Think carefully about the audience's language skills, especially when writing or speaking:
   - for children
   - for speakers of English as a second or foreign language
   - for a general audience who may include a wide range of readers
   - about subjects where it is vital that every word is clearly understood—for example in matters of public safety

2 Make written text more readable by keeping sentence length down. 15–20 words per sentence is often considered to be a good average to aim for.

3 Difficult and 'long' words (three syllables or more) contribute to the difficulty of a text. When aiming for simplicity, either use shorter words or make sure that difficult words are explained or set in a context which helps the reader.

Knowledge and understanding

4 Make a careful assessment of:
   - how much your audience is likely to know about the subject
   - what background information you need to provide

5 In speech, check that you have got the knowledge level right by monitoring the reactions of your audience. In writing, consider the possibility of providing additional background information in a 'skippable' introduction or an appendix to which readers can refer.

Relationship with the audience

6 Decide how well you and your audience know each other and how close or distant you wish to be when you address them. This will determine how formal or informal your tone should be.

7 Make sure that your
   - vocabulary
   - use of long or contracted forms (e.g. *is not/ isn't*)
   - choice of pronouns (e.g. *I* or *one*)
   - standard or non-standard grammar
   support the decision you have made about tone.

11 Subject

The subject matter we wish to communicate affects the language we use. A number of considerations affect our final choice:

- The need to use language precisely.
- Avoiding confusing the audience by using words and expressions they do not understand.
- Making sure not to exclude them by the use of jargon.
- The risk of causing emotional offence and the dangers of euphemism.
- Problems caused by hackneyed expressions and clichés.

Naturally the subject we are talking about has a powerful influence on the language we use. For example, it is difficult to talk about using a computer without using words like *screen*, *mouse*, *cursor*, and *hard drive*.

Choosing the best words is thus an important part of effective communication. There are five factors that affect this process and determine how effectively you communicate:

- precision
- confusion
- exclusion
- emotion
- style

Precision

See also
- CHAPTER 18
Vocabulary
(p. 217)

Language should always be as precise as possible. So, for example, if you wish to refer to a *split-image rangefinder* when talking about a camera, then that is the phrase you must use.

Or is it? The use of such 'technical terms' is fine if your readers know and understand them. But what if they don't? Sometimes it doesn't matter too much if the reader does not know the precise meaning of all the words in a passage. Consider, for example, this short text:

> The music the children provided was exciting, colourful, and exotic. They used a wide range of instruments. The younger ones had fun playing simple percussion instruments like timbales and bongos. Others played ocarinas, maracas, and guiros, while the melody was provided by two older students playing a zither and a balalaika.

Many readers will not know *exactly* what all these instruments are or what kind of sound they make, but it doesn't really matter; the overall impression is clear and ignorance of what a *guiro* is does not spoil it.

On the other hand, consider these sentences:

> When you move up from a simple point-and-shoot camera to a DSLR, you discover a whole new world of controls and complexity. To begin with, you have to decide what ISO to use, and whether to go with programmed exposure, aperture priority, shutter priority, or fully manual control.

If readers don't know what 'exposure' and 'ISO' mean, they are lost. The writer could argue that they will just have to look the words up in a dictionary. The *Oxford English Dictionary* offers the following for 'exposure':

> **exposure**, Photogr. The exposing of a sensitized surface to the action of actinic rays; also, the time occupied by this action. Also attrib., as exposure meter n. a device that indicates the correct time to allow a film, etc., to be exposed.

which is fairly heavy going. However, the dictionary offers no help with 'ISO'. For this, you need to go to a dictionary of photographic terms, such as that available on the PhotoNotes.org website (<http://photonotes.org/ dictionary/>), which explains that 'ISO' refers to:

> International Organization for Standardization. (yes, it's not IOS) The Swiss-based international agency responsible for coordinating every kind of international standard imaginable, including film speed standards. Most exposure indices or film speeds today are described by the ISO system, which uses the same numeric values as the old ASA system (eg: ISO 100, 400, 800). The slower the film the lower the number. By today's standards ISO 100 is slow film and ISO 800 or 1600 is fast film. Though it should be noted that these speeds represent technical advances in film technology—as recently as a couple of decades ago, 64 was slow and 200 or 400 was thought of as fairly fast.
> Technically the ISO standard seems to list both the ASA-style film speed and the DIN-style film speed (eg: ISO 100/21°) which is an

informationally redundant compromise. To the undoubted dismay of the Germans, however, hardly anyone uses the DIN numbers anymore.

Digital cameras do not use film and so cannot have film speed ratings as such. However, many digital cameras have adjustable light sensitivity levels, and these adjustable levels are stated as ISO film speed equivalents, simply because the ISO film speed numbers are a well-understood and handy convention.

Again, this is detailed and complicated information to take in. So it is important to consider carefully how much background knowledge readers may have, and how much technical terminology you need to include. Precision is desirable, but not if it leads to confusion.

Confusion

Confusion is caused when the writer or speaker assumes a higher level of expertise than the audience actually possess. This has already been touched on in Chapter 10, but the point is worth pursuing.

Essentially you can do one of three things:

- avoid using words your audience may have difficulty with
- use them and explain them at the time, or in a glossary
- use them and not explain them

The first approach is suitable for some kinds of writing and speaking for children (although if they never hear the 'difficult' words for things they have no chance of ever learning them). This approach can also be used when presenting simple (or simplified) material for adults, but it is important to be sure that you are not talking down to your audience, which quickly gives offence.

The second approach is more useful for a wide range of writing and speaking for adults. Care is needed to make sure that too many explanations and definitions do not obscure the main thread of what is being explained.

The third approach might seem rather off-putting, but it depends on the situation. Many general readers, for example, might find the following text fairly impenetrable:

Every lens projects a disc of light, the base of a right circular cone whose apex is at the centre of the exit pupil of the lens (page 48). The illumination of this disc falls off towards the edges, at first gradually and then very rapidly. The limit to this circle of illumination is set by the rapid fall-off due to natural vignetting (page 52) as distinct from any concomitant mechanical vignetting. Also, owing to the presence of residual lens aberrations, the definition of the image within this disc deteriorates from the centre of the field outwards, at first gradually and then more rapidly. By defining an acceptable standard of image quality, it is possible to locate an outer boundary defining a circle of acceptable definition within this circle of illumination.

The text is intended for professional photographers. If the authors were to explain every single term used, the book would become impossibly long and most of its intended readers would be irritated by being told things they already knew.

So it is a matter of judgement. When you are speaking to an audience you can work out from their reactions whether you are getting it right. In a book this is impossible, but it underlines again the importance of giving very careful thought to exactly who your audience are.

These two extracts are about similar subjects. How do they differ, and could either be written more clearly and/or contain more explanation?

A **Benefit Value**

(a) At the Pension Date, Investment Units allocated to each Arrangement to be vested will be cancelled and the value calculated in accordance with Condition 27(b). The amount so calculated is the 'Benefit Value'.

The Benefit Value will be applied at GA Life's immediate annuity rates (taking account of any relevant charges) current at the date Investment Units are cancelled to secure an annuity payable during the Member's lifetime by monthly payments in arrear from the Pension Date without proportion to the date of death.

B The biggest-ever pensions shake-up comes into force on Monday, when all firms have to start enrolling workers into company schemes.

It will mean many lower-paid workers will have the chance for the first time to put cash away towards their retirement and have contributions from their employer to boost funds.

The Government is singing the praises of the new scheme, saying that it will mean more than a half a million will be saving into a pension for the first time by Christmas.

→

> But the reality could mean little difference to the historically low numbers of workers saving for their future—less than one in three adults currently save into a pension.
> While we need something drastic to lift the pensions system out of crisis and to encourage younger workers to put something away to fund their retirement, auto-enrolment may not be the saviour the Government is hoping for.

See page 374 for comments.

Exclusion

A text that is confusing because of the technical language it uses excludes readers or listeners who cannot understand it. It is also possible to exclude an audience—deliberately or unintentionally—by using 'insider' language:

> **Does your bandwidth need a boost?**
>
> If you want to deliver your files at warp speed, add a little rocket fuel to your workflow with iSDN Manager™ Primary Rate.
>
> Utilizing all 30 channels, iSDN Manager™ Primary Rate delivers even a 100MB file anywhere on earth in just 10 minutes; or up to 15 simultaneous transfers makes iSDN Manager™ Primary Rate the obvious solution for even the busiest of pre-press departments.
>
> Boldly delivering your files with the simplest drag & drop, iSDN Manager™ comes in many guises: single or multi user, internal or external ISDN hardware devices, portable or desktop machines, MacOS, Windows 3.1, '95 or NT. And if ISDN 30 at 12.5MB per minute is too far into hyperspace, there's always ISDN 2 or ISDN 8 to choose from.

 See also
• CHAPTER 18
Vocabulary
(p. 217)

This is computer **jargon** and is designed to appeal to potential purchasers who use, or are entertained by, such language. If it puts off other people because they find it irritating, that doesn't matter, because it was not intended for them anyway.

There are occasions, however, when it is possible to exclude people with whom you wish to communicate by using language they regard as irritating jargon. It is often said that one person's technical term is another's jargon. This is a little extreme; in many fields there are certain technical terms which cannot be avoided, as we have seen. But excessive use of technical terminology and certainly use of 'insider talk' *is* jargon and *does* put people off. So it should be avoided.

You try

The writer of this report probably did not think he was using jargon. What do you think? If it is jargon, how could it be made more 'reader-friendly'?

These principles underpinning effective performance appraisal have wider relevance than simply improvements in individual performance. They are also concerned with the development of a participative organizational culture by contributing to the broader goals of creating satisfying, effective jobs, encouraging the involvement of people in the organization, and the development of people.

Failure to view the performance appraisal strategically as an important element in an involved organizational culture committed to the development of its individual members has resulted in problems. The early emphasis on the feedback principle, i.e. letting people know how they are performing, neglecting the involvement of the individual in the process, cast appraisers in the uncomfortable role of judge and often resulted in damage to individual development and involvement and commitment to the organization.

See page 374 for comments.

Emotion

➤ See also
- CHAPTER 18
  Vocabulary
  (p. 217)

There are situations in which we may not wish to use the most technically accurate language because it could hurt or offend our audience. For example, when breaking the news of a death to a close friend or member of the family, many people avoid blunt words such as *died* and prefer expressions such as *passed away*. This use of language is referred to as **euphemism**.

Euphemistic language is commonly used by people when talking about death, certain kinds of illness (e.g. cancer), sex, and other bodily functions such as excretion. It even affects the language used to describe certain parts of the body. For example, that part which is most accurately referred to as the *belly* is much more frequently called the *stomach* (inaccurate) or *tummy* (euphemistic).

We should, however, be wary of excessive use of simple or childish language. Doctors are sometimes accused of underestimating the linguistic maturity of their patients and of using unnecessarily euphemistic language. ('Any problems with the waterworks, Mrs Green?') This can not only be insulting, but may simply lead to further confusion, as in the famous story of the doctor who was explaining to a patient how to use a suppository and told him to 'place it in the back passage'. 'I did as he said,' the patient told a friend, 'and put it just outside the back door, but I might as well have stuck it up my arse for all the good it did.'

Once again, it is a question of balancing the requirements of the subject matter with the needs of our audience. It is desirable not to cause unnecessary offence, but it is important to make sure that the message is communicated accurately. If the message is essentially one of sympathy, then we can speak sensitively and avoid hurtful bluntness. If it is essentially factual, then it is important to use words that leave no room for confusion, and any concern about the emotional impact of what is said has to come second.

Style

There is another way in which you can unintentionally offend your audience, and that is by exhibiting linguistic 'tics' and using hackneyed phrases, or tired once-fashionable expressions, known as **clichés:**

> In the good old days it was all down to the private individual to earn an honest penny and make ends meet, but in this day and age all that's gone by the board. Life's a lottery and when push comes to shove, it's every man for himself.

Everybody uses clichés from time to time. They are formulae that save time and thought. Often they add little of substance to what we are saying, and just give a general impression of the line we are taking or the attitude we are presenting. They have little or no real meaning and if we use them too much we not only diminish the content of what we are trying to say, but run a severe risk of alienating our audience. Indeed, many people have a personal list of clichés they hate; if they hear another person use one of them, then that person immediately goes down in their estimation.

Guidelines

1 Choose language carefully to convey the precise meaning required.
2 Be aware of the problems your audience may have with technical terminology.
3 Don't use jargon or insider language unless you are sure that your audience will appreciate it.
4 By all means avoid hurting people's feelings or giving offence, but avoid relying on euphemism. It is better to speak plainly and communicate clearly even at the risk of causing offence than to fail to communicate at all.
5 Watch out for over-reliance on clichés: hackneyed expressions and other tired, once-fashionable turns of phrase.

12 Time and place

Time and place affect the language we use and the messages we pass to each other.

- Many situations in life are like scenes in a play, scripted by one or more of the people taking part.
- Some institutions take advantage of this to control the way in which people behave.
- A major element of this control is their use of language.
- Understanding how this works can help us to communicate with more confidence and success.

It may seem unlikely, but time and place affect what we say or write and how we do it. The physical setting determines what we can and cannot say.

An example: selling clothes

- The time: mid-morning on a wet weekday.
- The place: an open-air market in the centre of Birmingham.
- A crowd of people are gathered around the open side of a long lorry piled high with clothing and household linen. In the centre a small stage provides room for an energetic market trader and his two assistants. The trader is in full flow. He shows his audience a page in a mail-order clothing catalogue:

Will you just raise your hand in the audience if you like that dress, I'm not asking you to buy it, if you like it. You can all see it there in the picture, with the price, 24.99. Yeah? What I'm going to do with you, is this: if you buy that dress, there is another one on that page, I'm gonna have a right little deal with you if you buy that dress. OK? Hands in the air if you said you liked it. Then put your hands back up if you could afford a fiver . . . You could? Well I'll tell you what I'm going to do with you. You know who I am don't you? I'm Mick and I work on Birmingham Market on a Tuesday, Friday, and Saturday and I'm the cheapest in the country, OK? Get your money out—have a look in your pockets, have a look in your bra, in your knickers wherever you keep your money—shoot your hands up as fast as you can, and give me 2 pounds 99 . . .

25 pounds that dress my price 3 quid and on the top I'm going to do something now that is totally immoral and against all good trading practices and I'll do it and get away with it. It's only me who could. Did I say to you I always keep my promise? Did I say to you that there was another dress on that page that I was gonna give you free of charge? Yes? All those people who can show me a dress they've already bought is in for that.

This text could only exist in this particular setting. Mick can only use the words and sentences he does in this particular place and time.

If the women in his audience went round the corner to a large department store at sales time, they would not expect the shop assistant to speak to them in this way. They might well have a conversation about price and value for money, but it would be in very different terms.

The setting allows Mick a number of 'liberties' with his audience, some of whom are regulars, but many of whom are hearing him for the first time. He can joke with them, speak in his highly individual, racy style, and even use language which some of them might, in other settings, find mildly embarrassing or even offensive. The context gives him his licence to do this—and if anyone doesn't like it they have only to walk away to another stall and another trader.

Theatres of life

 See also

- CHAPTER 4
  Job applications
  (p. 41)
- CHAPTER 9
  The media
  (p. 105)

Mick has set up his own theatre in which he is not only lead actor but scriptwriter and director as well. The rest of us are both audience and bit-part players. We can, admittedly, take it or leave it, but we would find it difficult to change the script of the drama. You might argue that this is an extreme case, but it isn't really. There are many much more ordinary situations which work in a similar way: in a job interview, for example, the script is largely written by the person(s) conducting the interview and the interviewee has little choice but to accept the role allotted to him or her in the drama.

Institutions

Sometimes we are so weak that 'the scriptwriters' take advantage of their power and use it to control all our behaviour. It is a common complaint about hospitals that they deliberately cast patients in a very subordinate role so that they will behave in ways that are convenient to the staff. This is satirized in the following extract from an American novel. The narrator is in a private ward, recovering from a car crash:

> A middle-aged nurse nurse popped her head through the door, 'How are we doing?'
>
> 'Some of us are doing better than others. Do you know when Dr Herschel is coming back?'
>
> 'Probably around seven.' The nurse came in to feel my pulse. If there isn't anything else to do, make sure the patient's heart is still beating. Gray eyes twinkled with meaningless jollity in her red face.
>
> 'Well, we're certainly a lot stronger than we were a few hours ago. Is the shoulder giving us any pain?'
>
> I looked at her sourly. 'Well, it isn't giving me any—I don't know about you.'

The writer picks up the nurse's use of *we* instead of *you* as part of the way in which some medical experts attempt to depersonalize the interaction. (If the nurse can thus avoid having a 'you and I' conversation, she can avoid becoming personally involved with the patient's suffering.) The use by health workers of the patient's first name, rather than title plus family name, can also diminish the individual's status. The practice is significantly less common in private hospitals. A similar set of institutional pressures is often at work when an individual visits a large government or local authority office, or a large company.

Telephone calls

It might be objected that all this is well known but that the knowledge that the individual is likely to be weak and manipulated when up against a large institution is of little practical use. But this is not so.

First, it is important to remember that the main means used to achieve and control these situations are linguistic. So it is helpful to pick up the ways in which language is being manipulated—such as the use of 'we' in the extract quoted earlier. Secondly, if one can observe the ways in which the script of the situation has been written, it may be possible to take it over and rewrite it to one's own ends. A common technique used by companies dealing with telephone complaints goes like this:

CALLER:	Could you put me through to the Customer Services Department, please?
SWITCHBOARD:	Who shall I say is calling?
CALLER:	Jane Pershore.
SWITCHBOARD:	And what company is it?
CALLER:	Well, it isn't a company, it's just—
SWITCHBOARD:	Putting you through…

The caller is made to feel inferior because she isn't calling on behalf of a company, but is 'just' a private individual—and when she starts to explain is cut off by the switchboard in mid-sentence.

It is important to understand what is being done and the way in which the switchboard operator's language has—or can have—the effect of diminishing the caller's confidence and effectiveness. If you remember this, then it can help you to remain confident and focused on the task in hand. It is also helpful to have found out the name of the person who deals with the type of enquiry you are making.

Of course you can always go one step further and make up a company name—preferably as long and impressive-sounding as possible:

CALLER:	Could you put me through to Mark Wood, please?
SWITCHBOARD:	Who shall I say is calling?
CALLER:	Jane Pershore.
SWITCHBOARD:	And what company is it?
CALLER:	(*Speaking very quickly*) Amalgamated Inshore Biotechnology Computer Services
SWITCHBOARD:	Amalgamated Inshore Bio—Sorry what was that again?

Written texts

One of the commonest ways in which institutions manipulate individuals in written texts is the use of forms. If you want to apply for a job, apply for a payment of some kind, or even tell a company what you think of their products, you have to fill in a form. Forms inhibit freedom of expression:

- They control what you can write about. If there isn't a question about a topic, you cannot write about it.
- They decide the structure and sequence of your writing. Having to present information in a particular order can sometimes change the complete message.
- They determine how much you can write on a given topic.

On the other hand, forms are a convenient way for organizations to collect information in a format that enables them to process it quickly and efficiently. So how you respond to being asked to fill in a form depends on:

- the message you wish to communicate
- your judgement of how the reader will react
- how much this reaction matters to you

It is easy enough to overcome all the restrictions and subvert a form: you can ignore questions, add more information than has been allowed for (by pasting on flaps of paper), and give information that has not been requested. You can even redesign the form and produce your own 'reconstructed' version. More conventionally, you can refer the reader to an additional sheet of information enclosed with the form itself.

On the other hand, if you are completing a passport application form, or completing a tax return, it is advisable to 'do as you are told'. Otherwise the only result will be that your application or tax return is rejected and you have to start all over again.

With something like a customer satisfaction form you can do whatever you like. All you risk is that your form will be thrown away and you will not be entered for the prize draw—if there is one. A job application is rather different. By demonstrating your independence you may go up in the estimation of your prospective employer; or you may be marked down as a potential troublemaker.

Working on the inside

Institutions can also put linguistic pressure on those who work within them. They can require the individual to speak in a particular way when addressing others. The army requires other ranks to use particular language when addressing officers; nurses are expected to speak to doctors in an 'acceptable' way; schools require the same of pupils and teachers. Similar expectations may apply with written texts. The institution may produce its own forms which have to be completed by employees; reports and memos may have to be written using a specific vocabulary and sentence style.

Often these expectations are made clear when the individual joins the institution. It does not take long to work out the extent to which you have to adhere to the rules, and how far you can bend and use them for your own purposes. Sometimes, however, there are no clear guidelines. The institution appears to operate a kind of code but what this is and the rules which govern it are not made clear to the newcomers. They have at first to operate like anthropologists meeting a completely unknown tribe, noting behaviour patterns without initially knowing what they mean.

Guidelines

1 Whenever you are in a new language situation—even if it only involves one other person—try to assess how far it is being 'scripted' by someone else, and how this is being done.

2 If it is being scripted, decide how happy you are about this, whether you want to change the script, and how this can be done.

3 When contacting an organization or institution as a member of the public, be aware of how language may be used to control the situation.

4 Again, decide whether you want to go along with this, or to seek to change the situation. But also be aware of the risks involved. (You can, for example, make hospital staff address you in the way you want, but the cost may be that you are labelled as 'difficult'.)

5 As a new member of an institution take trouble to find out what 'the rules' governing language are and how well they are kept. Then assess how you will respond.

(13) Purpose

There are seven main purposes for writing and speaking:

- to interact
- to inform
- to find out
- to influence
- to regulate
- to entertain
- to record

It might seem obvious why people write or speak to each other: they do so to communicate. Communication involves conveying information, feelings, and ideas from one person or group to another. The more precisely and clearly we do this the more effectively we are communicating.

Everyday experience, however, suggests that things may be rather less simple. This is the beginning of a very ordinary telephone conversation between two neighbours:

> A: John—Anthony here.
> B: Hullo.
> A: How are you?
> B: I'm fine.
> A: Good. I've got your keys which I must remember to bring round.
> B: Yes...
> A: Er, they're spare keys are they?
> B: Yeah...er, yes...they're...sorry, there's no problem. There's no need for you to bring them round—I'll pop over.
> A: Or I'll pop them through or something...

The conversation contains about sixty words. It is true that some information and ideas are communicated: 'Anthony here' is essential information at the beginning of the conversation, unless B is to be left to work out who the speaker is. It might seem, too, that 'I've got your keys' is useful information, too, until we reflect that presumably B knows that A has got his keys. And what information or ideas are conveyed by this exchange?

B: ...I'll pop over.
A: Or I'll pop them through or something...

It really does not matter to either of them exactly what is done about a spare set of keys and indeed the whole purpose of the phone call is something of a mystery until A gets to the point:

A: Or I'll pop them through or something...um, what kind of broadband router have you got?

He wants to discuss computers, so why did he begin by talking about keys? In fact the beginning of the conversation is not about communicating information or ideas at all, but is to establish (or re-establish) the channel of communication between two people. The language is a kind of code; A and B are really saying to each other: 'Look, we are two people who know each other fairly well and last time we met it had to do with keys. This conversation continues from there.'

You might ask, 'Why do it?' If we remove the 'chat' from the conversation, we see why:

A: John.
B: Hullo.
A: What kind of broadband router have you got?

While this would achieve A's purpose in calling, it would seem abrupt and even rude. Social intercourse often requires a more leisurely approach.

The seven purposes

We use language for a wide variety of purposes, which include communicating information and ideas, and when we speak or write—especially in more formal situations—it is helpful to reflect on what our main purposes are. This chapter examines the more common purposes for speaking and writing.

To interact

As we have seen, an important function of language is to help us get on with other people, to interact. In the example above this formed part of a larger purpose: the caller A wanted to enquire about types of computer modems. He was using language to find out.

Sometimes language is used primarily to interact:

Subject: Re: Mislaid friend!

Dear Anne,

It is really good to hear from you again specially as I had mislaid your postal address and only had your old email address. Must store this one safely. It seems ages ago since you moved.

Have just had an unexpected Bank holiday visit from Maria. We had some lovely walks – even in the rain – and did 14+ miles in all. I feel much better for it. I've got some excellent books of walks and you go through all sorts of villages you would otherwise not visit – also some beautiful and interesting churches. She went back to London just after lunch yesterday as she had an invitation to a champagne party followed by a prom concert at the Albert Hall. Every now and then she gets this sort of invitation. I once went with her to a preview of the Chelsea Flower Show.

Jane is in Mexico with Jessie and family at the moment – she will be there for 6 weeks before returning to Indonesia. Have just had an email from her and they've been to all sorts of parties. Jane reckons the Mexicans really know how to enjoy themselves. When her contract at the International School ended she didn't renew it as she was fed up with teaching there and also got back all the income tax she had paid the Indonesian Govt – extraordinary arrangement. James has signed on for another year and after that they may well end up in Kenya. She is busy writing and illustrating a children's book – apparently she has long wanted to do this. She may well do voluntary work when she gets back to Jakarta.

Even here information and ideas are being communicated as well. Normally this use of language takes place between people who have met or had some kind of contact even if only by email or telephone. But it can also take place when the speaker and the listener are completely unknown to each other, as in many local radio phone-in programmes.

This kind of language use is sometimes referred to—dismissively—as small talk: 'I'm afraid I'd be no good at that; I've got no small talk.' Yet interacting with others forms an important part of most people's lives and the ability to talk to people one does not know (or, perhaps, to those whom one has no reason to like) is a valuable social skill. Of equal value is the ability to write in a variety of social situations. As W. H. Auden put it:

Letters with holiday snaps to enlarge in,
Letters with faces scrawled on the margin,
Letters from uncles, cousins and aunts,
Letters to Scotland from the South of France,
Letters of condolence to Highlands and Lowlands...

These days he would have written about emails, Facebook, or Twitter, rather than letters.

To inform

Every day of our lives we communicate information and ideas to other people. Sometimes such communication is official, formal, businesslike:

Claiming the State Pension

 The Pension Service will write to you before you reach your State Pension age. They will explain your options, including how to claim your State Pension or how you can put it off until later. Find out what to do if you are not contacted.

When to claim your State Pension

You can claim your State Pension when you reach your State Pension age. Not everyone has the same State Pension age so you need to find out what yours is.

› Calculating your State Pension age

Four months before you reach your State Pension age, The Pension Service will write to you. The letter will tell you if you need to claim your State Pension. If you're getting certain social security benefits you may not need to make a claim.

How to claim your State Pension

The most convenient way to claim your State Pension is online. This is a secure protected service that is available 24 hours a day. It allows you to make your claim at your own pace and you can save your claim at any time and return to it later.

You can claim your State Pension online if:

 • you live in England, Scotland or Wales
 • you have received your letter from The Pension Service

How to claim your State Pension if you live in Northern Ireland or abroad.

› Apply for a State Pension in Northern Ireland ⏎
› State Pension for people living abroad ⏎

If you are getting certain social security benefits you may not need to make a claim.

Claim your State Pension online ➡

but this text contains more than a 'straight' communication of facts. The writer is 'selling' something to the reader. It concerns how to claim a benefit to which citizens of a certain age are entitled. However, before they can receive it, they have to make a claim. The government would much prefer it if these claims were made online, since it requires a lot less work for its employees. On the other hand, it is aware that many people in their sixties are still apprehensive about doing such things online. So it uses language that (it hopes) will calm their fears. The online service is 'the most convenient way'; it is 'secure' and 'protected'. What's more, users don't have to complete the process all in one go: they can, if they wish, save what they have done in a session and then complete it later.

Although we may be suspicious of the government, 'even bearing gifts', at least the communication of this information is clear and to the point. Some people find it difficult to convey a clear and simple message, as in the following transcript of a telephone conversation. A representative of a mail-order company is answering a query from a customer who has not received the whole of an order. A parcel containing a computer scanner has gone missing.

Apparently on the discrepancy report that scanner hasn't actually come up so what Business Post are doing—they are chasing this still and they want to work out whether it was stolen from us to them or whether or not it went out from their hub...uum...so they are looking into this. What we're going to be doing is that we're obviously waiting till they get some feedback to us—or whether or not it's gone off to another hub by mistake. Normally what would happen is that this would be on the discrepancy report but obviously it's only been a day I understand...that um...it could've been that...um...it still hasn't been received by another hub as yet so they won't know until the end of the day before we can find out what the situation is with that...uuh what we're going to be doing is that as soon as we get some report from them we'll get in touch with you. If we don't hear anything by the weekend we'll be chasing this ourselves.

The speaker is clumsy and difficult to follow. When you boil his message down it is that he does not know where the goods are and is still trying to find out. His secondary purpose is to calm the customer down and persuade him to wait a little longer so that the company can sort things out. (You could even argue that his very incoherence and use of technical terms like 'hub' are intended to contribute to this. The message is certainly so mind-numbingly confusing as to inhibit further enquiries.)

At least in a telephone conversation it is possible to question a speaker who is confused or confusing. In a radio talk or television commentary, as well as in most written texts, this is not possible and it is vital for the speaker or writer to consider the needs of the listener or reader. When a writer fails to do this, there is little the reader can do. Writing or speaking to inform needs to be clear and this means not only knowing the facts, but also being aware of the needs of your audience.

To find out

Not only do we use language to inform, we also use it to find out information. The ability to ask questions and then follow them up with further enquiries is very important in both work and leisure. Its importance in human development is shown by the behaviour of young children who, as soon as they can frame questions, bombard their parents with enquiries about—literally—everything under the sun.

For adults too, the ability to ask the right question is essential. Often it is just part of the everyday business of living:

A: I've managed to get one of those zoom lenses you were asking about—for you to have a look at...I borrowed one from Birmingham...

B: So I need to come in and have a look at it.

A: Yes please, yes.

B: How long do you reckon you can hang on to it?

A: I'll probably send it back on Monday.

B: Monday...so I need to come in by the end of the weekend, in other words by the end of Saturday.

A: Yes.

B: OK. What time are you open to in the evenings?

A: Half-past five.

➤ See also

• CHAPTER 12
Time and place
(p. 137)

In this brief conversation B speaks four times. Only two of these utterances are framed as questions, specifically asking for information, but the other two are also in effect requests for information—or at least confirmation that he is thinking along the right lines ('...so I need to come in...by the end of Saturday...').

There are other occasions when the pattern of question-and-answer is part of a more formalized situation. When you fill in a form, for example:

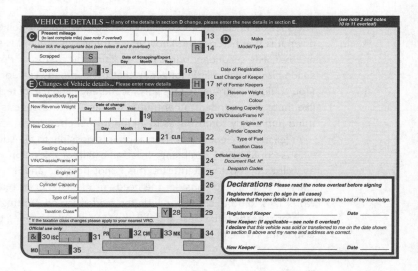

Even when the subject matter is more light-hearted, the situation may still be 'formalized':

➤ See also

• CHAPTER 9
The media
(p. 105)

RADIO INTERVIEWER: Are you at all concerned about hair loss?

A: Er...no, not really. I think it's something I can't avoid, so I try not to worry about it.

RADIO INTERVIEWER: Do you do anything to try and ease the situation?

A: No.

RADIO INTERVIEWER: But have you lost—you've obviously lost a little bit of hair...

A: Just a little bit, yes!

RADIO INTERVIEWER: What does your wife or partner think about that?

A: She doesn't mind. No, she still loves me.

By answering the interviewer's first question, the respondent is agreeing to take part in the 'game' of being interviewed and to play according to the rules. This may seem an odd way of describing it, but imagine what might happen if the person being interviewed did not play according to the interview rules:

| RADIO INTERVIEWER: | Are you at all concerned about hair loss? |
| A: | No. Are you? |

or

| RADIO INTERVIEWER: | Are you at all concerned about hair loss? |
| A: | Don't you think you're rather overweight to be asking me questions like that? |

or

| RADIO INTERVIEWER: | Are you at all concerned about hair loss? |
| A: | Tell you what, why don't we just slip down to my place and I'll give you a full and frank run-down on my hair loss situation. |

Of course such responses may occur, but if they do, they tend not to be broadcast.

To influence

➤ See also

• CHAPTER 14
Different ways of communicating (p. 155)

Whether I look at life as a private individual, as a worker, or as a citizen, it is important that I should be aware of when others are trying to influence me, and of how they are trying to do it. This covers a wide spectrum of writing and speaking. At one end of this we are fully aware that different points of view are being expressed and are free to make up our own minds. Sometimes a writer or speaker may even express two contrasting view points without offering his or her own opinion. Frequently, however, the writer chooses to put an argument as strongly and persuasively as possible:

> **Just think about it**
>
> Nuclear power involves splitting atoms to create some of the deadliest materials on Earth, then using the water they heat to drive a turbine. And then these lethal materials are removed from the reactor—what then? What do you do with this poisonous waste?
>
> Nobody's ever worked out a safe way to deal with these 'spent' fuel rods, which are now even more dangerous than they were to start with. The result? Since the first commercial nucelar power station opened at Calder Hall at Sellafield in 1956, there has been no way of getting rid of any of the fuel rods or other dangerous radioactive waste. It has simply been stockpiled and will be left for future generations to clean up.
>
> Isn't it time to say 'enough is enough'?
>
> Don't you think it's time to close these death traps down now, before there's another 'accident'?

Although this text was written some years ago, it describes a situation and presents an argument still relevant today. It does so, however, in a very one-sided way—as is the writer's intention. It is interesting to examine how this has been done.

Firstly, the subject has been completely decontextualized. A balanced argument would look at the current energy situation and consider what the alternatives are. If nuclear energy is a bad option, then what are the alternatives? In a world increasingly concerned with the problem of global warming, it is regarded by some as much cleaner than any of the alternatives.

This is, of course, related to the writer's strategy of only presenting one side of the story. A balanced argument, such as that presented on pages 167–8, sets out the cases for and against a proposition. This writer deliberately ignores all contrary arguments and drives the message home with full force.

The impact of that message is strengthened by the choice of language. The vocabulary is frequently emotive. Nuclear fuel consists of 'lethal materials'; spent fuel is 'poisonous waste'; and nuclear power stations are 'death traps'. There are rhetorical questions: 'Isn't it time to say "enough is enough"?' and the tone is conversational and informal. The writer's intentions are clear throughout.

At the other end of the scale language is used to influence without the audience being conscious of it. This often happens in advertising. Consider the way in which the text of this advertisement uses words:

> **Introducing BeoSystem 3**
>
> The highly advanced, versatile 'stage manager' for your personal home theatre. Not only is it the most sophisticated picture engine on the market today, it is also modular and flexible, giving you the possibility to continually upgrade your home theater. For use in advanced setups, BeoSystem 3 is capable of simultaneously controlling both a flat screen monitor, such as BeoVision 4, and a projector. If you're planning a home theater, the first thing you need is BeoSystem 3.
>
> All the right connections
>
> You can connect almost any source to BeoSystem 3: it will play most formats you can think of, and your Beo 4 remote control will most likely be able to control it. There are more than 70 connections on the front, hidden behind sturdy front plates. In goes HDMI, Cable, Satellite, High-Definition DVD, Hard Disc Recorders, Surround Sound, content streamed over Broadband, game consoles, digital cameras, MP3-players, and out comes Dolby Digital 5.1, and 6.1/7.1 Ex, DTS 5.1, DTS ES Matrix/Discrete 6.1 or Dolby Pro Logic IIx. Digital processors adjust the picture according to both the source and the screen connected.
>
> Put your BeoVision 4 and your projection screen on different walls and still enjoy perfect surround sound. BeoSystem 3 will turn the sound around for you to set the perfect stage. The built-in 'Home Cinema Control Module' completes the experience, adding advanced control over lighting, curtains and projectors.

See also
• CHAPTER 18
Vocabulary
(p. 217)

Here words are chosen not simply for their meaning, but for their connotations, their emotional effect. This isn't just a piece of electronic equipment, it is a 'stage manager', a 'sophisticated picture engine' that is 'sophisticated', 'modular', and 'flexible'. The writer's aim is not to persuade by argument, but to carry the reader along on a magic carpet of words which are, on analysis, rather meaningless. Politicians often use language in a similar way when addressing the public.

To regulate

Advertisers and politicians may try to persuade us of the rightness of a particular course of action; legislators tell us what to do. They use language to regulate our actions. So do school teachers (at times), doctors, and many others:

1 Remove the red mouthpiece cover and check that the mouthpiece is clean. If the inhaler is cold, warm it in your hand before use.
2 Shake the inhaler well (at least 5 times). If the inhaler has not been used for a while or you are using it for the first time, release one puff into the air to make sure that it works.
3 Holding the inhaler well away from your mouth breathe out gently but not fully, to avoid condensation and blockage of the spray. DO NOT breathe out through the inhaler.

To entertain

Fortunately language isn't all work. There is also play. And the playful use of language is both important and widespread. The way in which we use language in entertainment also varies widely, from simple jokes:

A famous Washington columnist, dining in the old quarter of Montreal, raved over the trout Marguery. He summoned the proprietor of the restaurant and said, 'I'd like to have the recipe for this dish.' The proprietor smiled and answered suavely, 'I'm sorry, m'sieur, but we have here the same policy as you journalists. We never reveal our sauce.'

to poetry:

Shall I compare thee to a Summer's day?
Thou art more lovely and more temperate:
Rough winds do shake the darling buds of May,
And Summer's lease hath all too short a date:
Sometime too hot the eye of heaven shines,
And often is his gold complexion dimm'd;
And every fair from fair sometime declines,
By chance or nature's changing course untrimm'd:
But thy eternal Summer shall not fade
Nor lose possession of that fair thou owest;

Nor shall Death brag thou wanderest in his shade,
When in eternal lines to time thou growest:
  So long as men can breathe, or eyes can see,
  So long lives this, and this gives life to thee.

These two examples may differ in their profundity, but both make playful use of language and draw attention to the fact that they are doing so. Even in more practical applications of language we may sometimes wish to do this.

To record

The previous six purposes all presuppose an audience other than the speaker or writer. There is one use, however, that does not. It is predominantly a purpose for writing, although it can be spoken. In many different situations we need to make a record of something. From a shopping list to a school attendance register, from Domesday Book to a ship's log: the primary intention of such texts is get something down on paper so that it is not forgotten. If we have an audience in mind when we write to record, then that audience is often unknown to us, and usually at some distance in the future.

Diaries are a rather specialized form of this. Many diarists write purely for themselves and to keep a record. Most of the diaries we get to read, however, have either been written with an audience in mind or have been 'tidied up' for an audience:

Ministry of Defence	Wednesday 23rd January

We're five days into the air war, but I am unhappy about the strategy. Attacking missile sites is always wasteful, has very little tactical effect and occurs mainly in response (as most obviously now) to political demands. We lost another Tornado last night. That's now five. I can't help noticing that traditions (ancient and revered) of Bomber Command are reasserting themselves. From the Tabuk mission last night, out of ten sorties six either aborted for technical reasons, or 'jettisoned ordnance while manoeuvring to avoid (sic) SAMs', or took targets of opportunity. (Uh? At night?) The sad thing is that it's always the brave ones, the true grit, who press on regardless (the contravening tradition) and get killed. Of the Italian flight of six, five turned back and only one brave boy went ahead. They got him. It's the difference between James and Andrew. But I want James to survive, don't I?

MGO has been here for an hour and a half. There's a potential ammunition crisis in some calibres. Unbelievably our NATO 'partners' are being most reluctant to pool their stockpiles, even though we're paying cash. The smelly little Belgians, who would never fire a shot at anyone and never have, and who did their best to shaft the BEF in 1940, have actually refused to let us have anything, except 'humanitarian supplies'—bandages and general past-its-sell-by-date detritus we don't need.

What would you say was the main purpose of each of these texts?
Checklist

- to inform
- to find out
- to interact
- to influence
- to regulate
- to entertain
- to record

A Don Quixote was enraged, when he heard such blasphemies uttered against his mistress Dulcinea, and lifting his lance, without speaking a syllable, or giving the least notice of his intention, discharged two such hearty blows upon the squire, as brought him instantly to the ground, and had not Dorothea called aloud and begged him to forbear, would certainly have murdered poor Sancho on the spot.

B The study showed that foreign business activity was important to industry: over 60 per cent of the survey companies conducted some form of business with foreign-speaking clients and this was of major importance to over 40 per cent of respondents. Such business was highly concentrated in a few language areas: about two-thirds each of companies with foreign business dealt with French or German speakers, about one-third each with Spanish and Italian speakers. Otherwise Japanese, Arabic, and Dutch were the only languages of clients of 10 per cent or more of companies.

C To install the application software:

1 Switch on your computer and wait for the desktop to be displayed.
2 Check that the CD driver is correctly installed.
3 Insert the floppy disk into the floppy disk drive slot.
4 Drag the contents of the floppy disk to your hard disk.

→

You try

Continued

D Within minutes of the shelling of the UN base near Tyre in Southern Lebanon, the Red Cross was on the spot providing vital medical care to the injured.

The Red Cross is currently the only international aid agency providing assistance throughout Southern Lebanon. We are distributing supplies to medical centres and clinics. We are giving mattresses, blankets, and vital food aid to people who have left everything behind. And we are deploying 32 ambulances and 25 mobile Red Cross clinics to the areas of greatest need.

Now we need your help to ensure aid continues to reach those who need it desperately. Please give as much as you can today. Your donation can save lives. Thank you.

For possible answers, see page 375.

Guidelines

1 When writing and speaking it is often useful to remember that you almost certainly have a primary purpose, which will usually come from this list:
   - to interact
   - to inform
   - to find out
   - to influence
   - to regulate
   - to entertain
   - to record

2 You will often find that you have more than one purpose; other, secondary purposes will run alongside your main purpose.

3 When writing, check that the language you have used—especially your tone—contributes to your purpose rather than detracting from it.

4 When you are listening to a speaker or reading what someone else has written, it is often useful to analyse their purposes, especially if they are seeking to influence you in some way.

14 Different ways of communicating

There are four main ways of communicating:

Narrative

A narrative is a sequence of events recounted either in the order in which they happened, or in an order chosen to emphasize certain aspects of the story.

Description

Descriptive writing deals with appearances: what things look, sound, feel, taste, or smell like. Observation and selection are key skills in effective descriptive writing.

Exposition

Exposition involves explanations: it may require the description of patterns, accounting for how things work, how processes take place, or a more theoretical analysis of a situation.

Argument

Argument requires the expression of one or more points of view, often to persuade or influence others. It usually requires the writer or speaker to give an explicit or implicit explanation for the views expressed, based on evidence and/or reasoning.

It is often the case that a written text or a piece of speech will involve a mixture of two or more of these **modes of discourse**.

Much of what we say or write is composed of four 'building blocks', known traditionally as modes of discourse:

Mode	Example
narrative	telling a story
description	saying what something looks like
exposition	explaining how something works
argument	expressing an opinion and giving the reasons for it

Narrative

A narrative deals with a sequence of events in time. Typical formats for narrative are:

>● See also
· CHAPTER 7
  Reports
  (p. 81)

- novel and short story
- biography and autobiography
- diary
- newspaper, radio, and TV news report
- other forms of report
- conversational anecdote

In this extract from an autobiography, the writer remembers an incident from his schooldays.

> One night, as I slunk along Church Hill in Harrow, dodging from the mouth of one alleyway to the next, I noticed something which had escaped my attention before. At the back of the Old Schools, one of the original buildings, dating in part from 1615—lay an expanse of lawn. Between the back of the Old Schools and the retaining wall across the end of the garden there was a gap about two feet wide, running away into the hillside at right angles to the street. Although this gap was closed by a cross-wall along the pavement, I spotted a small opening in it, two feet high by one wide, some four feet off the ground. A man's body would not have fitted through the aperture, but I was small and slim.
>
> In a flash I had jumped up and wriggled through the gap. I found myself in a tunnel with an arched brick roof, separating the Old Schools from the garden. Suddenly my adrenaline ran faster. In the wall of the school building was another small opening, blocked by an iron grille. Inside the building, I knew, was the Armoury, where all the Corps rifles were kept. This second opening appeared to lead straight into the Armoury. If only the grille were loose...
>
> It was. In a second I had lifted it clear and was wriggling through the aperture. Sure enough, I was in the heart of the Armoury.

Writing narrative

Telling stories is one of the commonest modes of speaking and writing. Because it 'comes naturally' it is easy to take it for granted and to write narrative without giving it sufficient thought, but there are important choices to be made and if the writer is unaware of these, the writing will be the poorer.

The story you have just read continues with the following information:

1 In the nights that followed he made more visits to the armoury.
2 He decided to 'borrow' a .22 rifle.
3 He already had illicit .22 ammunition taken from practice sessions on the rifle range.
4 As an experiment he took a shot at the window of a room belonging to one of his fellow pupils at the school.
5 No one heard the shot or realized what had happened.
6 On the last day of term he repeated the exploit. He chose the window of a room being used for an illegal party by sixth formers.
7 The curtains were open and the light on. He fired two rounds at the light bulb, but missed. The people in the room realized what was happening and put the light out.
8 Shortly afterwards the police arrived and he escaped to the armoury to return the rifle.
9 The school authorities took it as the work of outsiders and nothing was done. He later realized that his actions had been very foolish.

Order

These events could be narrated in a number of different ways. Unless there are strong reasons for changing things, it makes sense to tell the story in the order in which it happened. As the King told the White Rabbit in *Alice in Wonderland*:

> 'Begin at the beginning, and go on till you come to the end: then stop.'

Filling in the background

In the sequence above the events are listed in the order in which they happened with the exception of number 3, which is necessary at some point to explain why he had ammunition for the rifle he took. This need is a common one in narrative—since many stories are not entirely 'freestanding'. The problem is how to integrate such background information without interrupting the flow of the narrative too much.

One solution is to begin with this information:

> Before I begin I should explain that the school cadet corps used to go to the firing range regularly to do target practice with .22 rifles. There was little proper control over ammunition on these occasions..., etc.

This can be satisfactory, although it tends to give a narrative a rather flat beginning. An alternative is to weave such explanations into the narrative itself—as was done by the original writer:

> ...But I told nobody that I had conceived an ambitious plan. Whenever we had a shooting practice on the .22 range, control of ammunition was

> slack, and I found it easy enough to carry off a few spare bullets each time. I had already amassed a stock of these, and used to amuse myself by dropping into a boy's room for an apparently casual visit in the evening, surreptitiously scattering a few bullets on to his coal fire, and then taking my leave; a few minutes later, sudden explosions would shower red-hot coal all over his floor. Now I had a better use for this smuggled ammunition.

Skilfully handled, as here, this technique works well, but if there are too many interruptions to the flow of the story, or if the teller appears to be going off at a tangent, it can ruin the impact of the narrative.

Subverting the order

Sometimes it is useful to subvert the sequence and present events in a different order from that in which they occurred. A common reason for this is to achieve a dramatic effect. By plunging into the middle of the story with a startling, amusing, or dramatic event we hope to grab the reader's or listener's attention. This approach is popular with newspaper journalists, who rarely 'begin at the beginning':

> **PLAYING WITH FIRE**
>
> **Stupid prank at public school**
> A teenager fired two shots at sixth formers at Harrow School last night. In an extraordinary incident a fifteen-year-old boy broke up an illicit party by firing live rounds at the room where it was taking place.
>
> **Stolen rifle**
> Earlier the boy—whose name is being withheld—broke into the armoury belonging to the school cadet corps...

See also

• CHAPTER 9
The media
(p. 105)

A common pattern for such reports is:

1 **Lead paragraph**
   This tells the key part of the story in brief.

2 **Story**
   The details of the story following the main sequence of events.

3 **Background**
   Further background information.

4 **Comment**
   Selected comments from people involved, 'experts', politicians (and anyone else who can be persuaded to say something eye-catching).

Since newspaper readers often only read the beginning of a report, this approach ensures that they can grasp the essentials of a story by reading a few paragraphs. Those who wish for further detail can read the remainder at their leisure.

Special formats

A similar alteration of the order of events is found in other kinds of report. If the head of the school had made a report of the incident to the governors, he might have begun with a brief summary of the main events:

> Events of Tuesday 14th July
>
> At 11.15pm on 14th July, the last day of the Trinity Term, two shots were fired at a study window in New Block. No one was injured and no serious damage was done. The shots were fired by a fifth former using a rifle he had stolen from the armoury that evening and ammunition taken on a normal cadet firing day at the indoor range.
>
> Theft from the armoury
>
> Earlier in the term the fifth former,...

Emphasis

Even when writers keep the same sequence of events, they can give the story a very different emphasis, and therefore meaning, by putting greater weight on some incidents and less on others. This can be seen any day of the week by comparing reports on the 'same' event by different daily newspapers.

These two reports of the same event come from different daily newspapers. What would you say are the chief differences in the ways the two papers have treated the story?

Driving ban for nine-in-car son of millionaire MP

THE son of a multi-millionaire Tory Minister was banned for drink driving yesterday after being arrested with eight other people in his car, including two in the boot.

Alexander Bonsor, 20, spent the night in police cells and had to call his father—Foreign Office Minister Sir Nicholas—to tell him what had happened.

Bonsor, whose father is said to have a £13 million fortune, was banned for 14 months and fined £600 with £40 costs. The money will not unduly trouble the Bristol University politics student, full name Alexander Cosmo Walrond Bonsor.

Robert Davies, defending, told the city's magistrates: 'He has money. He is not a student who lies awake at night worrying about where money for the next curry or pint of beer comes from. He does not have to mark his milk to stop his friends taking it out of the fridge. He is given £500 a month to cover all his expenses.'

The court heard Bonsor and his friends had spent the evening in a Bristol pub watching the England v Italy World Cup qualifying match. Afterwards eight people climbed into his Ford Sierra—two in the boot, two in the front passenger seat and four in the back—and he drove off. Police stopped the car because it was so low on the ground that sparks were flying from it. Bonsor was breath-tested and found to be more than twice the limit.

He admitted driving with excess alcohol and using a vehicle where the number of passengers carried was such that it would cause danger of injury.

Mr Davies said when Bonsor and his friends left the pub he had no intention of driving home, but 'the red or blue mist descended on all nine of them'.

Sir Nicholas, who was in court, said afterwards: 'It was a very fair verdict and I hope he will learn a lesson from this.'

Eton-educated Sir Nicholas, a father of five, lives in a 14-bedroom mansion on an 800-acre Bedfordshire estate with Nadine, his wife of 25 years.

9-1N-CAR TORY SON BANNED OVER BOOZE

The student son of Foreign Office minister Sir Nicholas Bonsor was yesterday banned for drink-driving with eight pals in his car—two in the boot.

Alex Bonsor, 20, boozed as he watched the England v Italy World Cup soccer qualifier on TV in a pub. Then he drove off in his J-reg Ford Sierra, which was so weighed down that sparks flew from the back of it.

His father was in court at Bristol to see him get a 14-month disqualification and £640 fine after admitting drink-driving and carrying too many passengers.

Magistrates were told that the Bristol University politics student had no money worries because he was paid a £500-a-month allowance by his dad, who is worth £13 million.

Young Bonsor's lawyer Robert Davies said: 'He is from a thoroughly decent and respectable family.'

Mr Davies added: 'The incident has caused embarrassment to himself, his father and his family.'

Sir Nicholas, 54-year-old Tory MP for Upminster Essex, said afterwards: 'I think it was a very fair verdict and hope he will learn a lesson from this.'

See page 375 for comments.

Description

Descriptive writing is used in many different situations. For example:

- travel writing
- biography, autobiography and other writing about people
- diary and personal letter
- technical and scientific works

Personal and impersonal

In some contexts, like scientific writing, the personality of the writer may hardly appear:

> *Mebnoleuca cognata: rather yellowish or tan coloration; stem tall; gills ochretan*
>
> In conifer woods on paths and clearings. Autumn. Uncommon. Cap 10 cm (2 in), convex then expanded and umbonate; smooth, ochre-yellow to tan, paler when dry. Gills becoming clearly pale ochre or tan when mature; sinuate-adnate, crowded. Stem tall, straight, slightly bulbous, colour as cap with darker fibrils...

In other situations, the writer's personality may be quite intrusive:

> **Ag Roumeli** (60km from Chania) Tel. prefix 0821. There was an ancient settlement here, as long ago as the 5th century BC, as evidenced by archaeological excavations to the left (Fsw) of the Gorge. In an attempt to hold down the locals the Turks built a fort (surprise, surprise).
>
> Ag Roumeli continues to resemble a hot, Alaskan shanty town, the only 'establishments' missing being John Wayne and a bordello! The rustic, doo-hickey ambience is accentuated by the wandering, foraging chickens, goats and sheep. Other animal life in situ include mosquitoes, and the dawn chorus of the village's stray dogs will doubtless wake the heaviest sleeper.
>
> The inhabitants ('Sfakiots') have had a pretty hard life for the last 1000 years or so, what with tending and skinning goats, and sheep, in order to earn a crust. But now they are engaged in tending and skinning the tourists...

Writing description

Clearly it is essential to have the necessary information available before beginning to write descriptively. Preparation may range from careful research (as in the case of the technical description of a fungus), a mixture of research and memory (as with the travel-book extract) or pure memory and reflection. Even where the writer is relying heavily on memory it is useful to make preparatory notes, which will help with the ordering of the material and will enable the writer to see where problems are likely to arise.

Key decisions How you structure a description and the tone and style you adopt depend heavily on the answers to these questions, already tackled in this section of the book:

> See also

• CHAPTER 10
  Audience
  (p. 117)

• **Who?**

You must think carefully about the background knowledge and needs of your audience. For example, the description of *Mebnoleuca cognata* is of no use to a reader who has no botanical knowledge and cannot cope with words like 'sinuate-adnate' and 'fibrils'. By the same token a reader who wants a straight factual account of a place will find the description of Ag Roumeli irritatingly jokey.

> See also

• CHAPTER 13
  Purpose
  (p. 143)

• **Why?**

All description has to some extent the purpose of providing information. This may, however, take place within a broader setting. The fungus text is nothing—indeed, is downright dangerous—if it does not inform fully and accurately. The guidebook is clearly intended to provide a large measure of entertainment. The description of fungi, on the other hand, is intended to convey information succinctly and impersonally.

Pattern and emphasis

The writer of the text about fungi had few problems to overcome when planning. His description of each fungus follows a certain pattern:

• brief description of appearance
• habitat and season of appearance
• distribution ('common', 'uncommon', etc.)
• cap

and so on.

The writer of the guidebook, for all the apparent spontaneity of his style, also follows a pattern:

• location/telephone code
• history
• general impressions
• the people
• a walk through the town

As with much writing, the ordering of a description is crucial. Once you have found the right pattern and emphasis for the text, your writing can proceed with greater confidence and facility.

These two descriptions are both about the same place. In what ways are they different?

A The greatest disappointment was Chandni Chowk. In the poems and travelogues, the Moonlight Bazaar is praised as a kind of Oriental Faubourg St Honoré renowned for its wide avenues, its elegant caravanserais and its fabulous Mughal gardens. Having read the descriptions of this great boulevard, once the finest in all Islam, as you sit on your rickshaw and head on into the labyrinth you still half-expect to find its shops full of jasper and sardonyx for the Mughal builders, mother-of-pearl inlay for the pietra dura crafts-men; you expect to see strings of Bactrian camels from Kashgar and logs of cinnamon from Madagascar, merchants from Ferghana, and Khemer girl concubines from beyond the Irrawaddy; perhaps even a rare breed of turkey from the New World or a zebra to fill the Imperial menagerie and amuse the Emperor.

But instead, as you sit stranded in a traffic jam, half-choked by rickshaw fumes and the ammonia-stink of the municipal urinals, you see around you a sad vista of collapsing shop fronts and broken balustrades, tatty warehouses roofed with corrugated iron and patched with rusting duckboards. The canal which ran down the centre of the bazaar has been filled in; the trees have been uprooted. All is tarnished, fraying at the edges. On the pavement, a Brahminy cow illicitly munches vegetables from the sack of a vendor; a Muslim ear-cleaner squats outside the Sis Ganj gurdwara and peers down the orifices of a Sikh nihang (gurdwara guard). A man grabs your arm and stage-whispers: 'Sahib, you want carpets hashish smack brown sugar change money blue film sexy ladies no problem!'

B Old Delhi (Shahjahanabad)

Although it's not in fact the oldest part of Delhi, the seventeenth-century city of Shahjahanabad, built by the Moghul emperor, Shah Jahan, is known as OLD DELHI. The original city walls spread for seven miles, enclosing the sprawling fort, Lal Qila, and the formidable Jami Masjid, or 'Friday Mosque'. Old Delhi's main thoroughfare, Chandni Chowk, a seething mass of hooting, pushing cars, tempos, cycle rickshaws and ox carts, was once a sublime canal lined with trees and some of the most opulent bazaars of the East. Today the city walls have crumbled, and houses and shops have long since spilled beyond the remaining five of the fourteen old gates.

On the west bank of the River Yamuna northeast of the modern centre, Old Delhi resembles an overgrown village of tight-knit communities, alive with intriguing contra-dictions and contrasts. Photographers huddled at the east end of Chandni Chowk using rickety equipment left over from the days of the Raj are overlooked by garish film boards and advertisements for sex clinics, while the bazaars in the back alleys have changed

→

little since the eighteenth and nineteenth centuries. It's a fascinating area, but you'll need stamina, patience and time to endure the crowds and traffic, and pursue a rewarding exploration of the city's streets, mosques, temples and guradwaras.

See page 375 for comments.

Exposition

Exposition is concerned with:

- the pattern of things
- how things work
- how to do something
- the underlying reality of a situation

At its simplest—and most practical—exposition deals with the physical world:

> Stratus is a low-level layer cloud (not to be confused with altostratus and cirrostratus, which are much higher). In appearance, it is usually a featureless grey layer. Sometimes, when a sheet of stratus is affecting an area, the cloud base will be right down to the ground and the visibility will be below fog limits. However, the usual base will be between the ground and 1,000 feet (300 metres), which means that hilltops may be obscured by cloud. Sometimes stratus will produce drizzle, snow, or snow grains, particularly over hills.
>
> Perhaps the most important indication of its low altitude is its apparent rapid movement across the sky in any wind stronger than a flat calm. For example, a stratus cloud at 500 feet (150 metres) moving at 20 miles per hour will appear to move much faster than altostratus with its base at 10,000 feet (3,000 metres) moving at 60 miles per hour.

Often such writing is impersonal and formal in tone. But it need not be. Here a writer explains a practical subject in a more relaxed and personal way:

> The Victorians were extremely frugal and parsimonious, watching every halfpenny. The staggering waste of anything and everything which we see today was the exact contrary to their world. It was because of this parsimony that they could afford to buy a thousand solid silver fish-knives—and pay in gold napoleons—and get something that would be polished daily for fifty years without wearing out. For this they had a system; in the kitchen called the System. Its exact French title—for the French were the most frugal of all Victorians—is 'Rien se Perd' which is translatable as 'Waste does not Exist'.

Exposition is either outside time, or—as in the extract above—covers a period of time. This type of writing and speaking to expound and explain occurs in many different situations, especially in areas of life that are practical and useful. For example:

- home decorating, gardening and other household books and radio and TV programmes
- the features pages of newspapers and magazines
- books, articles, and programmes about countries, institutions, organizations, and developing situations

Good exposition is clear, logically ordered, and hits exactly the right level for the reader; it provides the information required, but does not assume knowledge and understanding that the reader does not possess.

Writing exposition

It is not easy to write good expository prose. Most people can work their way through a story with considerably greater confidence than they can through an explanation. This is probably linked to the important part story telling plays in the lives of most people from an early age. By contrast, for many of us, explaining is something we learned to do when things went wrong and we were in some kind of trouble!

It will help considerably if you focus on a few key areas.

Background knowledge

> *See also*
- CHAPTER 10
Audience
(p. 117)

It is important to have a clear idea of:

- what background knowledge you can assume that your audience already has
- what additional background information they need before the main exposition can begin. This will include not only general information, but also the language needed to discuss the topic.

This information can be presented in different ways:

- **all at the beginning**

  This has the advantage that it gets it over with all at once, but if this intro-duction is extended, it may prove rather daunting, so that the audience may be tempted to 'switch off', which can be counter-productive.

- **in stages as required**

  This places the necessary background information at the point where it is needed and avoids an over-long introduction. It has the disadvantage that those who already know this material may find it rather trying.

- **in a supplement or annexe to which readers are referred**

  In a written text this leaves the main exposition clean and uncluttered, but some readers may not bother to turn to the back for information that they need.

<table>
<tr><td>

Taking your audience with you

</td><td>

Closely related to this are the twin questions of clarity and pace. Probably more so than in narrative and description, the elements of an exposition are closely linked and interdependent. If the audience fails to grasp one component it may well prove fatal to their understanding of the whole.

It is important to ensure that:

</td></tr>
</table>

- you have not assumed knowledge that does not exist
- each part of your exposition is properly 'keyed in' to what has gone before and there are no gaps
- you have got the pace right, so that all members of your audience can grasp what you are saying, but you are not going so slowly that some are bored or insulted

Argument

The key features of argument are that:

- an opinion or point of view is expressed—with which others may or may not agree
- the reasons for that point of view are stated—or at least implied

An argument may also seek to persuade—often we want other people to agree with us—but it doesn't have to. The following text does not seek to persuade. It presents both sides of a longstanding disagreement and leaves it to the reader to decide.

Foxhunting

For: hunts help protect wildlife	Against: cruel, divisive sport
1	1
Foxes are vermin which need controlling—the Royal Society for the Protection of Birds has to shoot them to protect endangered bird species at some reserves. There are about a quarter of a million foxes before the start of each breeding season and their numbers appear to be rising. They kill huge numbers of game birds reared for shoots and also slaughter some new-born lambs.	Foxhunting is the least effective way of controlling the fox population, probably accounting for less than one-tenth of foxes killed by humans. While the pro-hunting lobby argues that it is helping to curb rising fox numbers, across much of lowland England the hunts themselves effectively admit that this is not the reason they hunt when they say that a lower fox population would harm their sport. The Ministry of Agriculture says foxes may take large numbers of lambs on some farms but they are not 'a significant factor in lamb mortality nationally'. And foxes help to keep down the numbers of rabbits, a destructive farm pest.
2	2
Foxhunting is one of the main reasons why the traditional, diverse landscape of hedgerows, copses, and spinneys has been preserved across much of England. Farmers who enjoy or support the hunt plant or maintain woodlands to provide cover for foxes and hedges for horses to jump. This is good for other wildlife as well as the scenery.	Hunting is becoming less of a force in conserving hedgerows and spinneys, according to an Oxford University fox expert, Dr David Macdonald. Farmers have a more general interest in conservation, and a variety of state incentives now encourage them to protect landscapes and wildlife.
3	3
The sport is an important plank in the rural economy. According to a consultants' report commissioned by the hunting lobby, the hunts directly employ 9,500 people, while there are 7,000 jobs in associated trades such as grooms and stable staff. The report suggests a further 23,200 rural jobs would disappear if hunting were banned—in veterinary surgeries, feed merchants, saddle-makers, etc.	Hunting's opponents do not question that the bloodsport maintains large numbers of rural jobs but they say the hunts should switch to drag hunting, in which the hounds follow an artificial scent trail and no foxes are involved.
4	4

For: hunts help protect wildlife	Against: cruel, divisive sport
Hunting is a key part of rural society and recreation. Up to 250,000 people take part each year, most of them as on-foot followers. It brings a variety of professions and classes together and is adrenalin-boosting, traditional, fresh-air fun.	Hunting is a divisive issue in the countryside as well as between town and country; many farmers and rural dwellers oppose it. It may be fun but it is unacceptably cruel. The fox may be killed swiftly, but it suffers extreme stress and fear during the chase. A fox which has gone underground and is pursued by terriers, dug out and shot endures further anguish. Preseason cub-hunting in the autumn, when the hounds are familiarised with fox scent and kill cubs, is especially cruel.
5	5
The ban introduced by the Blair government in 2004 is riddled with contradictions. Police have found it largely unenforceable, and have made it a low priority. Between 2004 and 2012 there were only six prosecutions against registered hunts. Because of the loopholes in the legislation, foxes are still being chased and killed by hunts—just as they were in the past.	The ban on foxhunting introduced in 2004 expresses the will of the majority of people in this country at the time. It is the law of the land and should be observed by all. Hunts can still meet and follow trails laid down in advance and members apparently enjoy this sport. Indeed, membership of some hunts has doubled since the law was passed.

It is possible to use this 'ammunition' in a number of different ways.

Expressing a point of view

An important use of argument is to present one's point of view and the reasons for it:

> I find it bizarre that in the closing years of the twentieth century men and women should want to dress up in funny clothes and ride across farmland on expensive horses with a lot of tame dogs, chasing one wild dog.
>
> If you ask them what they are doing and why...

In expressing this point of view, the writer is not seeking primarily to persuade others to agree. It is the expression of a point of view. The vigour with which the view is expressed and the tone adopted may have that effect incidentally, but that is not the prime aim.

'Come and join us'

A step further is to take one point of view wholeheartedly and to try to sell it to anyone you can persuade to listen. This approach is used in posters and advertisements for organizations opposed to or in favour of hunting.

Sitting on the fence or near it	The old truism tells us that 'there are two sides to every argument' and sometimes we may genuinely have mixed feelings about an issue, perhaps because the arguments for and against are very evenly balanced, or because they are are very complex. In such a situation the speaker or writer may prefer to present both sides of the argument, much as was done in the text quoted earlier, and explain the weight which he or she attached to the different strands.

If you are writing or speaking in a personal context—explaining your thoughts and feelings to a friend, for example—this approach has much to recommend it. If, on the other hand, you have been asked to come up with a recommended course of action—in a business context, for example— then you not likely to find it helpful.

Presenting an argument

A successful argument, whether spoken or written, depends on three things:

Purpose	You need a clear idea of why you are presenting this argument. The commonest purposes are:

- **to inform**

  the text under the heading 'Foxhunting' on pages 167 and 168 informs the reader of the key arguments for and against hunting

- **to persuade or influence others**

  the text under the heading 'Expressing a point of view' on the opposite page sets out to persuade the reader that hunting is wrong

- **to interact**

  you may wish to express a personal viewpoint and the reasons for it as part of your relationship with someone else

Pros and cons	1 You must have a clear idea of the reasons for and against the viewpoint(s) you are presenting.

  2 Reasons can be either:
  - factual evidence which most people will accept:

    There are about a quarter of a million foxes before the start of each breeding season and their numbers appear to be rising...so they...need controlling.
  - a logical progression from a starting point that those who hold a different opinion should find it difficult to reject:

    While the pro-hunting lobby argues that it is helping to curb rising fox numbers, across much of lowland England the hunts themselves effectively admit that this is not the reason they hunt when they say that a lower fox population would harm their sport.

  3 You must somehow take account of contrary arguments. You can:

- present both sides of the argument and then come down on one side or the other, explaining why (or sit on the fence, if that is what you have decided)
- state your own opinion and the reasons for it. State the contrary arguments as you go and explain clearly why they are wrong.
- state your own opinion and the reasons for it. Do not refer to contrary arguments directly but 'rubbish' anyone who does not agree with you.

Tone and style

The way in which your argument is presented will be largely decided by the two preceding considerations. It is very important to adopt a tone that is suitable for your purpose and for the style in which you have decided to present your case. If you are addressing a group of senior managers on the argument in favour of purchasing an important piece of capital equipment, it is not advisable to adopt the tone of someone arguing about football in a pub—and vice versa.

How it works

The four modes that have been described are sometimes used separately, but often they are combined, as in this illustration:

> **Description**
> the writer sets the scene

> **Narrative**
> now he begins to tell the story of what happened

> **Exposition**
> he explains why this procession is taking place

The narrow street was crowded with people. Old men leant on sticks side by side with mothers holding babies; teenagers chatted in a relaxed way, and above them the balconies were crowded with spectators. Vendors of sweets, soft drinks and peanuts made their way through the throng.

A murmur began to work its way through the crowd. All heads turned towards the the church of St John the Baptist at the end of street. Suddenly silence fell as the great doors of the church began to swing open.

Behind me someone spoke, and all around a sibilant hushing demanded silence. We all craned towards the doors and then it began. A great procession of black-hooded figures, all wearing the tall conical hats of the penitents, made their way out of the church and into the street.

Behind them, high above our heads, came a gigantic statue of Christ on the cross. It stood on a platform covered with blue irises and was carried on the shoulders of perhaps as many as a hundred men, moving slowly in step along the street. As they approached we could see that some were blindfold and many were barefoot: a strange and moving sight.

This was Semana Santa in Malaga. In the week leading up to Easter there are processions all over Spain and other Catholic countries, to commemorate the events leading to Christ's Crucifixion. Those in Malaga are particularly elaborate. From four o'clock every afternoon until the early hours of the morning, the whole of the city centre is taken over by these massive processions.

It is difficult for an agnostic from a protestant and undemonstrative culture like ours to understand why people should behave in this way. I was told that many of these people, especially the men, never enter a church from one year's end to the next. Some say that they do the procession to atone for this. Cynics add that, like all Latins, they love a show. Whatever the reason, you have to accept that there is more to Semana Santa than a petrified relic of a dead belief. It still has meaning.

....
▶ **Argument**
the different arguments people give to explain the continuing popularity of these celebrations
....

What is the main mode of each of these texts?

A In Africa universities were seen, with some accuracy, as focal points for all the malcontents and ideamongers in the country. Along with the television station, they were the first to go in times of trouble.

B It had a rather insubstantial rear, which later models moulded into extravagant fish tails of chrome and steel. The driver rested one delicate arm, as muscled but fine as an antelope's, on the sill.

C I watched him pull the stick towards him and down for first gear. We drove smoothly along Victoria Road and turned into Zwane, past the church. The driver glanced at me from time to time.

D He is a remarkable broadcaster and someone I have admired since I was a child. Despite the fact that millions of people are listening to him, he always sounds as if he is having a one-to-one conversation; there is an intimacy there which, as a listener, whatever you are doing, you respond to without thinking. He also makes his broadcasts sound effortless.

Answers on page 375.

Guidelines

Narrative

1 Make sure you have a clear idea of the order in which events happened.
2 Think about:
   • audience
   • purpose

3 Decide what background information—if any—the audience need.

4 Decide on the order in which to present the background information and the events:

- chronological order is simplest to use and easiest to follow
- starting in the middle can be dramatic but needs careful handling
- different situations and formats may demand a particular ordering

5 Think carefully about audience and tone when presenting the narrative.

6 You can change the emphasis you give a story by giving more weight to some events than to others.

Description

1 Before beginning a piece of description think about:

- purpose
- audience

2 Then decide how personal or impersonal your writing should be.

3 Your preparation may involve research, memory, reflection, or a combination of these.

4 You should also give careful thought to the order and pattern of your description. This may be strictly logical or it may be more creative or intuitive. It must lead the reader through so that the relationship between the parts of your description is clearly seen.

5 Try to appeal to your audience's senses of sight, sound, smell, touch, and taste.

Exposition

1 Consider your audience carefully to work out what background material they will need:

- information
- terminology

2 Decide how this should be introduced:

- at the beginning
- as you go along
- separately—e.g., in the appendix of a piece of writing.

3 Use your knowledge of your audience to make sure that you take them with you. Try to imagine the problems they may have in following different elements of your exposition, and allow for these.

4 Build in revision and consolidation as you go, especially where the topic is large-scale or complex.

5 Use visuals to support your text and even to replace parts of it.

Argument

1 Decide on your approach:
   - a statement of your view with reasons
   - an attempt to persuade others to your point of view
   - a statement of the arguments on each side with a clearly stated preference and the reasons for it
   - a statement of the opposing sides without any final judgement

2 Support the planks of your argument with:
   - evidence
   - reasoning from an agreed position, or evidence and arguments already presented

3 Think about audience and purpose when deciding on the style and tone of your text.

C Communication tools

15 How we talk about English

This section is about how English works. But our language is very varied and always in a state of change, so before we can begin to look at the elements of English—grammar, vocabulary, and so on—we need to understand about dialects and standard English, and the ways in which English has developed and continues to change. It is also important to understand that there are two opposed approaches to grammar: the traditional, which seeks to lay down rules about what we should and should not do; and the modern, descriptive approach, which sets out to describe the ways in which language is actually used.

16 Introduction to grammar

This chapter sets out the main levels of language that grammar describes: words, phrases, clauses, and sentences. It then focuses on simple (one-clause) sentences and analyses their possible component parts: subject, verb, object, complement, and adverbial.

17 More about grammar

This chapter continues the analysis by looking at multiple sentences (sentences with more than one clause). Compound sentences contain two or more clauses of equal status joined by conjunctions like but and or. In complex sentences, one clause is more important, the main clause, while other clauses are subordinate to it. Such sentences can be constructed in a very large number of ways and some of the most important of these are analysed. The chapter concludes with an examination of some of the problems associated with multiple sentences.

18 Vocabulary

We all have a range of words we use in speech and writing, and there are many more words which we understand when we come across them. Our vocabulary can be extended by the skilful use of suitable word books such as dictionaries and thesauruses. It also helps to understand how words are constructed, with a stem, prefix, and suffix. Words are not just 'bundles of meaning'; people have attitudes to them and their use in particular situations. Some words are regarded as slang, or informal, while others are 'taboo'. We need to be sensitive to this aspect of vocabulary.

19 Spelling

An analysis of why and how spelling can be a problem, followed by advice on tackling difficulties. The main spelling rules are then set out, followed by lists of problem words, grouped by type.

20 Punctuation

This chapter lists all the punctuation points, giving detailed advice on their use.

21 Speech

Although speech seems perfectly natural, it is helpful to have a basic understanding of how it is produced and the ways in which our voices can express subtle shades of meaning. The introductory analysis of the individual speech sounds of English is followed by a consideration of stress, intonation, accent, and pronunciation.

15 How we talk about English

Which English are we talking about?

Talking about the English language is complicated by two important facts:

- **English is constantly changing**

English is the product of 1500 years' development and is continuing to grow and change.

- **There is more than one version of English**

English is not one monolithic language but a large number of dialects. Each major English-speaking country has its own version of the language and within countries there are regional dialects, too. Fortunately there is a **standard English**, which is widely used in writing and formal speech. In addition to dialects, we have to be aware of important differences between written and spoken English.

Which approach should we take?

There are two opposed views about how we should talk about language:

- **Traditional grammar**

Based on the grammar of Latin, this view prescribes how language should be used; believes that language is static not dynamic; and only focuses on formal English.

- **Descriptive grammar**

Modern linguists concentrate on how English is used by real people and do not set out to prescribe how it should be used. An understanding of the elements of grammar can be very useful to users of English.

Which English are we talking about?

The way in which people use their own language is the subject of much debate and disagreement. Some become very angry about the way in which others, especially those in the media and public life, speak and write. The linguist David Crystal invited listeners to his radio series about language to write to him describing language usage they liked or disliked. Hardly anyone wrote about usage they liked, but many—especially listeners over fifty—wrote at length about 'pet hates'. Crystal noted that the language his correspondents used was frequently intemperate. They referred to expressions they disliked as *abominations* and said they were *appalled* and *driven wild* by the way in which English was being *prostituted*.

There are three reasons why people disagree about language usage and why, as a result, the debate about English will continue to be heated:

1 English is not static but dynamic; its vocabulary and grammar continue to develop and change, as they have done for centuries. People who are innately conservative feel threatened by changes in 'their own' language.

2 There isn't just one version of English but many; in different geographical regions people use different vocabulary and grammar, and there are also variations according to social groupings. Language can be a sign of group membership, and some people are tempted to see others who use it differently as inferior in some way.

3 While academic students of language, linguists, insist on **describing** the ways in which English is used, many others who write and speak about it insist on **prescribing** how it should be used. The ways in which these two groups develop their arguments are completely different.

It is useful to look at these three points in a little more detail before we begin to examine how English works.

Our changing language

Without going into a detailed survey of the history of English, it is worth pointing out that the origins of the language we speak today go back over 1500 years. When the Angles, Saxons, and Jutes invaded Britain in the 5th century, they effectively imposed their language on their new territories. Much the same happened at the Norman Conquest 600 years later, and the first version of English that is recognizable to the modern reader developed out of this fusion of the Germanic language of the Anglo-Saxons with the French spoken by the Normans. But even that English is a long way from the language we speak today. When Chaucer writes,

> Whilom ther was dwellinge at Oxenford
> A riche gnof, that gestes heeld to bord,
> And of his craft he was a carpenter.
> With him ther was dwellinge a poure scoler,
> Hadde lerned art, but al his fantasie Was turned for to lerne astrologie...
>
> (There once lived in Oxford a wealthy lout who took in lodgers. He was a carpenter by trade. He had living with him a poor scholar who had studied for his degree but was obsessed with the idea of learning astrology...)

we can recognize it as English—but only just.

By the time we get to Shakespeare, some 200 years later, the language being used is much more obviously like modern English, but it still isn't the language we speak today. In this brief extract from *Twelfth Night*, Malvolio has been woken up by the drunken singing of Sir Toby and his friends:

> MALVOLIO: My masters, are you mad? Or what are you? Have you no wit, manners, nor honesty, but to gabble like tinkers at this time of night? Do ye make an alehouse of my lady's house, that ye squeak out your coziers' catches without any mitigation or remorse of voice? Is there no respect of place, persons, nor time in you?
>
> SIR TOBY: We did keep time, sir, in our catches. Sneck up!

While a modern reader can understand much of what is going on, some of the words are strange. For example, most readers will have a very good idea of what Sir Toby means when he tells Malvolio to 'sneck up', but they are unlikely to have come across the word 'sneck' before (it is a North British dialect word meaning to close a door).

Since Shakespeare's day some words have disappeared from use, while others have changed their meanings. New words have come into the language. It would be a mistake to assume that this process has come to an end, but it is a mistake that is commonly made. As long as people have discussed language usage, there have been those who deplore the ways in which it is changing, just as there have been people who want to be in the forefront ('ahead of the curve', to use a relatively recent expression) of that change.

Where you place yourself in relation to this process of change is a personal choice, made—as many other choices are—after a consideration both of how you feel about the ways in which the language is changing and of how other people will regard you. If, for example, you are a barrister arguing a detailed and complex civil case, then the use of a lot of 'fashionable' expressions may well not be appreciated. On the other hand, if you are an advertising executive you would probably not speak to your clients

1 The words and expressions in the list below all appear in *The Longman Register of New Words* 1989 edition. Try dividing them into three categories:

A: still 'new' or 'fresh'

B: current common usage, and so unremarkable

C: stale and dated

→

Continued

bratpack	card swipe
networker	pressing the flesh
wuss	crumbly
moral majority	infomercial
des res	mega

2 The following words had all recently been coined at the time of writing.

   1. How many of them do you recognize?

   2. How many of them could you put a meaning to?

baby-lag

flirtationship

mansplaining

selfie

omnishambles

See page 376 for comments.

in language suitable for the barrister. Language choice and expression are matters of awareness and sensitivity to the situation you are in.

Just as English vocabulary continues to change, so does English grammar, although at a slower pace. In the past, for example, it would have been frowned on to begin a sentence, *If I was you…* Now this is increasingly heard, even from the mouths of educated speakers. Some will argue that there is an important difference between

> If I *were* captaining the team, I'd…

and

> If I *was* captaining the team, I'd…

The first, they say, means that the speaker believes that there is not the remotest possibility of the situation arising, while the second regards it as unlikely, but possible. If language is developing towards the abandonment of *If I were*, however, it means that more and more people will simply not pick up this difference—so we shall have to find other ways of communicating the same meaning.

People who discuss how language is used take up one of three positions about the way in which English is changing:

1 They disapprove of change and hark back to a golden age when English was in some way purer. This is the spirit that made the French set up their Academy and later even passed laws banning the use of English words where there were French words that would serve.

2 They simply describe the changes without any comment about whether they are good or bad.

3 They describe the change and attempt to judge how far it has progressed and how people are reacting to it. The purpose of this is to help people to judge which usage they should adopt themselves.

The first group cannot, ultimately, win; their campaigns to 'defend the language' may give them some satisfaction but will not make any difference. The second group are safe but unhelpful to the everyday user. It is only the third group that can give the everyday user of English helpful advice: a mixture of factual information and balanced judgement. Here, for example, is Godfrey Howard in *The Good English Guide*:

> -related In the fast lanes of the 1990s there is a constant drive to speed up communication. As a word joined on with a hyphen, *-related* is a short cut. Instead of 'illnesses caused by stress', 'crimes caused by drink', 'negotiations about money', we have stress-related illnesses, drink-related crimes, money-related negotiations. It would be a pity to overdo this or, like any other useful linguistic device, it would degenerate into jargon.

How many 'Englishes'?

Most people are aware that people in the United States and people in Britain speak the same language but with important differences of vocabulary and grammar. An English reader would probably pick up that this message was written by an American:

> I would be happy to meet with you while I am in Oxford. Mornings are best because I will be teaching in the M.B.A. program in the afternoon...

Both *meet with* (for British *meet*) and *program* (for *course*) give the game away.

American English has a powerful influence ('impacts heavily') on British usage. Many people are fairly relaxed about this, but some purists resent this Americanization of English. It tends to be new words, especially technical and social ones, that transfer most readily. Despite the close contacts between the two countries a number of common words remain steadfastly different. Britons still speak of *taps, cupboards*, and *lifts* rather than *faucets, closets*, and *elevators*, for example.

Many other English-speaking countries, such as Australia and India, also have distinctive versions of the language, and even within Britain and the other countries there are important variations of dialect. To the academic linguist, no one dialect is better than any other; they are simply different. For the user, social attitudes are important and if you ignore them, you risk alienating those who hold different attitudes from yourself.

Standard English

Ever since the invention of printing there has been pressure to standardize English. When Caxton set up his printing press in the fifteenth century, he was aware of the problems caused by the variety of different dialects spoken in England. He had to choose which dialect and which spellings to adopt when publishing books in English. The period since then has seen the evolution of standard English, which may be only one more dialect of the language, but which has far more social prestige than the others and which is normally used in writing as well as being used in all formal or semi-formal speech situations.

Standard English is not, however, something fixed. When people who write about language describe a usage as 'non-standard', they are making a judgement based on experience, rather than a statement of scientific fact. This is perhaps easier to understand if one compares the possible alternatives.

➤ *See also*
· CHAPTER 10
  Audience
  (p. 117)

standard English:	*very frightened*
informal English:	*scared stiff*
regional dialect:	*frit*
taboo slang:	*shit scared*

The standard phrase will always work and will offend no one. The informal expression is acceptable in many situations and is on the edge of being standard English. Until the 1970s *frit*, on the other hand, would not have been heard in formal situations, being a dialect word—until it was used by the then Prime Minister, Margaret Thatcher. It would probably be regarded now as acceptable informal usage—which is certainly not the case with the fourth item in the list.

You try

Which of the following, if any, would you describe as standard English?

1 Let's get this show on the road.
2 He got down on his hunkers.
3 It happened in the dead of winter.
4 She had just argued herself into a corner.
5 Most of the women were only working there to earn some pin money.
6 When we got home my wife wrote them a bread-and-butter letter.

See page 376 for comments.

Speech and writing

The way in which we use language when we speak need not be different from how we use it when we write, but it often is. When we use speech in face-to-face conversation, our audience is present and we can adjust what we say according to their response. We have the advantage of being able to use gesture, facial expression, and vocal tone in order to help us communicate. Of course, speech takes place in 'real time', by contrast with a written text that can be revised and rewritten until we are satisfied with it. Spoken language is—apparently at least—spontaneous and made up as we go along. As a result we have to revise and recast our sentences even as they are being uttered. Alternatively we have to add other sentences which revise or clarify the meaning of what has gone before. Here, for example, are two students discussing how we judge people by the way they speak:

A: A lot of people—as soon as you open your mouth they judge you by what comes out.
B: My mother's from Birmingham and my dad's from Leicester—my mother especially is—is—it's obviously not deliberate—but because she works in the university she's got...she's—like—adopted over the years this quite stuffy accent really.

The standard English version of what A says would be written as:

> As soon as you open your mouth a lot of people judge you by what comes out.

In what B says, we can see the process of 'instantaneous revision' going on, with false starts and rephrasing as she sorts out what she wants to say.

This is not to say that spontaneous speech is just sloppy language. In ordinary conversation we cannot work out carefully in advance exactly how each sentence is going to be constructed. If we did, conversation would become boring and stilted. Instead of careful formal constructions we rely on the listener's goodwill and on our own ability to reconstruct and explain as we go along.

In situations where we cannot be sure of that goodwill, or where it is important to sound confident, prepared, and unhesitant, then some form of preparation is required and this produces speech that is less spontaneous and more like written standard English.

Which approach should we take?

▶ See also
· CHAPTER 12
Time and place
(p. 137)

We have already seen that different attitudes towards language affect the way in which we talk about it and the conclusions we draw.

Traditional grammar

In the past, many scholars attempted to describe the grammar of English in terms of Latin. They worked on the assumption that this was a universal grammatical structure which could be applied to all languages, including English. Since all languages work in different ways and their grammars have to reflect this, the attempt to impose a Latinate grammar on English was not a success. It led to a number of important side effects:

- Traditional grammarians tried to prescribe how the language should be used. Where the flexibility of English meant that it did not fit the imposed Latinate grammar very well, they said that this was because language was being used sloppily.
- They believed that language should be fixed and unchanging. Where changes occurred they were for the worse.
- They believed that only the standard form of the language should be used and that all other forms were inferior. Pushed to its extreme this meant that American English was inferior to British English.

As we have seen, some of these attitudes still linger on, but during the twentieth century a new approach to grammar has developed and been broadly accepted.

Modern descriptive grammar

The modern approach is to take a large selection of language, to study it scientifically and then to describe exactly how it actually works. Grammars of this kind also produce 'rules', but they are rules which explain how things work—just as the law of gravity does in physics—rather than telling people what to do. For example, traditional grammarians would object to splitting an infinitive. They would argue that the form *to go* constitutes a grammatical unit (since in Latin the infinitive *ire* [to go] is one word) so no words should come between *to* and *go*. To write *to boldly go*, therefore, is wrong. A modern grammarian, on the other hand, would say something like this:

> Infinitival *to* is a separate word, and therefore adverbials (especially single adverbs) sometimes intervene between it and the infinitive. The interruption results in what is traditionally known as the split infinitive.
> **Sidney Greenbaum:** *The Oxford English Grammar*

The writer does not say whether he considers it right or wrong, but explains, technically, that it happens and how it works.

Modern descriptive grammar, therefore, deals in facts. The conclusions it draws may be more or less accurate, depending on the skill of the practitioner.

But this is in stark contrast to traditional prescriptive grammar which deals in opinions, many of which are based on false information or false reasoning.

The need for guidance

All of this is of little help to the person who wants advice on how to speak and write. Traditional grammarians are too narrow and unyielding in the advice they give, which is often unscientific and unreliable; modern grammarians do not offer advice. It would be tempting to assume that as a result anything goes.

Tempting but wrong. This can be shown by three simple examples. Each of these sentences has something 'wrong' with it, but the reasons for that 'wrongness' are different.

1 Who was that girl I saw you with?
2 Several of my friends, including Jamie, has decided to have a holiday together this year.
3 I'll see her when I shall go to Bristol.

Number 1 is disapproved of by some traditionalists, who say that you should not end a sentence with a preposition. This is a matter of stylistic prejudice and is not based on grammar at all: there is nothing wrong with the sentence. Number 2, on the other hand, contains an error of grammar. The subject of the sentence, 'Several of my friends', is plural and the verb should agree with it in number: '**have** decided'. The speaker has presumably been confused by the fact that the singular 'Jamie' comes immediately before the verb. Sentence 3 is not one that is likely to be constructed by a native speaker of English, but contains an error often made by foreign learners. It is a literal translation of what might be said in French, for example. In English, even if a *when* clause refers to the future we use the present tense ('I'll see her when I go to Bristol') or the present perfect ('I'll see her when I've finished the shopping').

So some knowledge of grammar would help explain the mistake in sentence 2 to a native speaker and the mistake in sentence 3 to a foreign learner. A basic understanding of the general structure of English and a handful of technical terms with which to describe its main features are useful tools for any user of the language. They can be used to analyse writing and speech, and to help develop a sense of style.

A simple grammatical grounding, and the necessary technical terms, are the subject matter of the next two chapters. The grammatical content is kept to an absolute minimum and all the terms used are explained in the Glossary on pages 359–372, to which you can refer as necessary.

You try

Each of the following sentences would be objected to by some people. What are your feelings about each of them?

1 The car I have just bought is totally different to the last one I had.
2 I was trying hard to fully understand his problems.
3 Peter Davies was the person I sold my last car to.
4 I will send you the invoice next week.
5 None of my friends like Tom Cruise films.
6 The British media is dominated by a small number of wealthy men.
7 We hope to be able to finalize the deal in the next few days.
8 There are less Spaniards living in some sections of the Costa del Sol than expatriates.
9 I am really interested of impressionist paintings.
10 Her latest film is centred around the last earthquake to strike San Francisco.

See the commentary on page 374.

Guidelines

1 When thinking about language, remember that it is living, not dead. It continues to develop and change. To use English well, you need to be aware of how it is being used in different situations and for different purposes. Some changes don't 'take', but others last a long time, so it is impossible to have one single attitude towards all new words and expressions. How you react to change depends on who you are and the social contexts in which you write and speak.

2 Remember, too, that English exists in many different dialects. The 'official' form, **standard English**, is suitable for nearly all writing and for formal occasions when you are addressing people whom you do not know well, or in situations when people expect formality. At other times the use of a regional or social dialect may well be more suitable. But if in doubt, use standard English.

3 Do not expect modern grammatical writers to tell you how to speak and write; their function is to describe how English *is* used, rather than how it *should* be. Guides to usage can help you here, but they are based on the writer's judgement, so some are better than others. Look around in libraries and bookshops before selecting one that answers the questions you have in a way that you find helpful.

16 Introduction to grammar

Grammar analyses language at different levels. In particular it is concerned with:

- sentences
- clauses
- phrases
- words

There are four sentence types:

- statements
- questions
- directives
- exclamations

Simple sentences contain one finite verb. The five elements they can contain are:

- subject
- verb
- object
- complement
- adverbial

Sentence length and variety are important when writing. Verbless ('minor') sentences can have their place but need to be used sparingly.

Introduction

To many people, grammar appears threatening and even impossible to understand. This is often because of the way in which it has been presented to them, whether at school or later in their lives. The purpose of this chapter is to provide a simple introduction to what grammar is and how a basic understanding of it can be used to see how simple sentences are constructed. Chapter 17, *More about grammar*, as its name suggests, goes into more detail.

Grammar is a set of rules which describe how a language works. These are rules in the sense that scientific laws are rules: general statements that describe how things are, not moral regulations like the Ten Commandments. Grammar can be divided into two:

- The rules which describe how words are arranged to make sentences. The technical name for this is **syntax**. Syntax explains why these two sentences have different meanings:

  The cat sat on the mat.

  The mat sat on the cat.

- The rules which describe how words are changed to fit into sentences. Linguists call this **morphology**. Morphology explains why these two sentences have different meanings:

  The cat sat on the mat.

  The cat sits on the mat.

Levels

One of the difficulties of grasping grammar is that there seem to be so many things going on at the same time: are we supposed to be looking at the whole sentence, or bits of it? And if the answer is, 'Bits of it,' how do we know which bits to look at?

Grammar answers this by working at a number of different levels. They can be illustrated by this sample sentence:

The cat sat on the mat, while the dog ate its dinner.

We can divide this **sentence** into two **clauses:**

The cat sat on the mat	*while the dog ate its dinner.*
MAIN CLAUSE	SUBORDINATE CLAUSE

Each clause is composed of different **clause elements**, each of which has a particular job to do:

The cat	*sat*	*on the mat*
SUBJECT	VERB	ADVERBIAL

Each clause element can be considered as a **phrase:**

The cat	*sat*	*on the mat*
NOUN PHRASE	VERB PHRASE	PREPOSITIONAL PHRASE

Each phrase in the sentence is made up of words and each word belongs to a particular **word class:**

The	cat	sat	on	the	mat
ARTICLE	NOUN	VERB	PREPOSITION	DETERMINER	NOUN

So there are all these different levels to think about when talking about grammar:

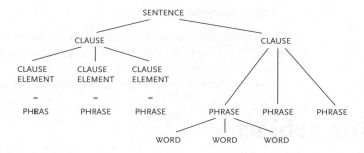

Definitions

It would seem reasonable at this stage to proceed to a simple definition of each of these levels: 'A sentence is...' and so on. Unfortunately the experts find it difficult (many would say impossible) to give a simple definition of what a sentence is. This can give writers about grammar a slightly shifty air, as they try to avoid answering that 'big question'.

The approach in this chapter is as follows. Most people who speak English have in fact got a fairly good working understanding of sentences. Much of the time they have no difficulty in telling you what is and what is not a sentence. Problems arise when they write a sentence that they think may be questionable and they want advice about how it should be put right. The focus in this book is on just such problem situations. Usually they can be resolved by understanding how the components of the sentence work together. For example, a large proportion of such sentence problems have to do with the relationship between the subject and the verb. So it is important to be able to identify the subject and the verb and to understand a number of key features about them.

In this chapter we concentrate on simple sentences. These are sentences that consist of a single clause, with one subject and one verb. Chapter 17 then looks at more complicated constructions and their related problems.

Types of sentence

The sentences we use can be divided into four types, according to their purpose:

- **Statements**

  Mr Sanderson is leaving the company next month.

- **Questions**

  Why is Mr Sanderson leaving the company next month?

- **Directives** (sometimes called commands or requests):

  Clear your desk before leaving.

- **Exclamations**

  What a worker she was!

The grammatical explanations that follow are based on statement sentences. These are by far the commonest type, and the other types can be derived from them.

All simple statement sentences contain **one subject** and **one verb**.

The subject

Position and meaning

In a statement sentence, the subject normally comes before the verb. It often (but not always) tells us what the sentence will be about, or where its focus will be, as in these sentences:

> *Success drives many managers.*
> *Many of my friends are unhappy in their work.*

This is not always true, however. Sometimes the subject gives little away:

> *It is not always easy to spot a successful product.*

The subject of a sentence may be:

- **A noun**

  People are strange.

- **A noun phrase**

  This is a group of words based on a noun:
  The people in our department will miss Mr Sanderson.
  The noun phrase printed in bold is based on the noun *people*.

- **A pronoun**

  This is a word which 'stands for' a noun, a noun phrase, or some other group of words which has recently been mentioned.
  They say the strangest things.

- **An infinitive**

  This is the 'to...' form of the verb:
  To err is human.

- **A verbal noun**

  Sometimes called a gerund, this is the '...ing' form of the verb:
  Swimming *is an excellent form of exercise.*

The verb

The grammatical term 'verb' can be used to refer to a class of words, like *be, happen*, and *kill*. It is also used to refer to one part of a clause or sentence (when it is sometimes referred to as the **verb phrase**). This second way is how it is being used in this section.

Position

In a statement sentence the verb usually comes after the subject:

> Mrs Hart **hates** ice cream.

It does not necessarily come *immediately* after the subject. In this sentence the words in brackets come between the *subject* and the **verb:**

> *She* [only recently] **started to eat** yogurt again.

In exceptional cases the verb may come before the subject:

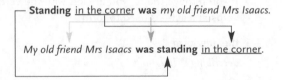

Meaning

The verb provides important information about the subject. It usually refers to:

- **an action**

  The volcano **destroyed** the village.

- **a state or condition**

  I **was dreaming**.

Or it may act as a **link** between the subject and the rest of the sentence:

> My father's first name **is** Peter.

The form of a verb phrase

The verb in a sentence may be one word or several:

> I **visited** Paris last week.
>
> I **should have been visiting** my grandfather today.

When the verb phrase consists of several words, these are all verbs. They are either:

- **full (or 'main') verbs**

  These are verbs that can stand on their own in a sentence, without reference to any other verb. They are mostly words with a 'dictionary meaning'. For example:

  collect   make   send   suggest

- **auxiliary verbs**

  These are verbs which work with the full verb. They are:

  shall   should   will   would   may
  might   can   could   must   ought (to)

- In addition there are three verbs which can work either as auxiliaries, or as full verbs:

  be/is/am/was, etc.   have/has/had   do/does/did, etc.

  These are called **primary verbs**.

Parts of a verb Verbs exist in these forms:

- **the infinitive**

  This is the 'to' form of the verb:

  *...**to sleep**, perchance **to dream**...*

  If you remove the *to*, you are left with the verb **stem**, which—in regular verbs at least—is used to form:

- **the -ing form**

  describing   laughing

- **the -ed form**

  described   laughed

    This is used in a number of different **tenses:**

    I described   I have described   I have been described

Many common verbs are irregular, however:

to walk	she walked	she has walked
to sing	she sang	she has sung
to go	she went	she has gone

Tense English has a wide variety of tenses, which give information about **when** something happened, and also the **aspect** of the action we wish to focus on. For example:

SIMPLE PAST		*I **walked** to the office this morning.* (Action in the past, attention focused on the fact that it is a single completed action.)
PAST CONTINUOUS		*As I **was walking** I saw a swan.* (Action in the past, attention focused on the continuing nature of the action—it was going on when something else happened.)

Agreement

The verb has to agree with the subject in number and person:

SINGULAR	FIRST PERSON	I walk
	SECOND PERSON	you walk (*thou walkest*)
	THIRD PERSON	he/she/it walks
PLURAL	FIRST PERSON	we walk
	SECOND PERSON	you walk
	THIRD PERSON	they walk

Sentence problems

One of the causes of problems when writing sentences, especially long sentences, is the verb.

Finite verb

A sentence must contain a complete, or **finite** verb. This is a verb that shows **tense, number**, and **person**. If a sentence does not contain a finite verb, then it isn't a sentence:

> In late September in Herefordshire, during those last magic days of summer, **walking** through the fields down by the river Wye!

It is typical of sentences like this, that the reader is left waiting for something to happen, but nothing does and then the sentence ends. We want to know **who** the sentence is about and exactly **what they were doing**. It might mean, for example:

> In late September in Herefordshire, during those last magic days of summer, **I used to love walking** through the fields down by the river Wye!

Otherwise we cannot know what the writer meant, because the sentence does not contain a finite verb.

Lack of agreement

Another possible reason why sentences sometimes don't work is that the subject and verb fail to agree. As we have seen, they should agree in number and person. If the subject is short and simple, there is usually no problem, but when the subject is complicated it becomes more difficult to keep track of exactly what the whole subject is:

> Several representatives of the Board, including the Chair, **has visited the region in the past year.**

The trick is to ask yourself 'How many: one, or more than one?' In this case the answer is 'More than one', so the verb should be *have visited*.

The question of agreement is particularly vexed where **either** or **neither** are used in the subject. If both items are singular, then there is no problem; the verb is singular:

> Either the sales manager or his assistant **is** the person to take charge of this assignment.

If one of the two is plural, then the verb should agree with the one that comes immediately before it:

> Either the prime minister or his ministers **are** to blame.

The same applies to the *person* of the verb:

> Either Peter or I **am** going to look after it.
> Either you or Peter **is** going to look after it.

You try

Pick out the subject and the verb in each of the following sentences:

1 Making good coffee is an art.
2 The occasion of my last visit to see my Great Aunt Annie could have been a disaster.
3 This time next month I shall have been living in Australia for ten years.
4 During the last years of his life, the composer had become increasingly eccentric.

In each of the sentences that follow, the verb is in brackets. Put it into the correct form so that it agrees with the subject of the sentence.

1 Both James and I (*be*) members of the local golf club.
2 After some time, all the members of the board of management, including our latest recruit, Mrs Greene, (*be*) happy about the decision.
3 Either your brother-in-law, or you (*have*) to decide what to do next.
4 Neither I nor my sisters (*be*) present when the will was read.

Answers on page 377.

Other sentence elements

Some sentences only consist of a subject and a verb:

SUBJECT	VERB
Mrs Howard	has left.
Most of our long-term problems	are being overcome.
This question	would have been foreseen.

However, many sentences have one or more elements after the verb.

Object

One definition of the object is that it describes 'what is affected by the action of the verb' and in this example that is clear enough:

The dog bit our visitor.

Often, however, there isn't much 'action' involved:

I like ice cream

so it is more accurate, if more complicated, to say that the object:

- normally comes after the verb
- refers to a person, place, thing, or idea that is different from the subject
- often describes something or somebody that has been affected by the action of the verb
- can be: a noun, a noun phrase, a noun clause, or a verbal noun.

Some sentences have two objects: direct and indirect:

Our visitor	gave	the baby	a rattle.
SUBJECT	VERB	INDIRECT OBJECT	DIRECT OBJECT

To distinguish these two kinds of object, remember that this kind of sentence can normally be turned round, with the addition of *to*:

Our visitor	gave	the baby	a rattle.
Our visitor	gave	a rattle	**to** the baby.

The commonest problem for writers concerns the **case** of the object. Some pronouns in English change according to whether the word is the subject or the object of the sentence:

SUBJECT (SUBJECTIVE CASE)	VERB	OBJECT (OBJECTIVE OR ACCUSATIVE CASE)
I	told	**him.**
He	told	**me.**

The pronouns concerned are:

I/me	he/him	she/her
we/us	they/them	who/whom (and whoever, etc.)

When a pronoun is governed by a preposition, you should use the objective case. So it should be *to John and **me*** not *to John and I*.

Problems can arise when there is a double object:

> After the accident the chairman visited **my wife and I/my wife and me in hospital.**

If you are in any doubt about which is correct, remove the other part of the object and see if it sounds right.

> After the accident the chairman visited **I** in hospital.

This can never be correct in standard English (although it is in some dialects); the objective or accusative case, **me**, is what is required:

> After the accident the chairman visited **my wife and me** in hospital.

You should also use the objective or accusative case after prepositions:

> The chairman paid several warm compliments to **my wife and me.**

Complement

A small number of verbs are followed not by an object but by a complement. The verbs, sometimes called **linking verbs**, include:

to be	to seem	to appear to	to become

In sentences containing these verbs, the subject and the complement refer to the same person or thing:

SUBJECT	VERB	COMPLEMENT
My uncle	became	a Roman Catholic.

The complement of a sentence can be a noun, preposition, or noun phrase (just like the object), but it can also be an adjective or adjective phrase:

SUBJECT	VERB	COMPLEMENT
My uncle	is	very happy.

Grammatically the complement should be the same case as the subject; hence the problem people have with:

Who's there? It is I.

Technically this is correct and, in formal written English, this is what you should use. But if you use 'It is I', rather than 'It's me' in everyday conversation people will probably think you are being a bit finicky.

Adverbial

Adverbials are much more varied. They provide information that answers these questions:

- **when/how long?**

  *I met her **yesterday**.*

- **(to) where?**

  *He placed a book **on the table**.*

- **why?**

  *They did it **for my sake**.*

- **how?**

  *The trick was performed **very very skilfully**.*

- **how much?**

  *I helped them **as much as possible**.*

As these examples show, the adverbial can be:

- a single word, an adverb: *yesterday*

- an adverb phrase (a group of words built up on an adverb): *very very skilfully*
- a prepositional phrase (a group of words that begins with a preposition): *on the table*

Position

Subjects, verbs, objects, and complements are fairly predictable: there isn't much choice about where you put them in the sentence. Adverbials can pop up anywhere; there is often a choice about where you put them. Both these sentences are possible:

> *We had our holiday in June.*
> *In June we had our holiday.*

The difference is one of emphasis and context.

Normally the adverbial should come as close as possible to the verb it modifies, though not between the verb and its object. There are, however, occasions when to follow this rule may itself cause confusion. If the object is longer and we place the adverbial after it, the adverbial may become attached to the wrong part of the sentence: This sentence:

> *The workman explained his reasons for leaving the site angrily.*

clearly does not mean the same as this one:

> *The workman explained angrily his reasons for leaving the site.*

Warning

Some common adverbials can cause ambiguity when wrongly placed. All these sentences have different meanings:

1 **Even** the scientists are concerned about traffic fumes.
2 The scientists are **even** concerned about traffic fumes.
3 The scientists are concerned about **even** traffic fumes.

1 means that **everyone including scientists** is concerned
2 means that scientists are **concerned about lots of things**, including traffic fumes
3 means that scientists are **concerned about all fumes**, including traffic fumes

To avoid ambiguity or wrong emphasis, *even* should be placed next to the word it refers to.

There are sometimes similar problems with *only*, but they are not so great and much of the time it is possible to place *only* in its natural place, next to the verb, without causing confusion:

> *I **only** read his letter last week.*

This clearly means 'It was only last week that I read his letter.' No one is likely to understand it to mean 'I could have torn it up or burned it, but all I did was read it.' Particularly in speech we can make our meaning clearer by tone of voice and emphasis, so normally *only* takes its natural place next to the verb and our voices do the rest. In writing, if there is any possibility of confusion, *only* should be placed next to the word(s) it refers to.

Each of the following sentences has one part printed in bold. Is it subject, verb, object, complement, or adverbial?

1 The mechanic placed the new carburettor **on the workbench**.
2 Later that year she became **leader of the local council**.
3 Our only local newspaper has just ceased **publication**.
4 I **should have preferred** a more interesting approach.
5 In a few years' time **everyone except us old folk** will be computer literate.

Is there any difference in meaning between the sentences within these groups?

1a Harry forgot even his grandfather's birthday.
1b Even Harry forgot his grandfather's birthday.
2a Originally I concentrated on black and white photographs.
2b I concentrated originally on black and white photographs.
2c I concentrated on black and white photographs originally.
3a Happily Peter gave Maria back her book.
3b Peter gave Maria back her book happily.
4a Only the Sales Department wants the new product painted pink.
4b The Sales Department wants only the new product painted pink.
4c The Sales Department wants the new product painted only pink.

Answers on page 378.

Sentence length and variety

Short sentences

Of course, most writing does not consist entirely of simple sentences, containing only one subject and one verb, but there are certain things it is useful to say at this point about written style.

A real strength of simple sentences is that they can be short and punchy. In the right place they can be very powerful. This paragraph contains one short simple sentence right in the middle:

> I had seen the collision coming, but when it happened the impact was so abrupt and stunning that it shocked the sense out of me, and for a while I sat quietly among the broken glass of the jeep as though I had been sitting there forever. In any case I found I could not move because of the dead weight of the soldiers on either side of me. **We had hit the bus head-on.** The front of the jeep was embedded under its bonnet, and the crash must have somehow distorted the wiring apparatus because the first thing I became aware of was a continuous metallic howl from the horn that nobody tried to stop. It seemed as though the machinery itself was screaming in pain, while all the people involved were spellbound and silent.

The first two sentences introduce the situation but by the end of the second we are still not clear exactly what has happened. Then the writer tells us, simply and brutally.

It is important not to overdo it, however. Too many short sentences can make a text seem jerky or immature (young children sometimes write in this way).

Minor sentences

In this chapter, a sentence has been partly defined as having a finite verb. We often encounter 'sentences' that break this rule. They are particularly common in public notices:

> One-way street.
> Parking for residents only.
> Fresh stock now in.

They also occur in speech:

> Lovely weather this morning!

They make complete sense, but they are grammatically incomplete. Linguists sometimes call them minor sentences. They can be used in continuous writing for a particular effect. A good idea? Possibly. Definitely capable of overuse, however. Like most things.

Sentence punctuation

Normally, of course, written sentences are marked off by punctuation, beginning with a capital letter and ending with a full stop. Occasionally writers fail to do this, running sentences together, or separating them with a comma, rather than a full stop:

> This type of of writing can be difficult for readers, their eyes are trained to see a comma as marking off parts of one sentence, when they come across writing where this is not done they become confused, it is important to remember this when writing.

This error is sometimes called the comma splice, because a comma is used to splice, or join, two sentences. There is, however, a punctuation mark which can be used for this purpose, the **semicolon**.

If you have two sentences which are closely related in meaning, they can be linked in this way:

> Writing clearly and simply is not easy; it requires practice.

This sentence reads slightly differently from:

> Writing clearly and simply is not easy. It requires practice.

In the first example we see that the two ideas are closely linked together. In the second they are offered as separate thoughts, one after the other, and the reader is left to make the link from the sense.

An easy way of remembering this is as follows. You shouldn't link two simple sentences with a comma. All you need to do is:

- replace the comma with a full stop, or
- put a full stop above the comma, turning it into a semicolon (;)

Guidelines

Subject

1 The subject of a sentence can be quite extended. Make sure that your readers do not lose track of the subject before they even reach the verb. This is particularly likely to happen if you put a participle before the subject:

Walking *down Exhibition Road, just by the Fire Station, my old and trusted friend from the good old days and now a wealthy property developer, Mr Patel, saw...*

Verb

2 Make sure that the verb is finite and agrees with the subject in both number (singular/plural) and person (*she is/we are*, etc).

3 Agreement is particularly tricky in these situations:
- where there is a multiple subject, joined by *and*
- where you are using *either* or *neither*

Object

4 Make sure that pronouns used as objects are in the correct, objective, case (*me*, not *I, him* not *he*, etc.).

Complement

5 In formal writing, pronouns used as complements should be in the subjective case (*It is I*).

Adverbial

6 Make sure that you have placed any adverbials in the best position in the sentence. Often this is next to the verb, but sometimes the adverbial must be placed to make the precise meaning clear. This applies particularly to *even* and *only*.

Style

7 Use short sentences sparingly for maximum impact.

8 Minor sentences can be used in written texts, but again only sparingly and for a particular effect.

9 Make sure that sentences are correctly separated by punctuation, normally a full stop and following capital letter. If two sentences are closely linked in sense they can sometimes be joined by a semicolon.

➤ *Further reading*

John Seely, *Everyday Grammar*
(Oxford University Press, 2006), ISBN 9780195679779.

John Seely, *Grammar for Teachers*
(Oxpecker, 2007), ISBN 9780955345128 (print and e-book versions).

17 More about grammar

Compound sentences

- Definition
- Coordinating conjunctions

Complex sentences

- Adverbial clauses:
  time
  place
  condition
  purpose
  reason
  result
  concession
- Noun clauses
- Relative clauses:
  defining and non-defining
  who or whom?

Problem areas

- Coordinating:
  joining items of equal status
  both
  either/or and *neither/nor*
- Subordinating conjunctions:
  as
  because
  so

In the last chapter simple sentences were defined as having only one verb. Technically such sentences consist of one **finite clause**. A finite clause is a grammatical unit that contains a finite verb; it can stand alone as a simple sentence, or be combined with other clauses into compound or complex sentences.

Compound sentences

The simplest way of joining clauses is by bolting them together like this:

Maybrick Ltd supplies bearings	and	ERICO fits them.
CLAUSE	+	CLAUSE

The two clauses are of the same status in the sentence (they are described grammatically as 'coordinated'—of the same level) and each could stand on its own as a simple sentence.

Coordinating conjunctions

The commonest conjunctions used to link clauses in this way are:

and	but	or	nor	then	yet

It is important to remember that although they all do the same job grammatically, they have very different meanings.

Then

Then is straightforward: the event described by the second clause must follow that described in the first:

Maybrick Ltd supplies bearings, then ERICO fits them.

Clearly it wouldn't make sense to have the clauses the other way round.

But/yet

In the example above, *and* simply joins the two clauses, but if it were replaced by *but*, the meaning of the whole sentence would be changed:

Maybrick Ltd supplies bearings, but ERICO fits them.

On its own, the sentence does not make clear why the speaker has said 'but', and this is sometimes true even when we know the context. *But* does imply some sort of contrast, conflict, or contradiction, however, even when its exact meaning is unstated. For example, if the speaker is the managing director of Maybrick Ltd he may be implying that once the bearings have left the factory his company has no responsibility for what ERICO does with them.

Yet is used in a similar way to *but*.

Or/nor

These two conjunctions only make sense when the two clauses they link are genuine alternatives. It would, for example, be nonsense to say:

Maybrick Ltd supplies bearings, or ERICO fits them.

On the other hand you *could* say:

> Maybrick Ltd supplies bearings, or ERICO purchases them from a company in the States.

where it is understood that the first clause means '... supplies bearings *to* ERICO...'.

Nor works in a similar way to *or*, but as a negative:

> I have never met Dominic McGhee, *nor* do I want to.

Beginning a sentence with *and*

It is sometimes said that you should not begin a sentence with a coordinating conjunction, because, as its name implies, it must come between the two things it is coordinating and should not, therefore, be separated from one of them by a full stop. This 'rule' may appear to be logical but it has cheerfully been ignored by writers across the centuries. Separating the two items being linked by *and* or *but*, for example, can be an effective way of giving additional emphasis to the item that is thus separated. But you should not do it too frequently. Or people will find it irritating. Then they will stop reading.

Complex sentences

You can only go so far by using compound sentences. Often we need to show more sophisticated relationships between two clauses. Each of the sentences that follows uses the same two clauses, but each expresses a different meaning:

1 If Maybrick Ltd supplies bearings, ERICO fits them.
2 Maybrick Ltd supplies the bearings that ERICO fits.
3 ERICO fits the bearings that Maybrick Ltd supplies.
4 Maybrick Ltd supplies bearings so that ERICO can fit them.

Which version is chosen depends on the context and the meaning you wish to convey. In this section of the chapter some of the main kinds of link between clauses are examined.

In grammatical terms, one clause in a complex sentence is more important than the others and is described as the **main clause**. The other clauses, the **subordinate clauses**, are grammatically less important and are nearly always introduced by a **subordinating conjunction**.

A complex sentence works in much the same way as a simple sentence. It contains similar elements: subject, verb, adverbial, object, and complement. In a simple sentence these elements may be single words or phrases. In a complex sentence some of them may also be clauses.

Adverbial clauses

Adverbial clauses are very useful and perform a wide range of different functions. They answer a number of different questions.

When? It is often important to show the relationship in time between two events. Perhaps one was completed before the other began; or one occurred during the period that the other was going on. English is particularly well supplied with ways of showing this.

The commonest conjunctions are:

after	as	before	since	until	when	while

These words do not do their work on their own, however. They work closely with the verbs in the sentence to convey their meaning. Each of the following sentences uses *when*, but each conveys very different meaning:

1 When she makes the cake she will listen to the radio.
2 When she was making the cake she listened to the radio.
3 When she had made the cake she listened to the radio.

Where? Time clauses are very common; clauses indicating place may be less common but can be very important—in instructions and descriptions, for example:

- Turn right where the speed limit ends.
- We parted where three roads meet.

The conjunctions used are *where* and *wherever*.

There is one special use of *where* which is worth remembering. It can be used to define conditions under which certain things can happen:

- Where there is shade and moisture, these plants will flourish.
- Where it can be shown that a contractor has damaged a road or pavement then the contractor, or the resident instructing the work, will be liable for the cost of restoration.

What if? Often we want to say that one thing depends on another happening. We frequently do this by using *if* or *unless*:

1 If he comes to the office, the manager will explain the situation.
2 If the company was to blame, then it would pay compensation.
3 If the cheque had bounced, the bank would have told us.

These three sentences all deal with 'one-off' situations: a single event and its possible results. Each suggests a different degree of possibility. Number 1 is open: the 'if' event may or may not happen. In number 2 the 'if' event is unlikely, but if it did happen, then the consequences would follow. These two sentences deal with something that has not yet happened. Sentence 3 is about something in the past and clearly the speaker believes that it has not happened. (But the bank hasn't told us, so the cheque hasn't bounced.)

There is a different kind of conditional sentence which does not deal with a single event, or a definite number of events, but which concerns 'things in general':

- If the company makes a profit, it pays a dividend to the shareholders.
- If babies are unhappy they cry.

As these examples show, it is important to use the correct form of the verb when using *if*. Failure to do so may mean that you do not communicate correctly your own view of the likelihood of the 'if' event—and when dealing with difficult situations, that could cause problems. So, for example, you may want to tell a client in a completely open way that you will help if she has a problem. You mean to say,

If your computer plays up, phone me and I'll come and put it right.

Company policy, however, says you should be more formal than this, so you end up saying:

If the product failed to operate properly during the first six months, then the purchaser would be entitled to free on-site service.

Not only does this lapse into unnecessary jargon ('on-site service'), but it makes the customer feel that the events described are extremely unlikely. Now that is fine if the machine is very reliable, but it may leave a lingering suspicion in the customer's mind that the *home visit* is very unlikely—even if it turns out to be needed.

Sentence 2 above can be expressed in two ways that are similar but significantly different:

- If the company **was** to blame, then it would pay compensation.
- If the company **were** to blame, then it would pay compensation.

The second of these uses a relatively uncommon form of the verb, the **subjunctive**. Its effect is to make the condition *impossible*, rather than just improbable, which is why it is used in sayings such as 'If I were you ...' (which is clearly impossible). Many people, however, do not observe this distinction; increasingly people say 'If I was you ...' and it may be that this use of the subjunctive is dying out.

Each of these groups of sentences looks at the same possible event in two or three different ways. Can you explain the differences between them?

1 a If I need to see you, I'll phone.
   b If I needed to see you, I'd phone.
   c If I had needed to see you I would have phoned.
2 a He'd have told us if he'd wanted to come.
   b He tells us if he wants to come.
3 a Please let us know if the party includes children.
   b Please let us know if the party is going to include children.
   c Please let us know if the party included children.
4 a If you experience difficulty cashing the cheque it is because the bank is in the process of transferring our account.
   b If you experienced difficulty cashing the cheque, it was because the bank was in the process of transferring our account.
   c If you had experienced difficulty cashing the cheque it would have been because the bank was in the process of transferring our account.

See page 378 for possible answers.

For what purpose?

Two common conjunctions enable us to explain the purpose behind an event: *in order that* and *so that* (sometimes abbreviated to *so*):

- The man was executed so that others would be discouraged from imitating him.
- We changed the design in order that health and safety regulations would not be broken.

Why?

'Never apologize; never explain' may be a popular saying, but we often *do* need to explain the reasons for an event. We do this by using *because, since*, and *as*:

- As I'm going to be in New York anyway, I thought I'd drop in on her.
- We made it of wood because that is the most suitable material.
- Since she is responsible for this project, she should be the person to make the presentation.

With sentences like these, you can often choose in which order to place the two clauses:

1 Since she is responsible for this project, she should be the person to make the presentation.
2 She should be the person to make the presentation, since she is responsible for this project.

The only difference is one of focus. Sentence 1 focuses on the reasoning process; sentence 2 focuses on 'her' and uses the reason as 'backup'.

Typical conjunctions here are: *so that*, *so*, and *and so*:

> Some of them have no qualifications in engineering so that they are
> looked down on by senior management.

Sometimes *so* and *that* are separated, with *so* referring to an adjective or adverb. The 'that clause' still describes a result:

- It all happened so quickly that I didn't realize what was going on.
- He was so fat that he could not get through the door to the dining room.

When reasoning or presenting an argument, we may wish to deal with alternative views or other possibilities. We do so using *although, though, even if, whereas*, and *while*:

- Although a pony and trap is an entertaining form of transport, a car is more reliable.
- While gas bills may have fallen during the past quarter, our general running costs have remained the same.

Noun clauses

Noun clauses can stand as subject or complement in a sentence:

> **What I cannot understand** is *how she got away with it.*

Here both subject and complement are noun clauses.
The object of a sentence can also be a noun clause:

> He told the Board that he wished to resign.

In these examples, noun clauses are introduced by *what*, *that*, and *how*. There are several other words which can introduce them, including *where, why, whether*, and *when*.

Relative clauses

Relative clauses act like adjectives or adjective phrases:

- I gave her a *red* scarf. (ADJECTIVE)
- I gave her a scarf *with a red pattern on it*. (ADJECTIVE PHRASE)
- I gave her scarf **that I bought in Amsterdam**. (RELATIVE CLAUSE)

Relative clauses can be introduced by the **relative pronouns** *who, whom, which, that, where, when* and, confusingly, nothing at all. Sentence 3 above could be:

> **I gave her a scarf I bought in Amsterdam.**

The relative pronoun is 'understood'.

Defining and non-defining

Relative clauses do not normally give rise to many problems for the writer. There is, however, one important distinction it is important to make. These two sentences are apparently the same:

1 Teachers who work long hours should be paid more.
2 Teachers, who work long hours, should be paid more.

In Sentence 1 the writer has two groups of teachers in mind: those who work long hours and those who do not. The former group should be paid more. In Sentence 2 the writer is making a statement about **all** teachers: they work long hours and so should be paid more. In the first sentence the relative clause **defines** or **restricts** the group (a 'defining—or restrictive—relative clause'); in the second it does not (a 'non-defining—or non-restrictive—relative clause'). When we speak we can make the difference in meaning clear by timing and intonation; in writing the difference is made by the punctuation.

It is also argued by some that the relative pronoun *which* normally introduces a non-defining clause. If we want to introduce a defining clause we should use either *that* or nothing. Like other such 'rules' this is quite often ignored, but the following guidelines may be of help:

- Use *which* rather than *that* to introduce a non-defining relative clause.
- Normally use *that* rather than *which* to introduce a defining relative clause.
- Only use *which* to introduce a defining relative clause to avoid repetition or for emphasis.
- Always use *which* rather than *that* after a preposition. (e.g. *The bank in which I placed my trust has gone bust.*)
- Use commas before and after a non-defining relative clause to emphasize what it is.
- Don't use a comma before a defining relative clause.

Who or whom?

The other problem area with relative pronouns is the question of when to use *who* and when to use *whom*. The traditional rule is simple—deceptively so:

1 **who** is used as the subject of the verb
   I had a word with the manager who is looking after the Neasden account.
2 **whom** is used as the object of the verb
   I spoke to our Neasden manager, whom I think you have met.

3 whom is used after prepositions

I spoke to Peter, from whom I received that interesting letter.

Modern usage, however, inclines more and more to the use of *who* in all three cases:

2 *I spoke to our Neasden manager, who I think you have met.*

3 *I spoke to Peter, who I received that interesting letter from.*

On the other hand, there are still traditionalists out there who object to this and certainly most people would still find it rather strange to hear:

I spoke to Peter, from who I received that interesting letter.

A sensible rule would be:

USE	FORMAL SITUATIONS	INFORMAL SITUATIONS
subject of verb	who	who
object of verb	whom	who
with preposition	whom, preceded by preposition[1]	who, with preposition at end[2]

1. ... from whom I received...
2. ... who I received that interesting letter from.

Problem areas

Coordinating

Many problems associated with conjunctions are linked to the fact that when we use coordinating conjunctions they must link two items that have the same grammatical status (i.e., both clauses—including a finite verb—or both phrases). When writers fail to remember this, they make mistakes:

He told us about the trip and that he had managed to make a number of important new contacts.

If you break the sentence down diagrammatically, it is easy to see what is wrong:

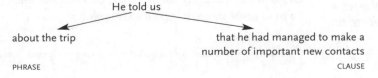

He told us

about the trip   that he had managed to make a number of important new contacts

PHRASE   CLAUSE

The sentence needs to be recast so that the two items joined by *and* have the same status:

> *He told us about the trip and the important new contacts he had made.*

Here *and* is joining two noun phrases:

> *the trip*
> *the important new contacts*

Both

Both is used to join two items and not more than two. It is wrong, therefore, to use expressions such as *Both Eleanor and the two girls* ... If it works with another conjunction, that conjunction should be *and*, so that this sentence is unsatisfactory:

> The company produces both PVA products as well as PVC.

It should be:

> The company produces both PVA and PVC products.

Again, it is important to remember that ...*both* ... *and* ... should only be used to join items of equal status.

> *He both performs in an orchestra and as a soloist.*

should be rephrased as:

> *He performs both in an orchestra and as a soloist.*

Finally, in expressions involving figures, *both* can produce ambiguities like this:

> *Both books cost £20.*

Did each book cost £10 or £20? Better to write either *Each book cost £10* or *The two books together cost £40*.

Either/or & neither/nor

Like other coordinating conjunctions, *either/or* and *neither/nor* must join items of equal status. It is poor style to write:

> *This argument neither explains what went wrong nor how it should be put right.*

It should read:

> *This argument explains neither what went wrong nor how it should be put right.*

A simple check is to remove the section of the sentence that begins with *either/neither* and ends with *or/nor*. If the rest of the sentence still works grammatically, then you have got it right. (The sense will have changed, of course.)

> *This argument explains ~~neither what went wrong nor~~ how it should be put right.*

Other problems with these conjunctions concern the agreement between subject and verb. The comments that follow all use *either* but apply equally to *neither*:

1 *Either* is singular when it acts as the subject of the verb:

   I have looked at both the Ford and the Peugeot; either is suitable for my purposes.

2 When *either/or* link two singular items, then the verb should be singular:

   Either the Ford or the Peugeot is suitable for my purposes.

3 When *either/or* link a singular and a plural item, the verb takes its number from whichever is nearest:

   Either oranges or ice cream is my choice for pudding.
   Either ice cream or oranges are my choice for pudding.

4 The same rule applies when there is a change of person:

   Either you or she has the best chance of winning.
   Either she or you have the best chance of winning.

5 Informally this 'rule of proximity' also operates when *either* is used without *or* to indicate a choice of plurals:

   Either of the cars are suitable for my purposes.

   but this is still frowned on in more formal situations.

The above rules also apply to *or* when it is used on its own.

Subordinating conjunctions

Subordinating conjunctions can cause problems, too, frequently because of ambiguity. Some of the commonest problems are listed here.

As

This small word can be tricky. It can work as a conjunction or as a preposition. As a conjunction it has a range of meanings, including:

1 while/when
2 because/since

The first two can sometimes be confused. For example:

> As I was going to the shops, I decided to buy some onions.

Does the writer mean 'I made the decision on the way to the shops' or 'Because I was going to the shops'? If the former, then it could be made clearer by writing 'While ...'; if the latter, then starting the sentence with 'Because ...' would be clearer.

Another common use of *as* is paired: *as ... as*. This construction can produce ambiguities, too:

> *I have visited Peter as often as Mary.*

This could mean:

- I have visited Peter as often as I have visited Mary.
- I have visited Peter as often as Mary has.

Because

When it follows a negative statement, *because* can lead to ambiguity, as in this sentence:

> *He didn't take up the option because he was hard up.*

This has two possible meanings so it should be rephrased:

- *Because he was hard up he didn't take up the option.*
- *It wasn't because he was hard up that he took up the option.*

Another possible cause of ambiguity occurs when the reason for coming to a particular conclusion comes **after** the conclusion:

> *I knew he was lying because I'd spoken to his wife.*

Here there are two possible meanings:

- As I'd spoken to his wife I knew he was lying.
- He knew that I had spoken to his wife and so he lied.

So

So can produce ambiguities similar to those of *as*, because it can mean:

- 'as a result'
- 'in order that'

This sentence, for example, is ambiguous:

> *He left home so his parents could get some peace.*

To make the meaning clear it should be rephrased:

- *He left home in order that his parents could get some peace.*
- *He left home and as a result his parents could get some peace.*

Guidelines

1 When you use compound sentences, coordinated with conjunctions like *and, or, but, nor, then, yet*, be aware of the limited range of meanings these can convey.

2 Remember that although complex sentences can convey a much wider range of meanings, they require more careful construction.

3 When you write *when* clauses make sure that the order of events you are describing is clear.

4 Remember that conditional (*if*) sentences require careful handling. (Check under the heading 'What if?' in this chapter (pp. 206–207) for the range of possible meanings.)

5 Relative clauses may be defining or non-defining, and you need to be clear which is which. (Check under the heading 'Relative clauses' in this chapter (pp. 209–211) for advice on when to use *which, that, who,* or *whom*.)

6 Take care with coordinating conjunctions like *both ... and*: they need to link items that are grammatically similar. (See under 'Coordinating', pp. 211–213.)

7 Make sure that *either/neither* and *or/nor* are correctly placed and that the verb agrees with the subject. (See under 'Coordinating', pp. 208–209.)

8 Subordinating conjunctions *as, because*, and *so* also need careful use. (See under 'Subordinating conjunctions', pp. 000 and above.)

> **Further reading**

John Seely, *Everyday Grammar*
(Oxford University Press, 2006), ISBN 9780195679779.

John Seely, *Grammar for Teachers*
(Oxpecker, 2007), ISBN 9780955345128 (print and e-book versions).

18 Vocabulary

All language users have an **active** and a **passive** vocabulary.

Getting help

In order to find words, and to understand their meanings and how to use them, we can use:

- dictionaries
- thesauruses
- other word books

Word formation and structure

A knowledge of word formation often helps in the understanding of unfamiliar words.

Word structure

- All words have a stem.
- Some also have affixes: a prefix and/or a suffix.
- A knowledge of prefixes helps in understanding the meaning of a word.
- Suffixes are used:
  - grammatically, to modify certain words before using them in a sentence
  - in word formation

Compounding

- Classical compounds are derived from Greek and Latin words, or parts of them.

Words and their connotations

- Social attitudes also have an important impact on which words can and cannot be used in different social contexts, especially in the areas of:

  taboo

  slang

  informal language
- Caution is also required when using language that can be described as jargon.
- Our use of language can also betray social attitudes and bias, especially towards minorities and vulnerable social groups.
- Even in more general situations language often carries emotional attitudes or 'colour'.

Most of the time we use words without conscious thought... until we are stumped either for the right word to use or for the precise meaning of a word we have read. While it is true that we all have a vocabulary of so many thousand words, our ability to use the words we know varies considerably. In my own experience I am aware of the following groups of words:

1 Those I know and use every day in conversation and casual writing.
2 Those I use with confidence when doing 'more serious' writing.
3 Those I use but need to think about a bit before committing myself to using—even to the extent of checking their meaning in a dictionary.
4 Those I understand clearly when I read them (and could define fully if challenged), but which I do not recall ever having used in speech or writing.
5 Those I understand well enough (I think!) not to hesitate over when I read them.
6 Those I have come across before, but the meaning of which I am very hazy about (and which, if it mattered enough, I would look up in a dictionary).
7 Those I have never encountered before.

Groups 1 and 2 are often combined and described as a person's active vocabulary. This includes all the words that person knows and can use confidently in speech and/or writing. Groups 4 and 5 are the person's passive vocabulary, the words that person can understand when listening or reading. Group 3 includes the words that are in the process of moving from being passive to being active (or possibly vice versa), while Group 6 includes those words that are beginning to enter the passive vocabulary.

You try

1 Look at the list of words below. Divide them into three groups:
  • those you would feel confident to use in a sentence
  • those you understand but would hesitate to use in a sentence
  • the rest

contract	compact	covenant	transaction	pledge
concordat	indenture	bond	undertaking	

Words in the first group form part of your active vocabulary, while those in the second group are part of your passive vocabulary.

→

Continued

2 Now do the same with this list:

fraction	fractionate	fractostratus	fraenum	fragile
fragment	fragrance	frail	fraise	frame
franchise	francium	francolin	frangible	frank

You can play a similar game online at <http://dynamo.dictionary.com/>, although the basis on which the site assesses your word knowledge is somewhat open to question.

Fortunately we do not usually encounter words in isolation; they are normally in the context of a sentence and often in a paragraph or longer text. The context frequently gives sufficient clues to help the reader with the meaning of a difficult word.

Determining the size of your vocabulary

It is difficult to say just how many words a person knows, but it is an interesting experiment to try to assess the size of your own vocabulary. This is one way in which it can be done:

1 Take a dictionary of between 1000 and 2000 pages.
2 Select 1 per cent of the total number of pages evenly distributed throughout the dictionary. (So, for example, if you were using a 1500-page dictionary you would need to choose 15 pages.)
3 Go through each page counting:
   • how many words you recognize and think you know the meaning of (your passive vocabulary)
   • how many words you think you have used in speech or writing (your active vocabulary)
4 Multiply each figure by 100 to get an approximate idea of the size of your active and passive vocabulary.

Getting help

If you go into a large bookshop or reference library, you will find a bewildering array of reference books offering information and advice about words.

The easiest way to describe word books is to break them down into three groups:

- dictionaries
- thesauruses
- the rest

Dictionaries

A large dictionary, such as the *New Shorter Oxford English Dictionary*, can provide a wealth of information, as this extract shows:

Headword
The word which the entry is about, and on which any derivatives listed at the end of the entry are based.

Pronunciation
This may use a phonetic alphabet, as here, or some other system. This will be explained in the introduction to the dictionary. With words of more than one syllable, the word stress is also shown.

Word class (part of speech)
This gives information on how the word is used in sentences.

Etymology
Information about the origins and development of the word.

Meanings
Many words have more than one meaning and here these are numbered and lettered.

sage /seɪdƷ/ aˡ ME. [(O)Fr. f. Proto-Gallo-Romance, f. L *sapere* be wise.] **1** Of a person: wise, discreet, judicious, now esp. through experience.   ME. **b** Of advice, behaviour, etc.: characterized by profound wisdom; based on sound judgement.   m16. **c** Of an expression, bearing, etc.: exhibiting profound wisdom. Now freq. *iron*. e19. †**2** Grave, dignified, solemn. m16–m17.
1b P. G. Wodehouse   The venerable old man was whispering sage counsel.   **2** Shakes.   *Haml*. We should profane the service of the dead To sing sage requiem to her.
sagely *adv*. lME **sageness**   *n*. the quality of being sage; profound wisdom: e16.

Quotations
Selected quotations illustrating a particular meaning of the word in use.

History
The dates or periods shown tell you when the word was first used in this way.

Derivatives
Other words that are derived from the headword.

Usage
Comments on the way in which the word may be used. Here we are told that this usage is often 'ironic', rather than 'straight' or 'serious'.

Smaller dictionaries provide correspondingly less information:

> *sage (1) noun*
> an extremely wise person
> *Word Family:* **sage**, *adjective*, wise; **sagely**,
> *adverb*; **sageness**, *noun*
> [Latin *sapere*, to be wise]
>
> *Heinemann English Dictionary* (for schools)

There are also specialist dictionaries that can be used for specific purposes. Some provide more detailed information about usage and are particularly useful for foreign learners and others who are uncertain about this aspect of language:

sage /seidʒ/, **sages**, 1 A	N COUNT
sage is a person, especially an old man, who is regarded as being very wise; a rather literary use EG *Homage was paid to the great sages buried in the city . . . . . . the Sage of Chelsea, Thomas Carlisle.*	= guru
2 A **sage** person is wise and knowledgeable, especially as a result of age and experience; a rather literary use. EG *They became sage parents anxious to dispense their wisdom* ◊ **sagely** EG *He nodded his head sagely, a smile of amusement appearing on his face*	ADJ QUALIT ◊ ADV WITH VB

Collins Cobuild English Language Dictionary

Digital dictionaries

Increasingly people expect to be able to look words up from their desktop computer, tablet, or smartphone. Computer operating systems themselves include a dictionary for spell-checking, and there are many online dictionaries, many of which are free. For example:

- <http://oxforddictionaries.com/>
- <http://dictionary.cambridge.org/>
- <http://www.collinsdictionary.com/dictionary/english>
- <http://www.merriam-webster.com/>

At the other end of the scale in both complexity and cost is the *Oxford English Dictionary*. Although this is a subscription service, many UK public libraries subscribe and their readers can often access the dictionary from their home computers. You can find out more about this at <http://www.oup.com/uk/academic/online/library/>.

Smartphone apps include offerings from Oxford, Cambridge, Collins, and Merriam-Webster, although frankly these are rather expensive for what they are. Cheaper and very usable is the offering from Chambers. At the time of writing, Amazon Kindle readers come bundled with, among other things, the *New Oxford Dictionary of English*.

The key question to ask any dictionary before relying on it is, 'Who says?' In other words: 'On what basis is the information provided?' Most dictionaries of any size are the work of teams of lexicographers working over a period of many years. They rely on a corpus of written and spoken texts from which they define the ways in which the word in question is used at the time they are writing. Some, like the *Shorter Oxford Dictionary*, also provide information about how the word was used at different points in the past.

➤ See also
• *Taboo, slang, and informal* (p. 230)

In all of this, lexicographers have to exercise judgement. This is even more true when it comes to making comments on usage. For example, the *Shorter Oxford* describes one usage of 'sage' as 'now frequently ironic', while the *Collins Cobuild* says it is 'literary'. Such divergences of opinion are frequently even greater when the word discussed is informal, slang, or taboo.

So dictionaries are time-bound and, to some extent at least, based on the personal opinions of those who construct them. As a result, simply having recourse to a dictionary to resolve some dispute about a word's meaning or usage may not of itself be enough. We also have to consider just how far we trust the lexicographer's judgement. And, of course, the bigger the dictionary, the more information it will provide to help us make up our minds.

Using a thesaurus

If you have an idea and want to find the exact word, a thesaurus *may* be what you need. The word *thesaurus* derives from the classical Greek word for 'storehouse or treasury', which describes it well. It is a storehouse of words. Some thesauruses are arranged alphabetically, providing lists of synonyms (words of similar meaning) and antonyms (words of opposite meaning) for any word you look up. A more traditional arrangement, however, is thematic. The original concept was developed by an English doctor, Peter Mark Roget, who developed a hierarchical classification which is still used (and explained) in contemporary versions of *Roget's Thesaurus*. Other thesauruses follow the same principle but have devised their own classification system.

A typical thematic thesaurus consists of two parts:

- the thematic presentation of synonyms and antonyms
- an index in which words can be looked up.

Index

The index is necessarily lengthy and detailed. It normally provides more than one reference for a word:

> **sage 45** Herbs and Spices, 4,
> 277.7 *deep thinking*, 413.5 *herbs*, 459.8 *intellectual*
> *person*, 459.10 *intelligent*, 501.6 *knowledgeable person*,
> 507.3 *wise man*, 517.8 *oracle*, 611.4 *bigwig*, 654.4
> *adviser*, 655.4 *skilled person*, 688.10 *person of author-*
> *ity*, 696.9 *educational leader*, 849.14 *awe-inspiring*

Each of these references leads to a list in the thematic section:

> 459.8
> **intellectual person**, intellectual, scholar.
> academic, academician, thinker, genius, wise
> man, sage, savant, master, guru, elder states-
> man, oracle, pundit, polymath, litterateur,
> illuminati, bookman, bookworm, bibliophile,
> bluestocking, highbrow, egghead (Inf), intel-
> lect (Inf), boffin (Inf), brainbox (Inf), know-all
> (Inf), know-it-all (US inf), clever clogs (Inf),
> swot (Inf), smart aleck (Inf), smarty pants (Inf),
> smartarse (Inf)

In the search for the *exact word*, you may strike lucky first time, or you may have to follow up several references in the index. When it comes to the moment of choice, however, you often find that what the thesaurus is doing is reminding you of words that you already knew. If so, then more likely than not you know how they should be used and when they are appropriate. Occasionally, however, the thesaurus will suggest words that you have never met before, or about which you are rather unconfident (possibly, in the list above, *illuminati* or *bluestocking*). Then it is necessary to follow up with a dictionary.

Digital thesauruses

As with dictionaries, there are many online thesauruses to experiment with. Most are similar to their printed counterparts (for example, <http://thesaurus.com/>), but some use interesting visual tricks to show you the inter-relationships between words. Examples can be found at:

- <http://www.visualthesaurus.com/> (Although this is only free for a limited number of searches; after that you have to subscribe.)
- <http://www.visuwords.com/>

Other word books

Most reading and writing needs are fulfilled by a good dictionary and the-saurus. There are, however, other specialist word books which may be needed from time to time:

- **Reference dictionary**

  In addition to definitions of words, reference dictionaries provide infor-mation about a wide range of topics, and usually include geographical place names and biographical information.
- **English usage**
- **Quotations**
- **Synonyms and antonyms**
- **Spelling**
- **Idioms**
- **Proverbs**

Word structure

One way of gaining a better understanding of English words is to look at how new words are formed. Some knowledge of word structure, compound words, and other types of word formation is particularly helpful when one is faced with a previously unknown word.

Some words are simple and cannot be broken down into parts. For example:

| grasp | settee | meander |

Many words, however, are composed of identifiable parts:

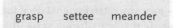

un	comfort	able
PREFIX	STEM	SUFFIX

Stem

The stem (or *base form*) of the word is what is left when any affixes (prefixes and suffixes) have been removed. Words like *grasp* consist of just a stem. *Uncomfortable* has the stem *comfort*, the prefix *un-* and the suffix *-able*.

Prefixes

Prefixes add to or change the meaning of the stem. A knowledge of how prefixes are used can be a great help when working out the meaning of unfamiliar words. Common prefixes include the following.

PREFIX	MEANING	EXAMPLE
a-	not, not affected by	amoral
ante-	before	antecedent
anti-	against	anti-pollution
arch-	chief	arch-rival
auto-	self	autobiography
bi-	two	bipartisan
bio-	(from biology)	biodiversity
circum-	around	circumference
co-	joint, together	co-worker
contra-	opposite	contradiction
counter-	against	counteract
crypto-	hidden	crypto-fascist
de-	making the opposite of	demystify
demi-	half	demigod
di-	two	dialogue
dis-	making the opposite of	disagree
du-/duo-	two	duologue
eco-	(from ecology)	eco-tourism
Euro-	(from European)	Eurosceptic
ex-	former	ex-husband
	out of	extract
fore-	in the front of, ahead of	forerunner
hyper-	very big	hypermarket
in-	not, opposite of	inexact
	in, into	insert
inter-	between	inter-state
intra-	inside	intravenous
mal-	bad(ly)	maladministration
mega-	very large	megastar
mid-	middle	midlife
midi-	medium-sized	midi-length
mini-	small	minimarket
mis-	wrong, false	misadventure
mono-	one	monogamy

multi-	many	multi-layered
neo-	new	neolithic
non-	not, opposite of	non-partisan
out-	beyond	outreach
over-	too much	overreach
para-	ancillary	paramedic
	beyond	paranormal
poly-	many	polymath
post-	after	post-election
pre-	before	pre-election
pro-	for	pro-gun
	deputy	proconsul
pseudo-	false	pseudo-intellectual
re-	again	rerun
	back	reverse
retro-	backwards	retrograde
self-	self	self-sufficient
semi-	half	semi-serious
sub-	below	sub-zero
super-	more than, special	superhuman
supra-	above	suprasensuous
sur-	more than, beyond	surreal
tele-	at a distance	telescope
trans-	across	trans-Siberian
tri-	three	tripartite
ultra-	beyond	ultraviolet
	very much indeed	ultra-careful
un-	not, opposite of	unnecessary
	reversal, cancellation	untie
under-	below, less than	underachieve
uni-	one	unitary
vice-	deputy	vice-chancellor

Suffixes

Suffixes have two functions:

- to inflect words for grammatical purposes (for example, -s and -ed added to verbs, and -s added to nouns)
- to form new words from other words, often, but not always, by changing its part of speech (so the noun *beauty* can be made into a verb *beautify*)

Suffixes are used to form verbs, adverbs, adjectives, and nouns.

Verb suffixes	-ify	beautify
	-ise/-ize	idolize

Adjective suffixes	-able/-ible	excitable
	-al/-ial	adverbial
	-ary	stationary
	-ate	insensate
	-ed	flat-roofed
	-esque	picturesque
	-ful	fateful
	-ic	Icelandic
	-ical	economical
	-ish	childish
	-ive	destructive
	-less	childless
	-like	blood-like
	-ous	analagous
	-y	dozy

Adverb suffixes	-ly	happily
	-ward(s)	westwards
	-wise	counterclockwise

Noun suffixes	-age	acreage
	-al	referral
	-ant/-ent	inhabitant
	-ation/-ion	examination

-dom	kingdom
-ee	addressee
-eer	auctioneer
-er	abstainer
-ery/-ry	effrontery
-ess	tigress
-ette	leatherette
-ful	handful
-hood	neighbourhood
-ing	mooring
-ism	impressionism
-ist	pianist
-ity	chastity
-ment	postponement
-ness	happiness
-ocracy	meritocracy
-or	escalator
-ship	directorship
-ster	trickster

Derivation families

As a result of the possibilities created by the use of prefixes and suffixes, one stem can be the 'parent' of a whole family of derived words:

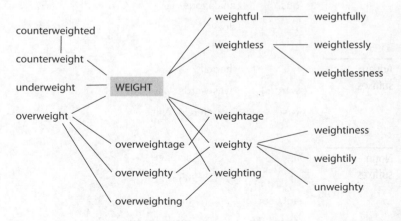

One or two of these words may look slightly strange (although all are recorded in the *Oxford English Dictionary*). Nevertheless, an understanding of affixes makes it possible to work out the meanings even of these. For example, *overweighting* is not a particularly common word, but, even if you did not know it, you could work out its meaning. The stem *weight*, as a verb, means *to load with a weight*; knowledge of suffixes will tell us that one effect of adding -*ing* is to change it into a noun meaning *the process of loading with a weight*. The prefix *over-* adds the meaning of *too much*; hence *overweighting* means *the process of loading with excessive weight*.

You try

1 This is a list of words derived from the stem ***clean***. Use it to construct a diagram similar to the one above.

clean	cleanable	cleaner	cleaning
cleanish	cleanlily	cleanliness	cleanly
cleanness	over-clean	reclean	self-cleaning
unclean	uncleanable	uncleanliness	uncleanly
uncleanness			

2 Make similar diagrams based on these stems:

| large | sail | wait |

See pages 378–379 for possible answers.

Classical derivations

There is a large group of words that come from Greek and Latin stems. Many of these are to be found in the fields of science and other academic specialisms. A knowledge of the common classical stems from which many of these words are drawn can help in gaining at least a rough idea of what an unknown word may mean. Although you may not feel that you know anything about classical Greek and Latin, you will find that words you already know which derive from them provide a useful starting point. For example, if you know the meaning of *geography* and *biology*, it isn't too difficult to work out the meaning of *biogeography*:

> The science of the geographical distribution of living things, animal and vegetable. (*OED*)

Use your knowledge of words derived from Greek and Latin to work out as many of these meanings as you can.

geocentric	geochemistry	geochronology	geodynamic
hydrogeologist	geophysicist	theogeological	geometrize
geoscopy	bioclimatic	bioluminescence	biomechanics
biosphere	bioscope		

See pages 379–380 for definitions.

More than just a meaning

➤ See also
• CHAPTER 10
Audience
(p. 117)
• CHAPTER 12
Time and place
(p. 137)

The decision about which word goes with which is, of course, a matter of experience—hence the problems encountered by foreign learners. Our experience of language is not, however, purely a matter of words and sentences. Linguistic knowledge is enmeshed with social experience. Words have dictionary meanings but they also have a range of social contexts in which they are habitually used and, in many cases, a range of contexts in which they are not used. This is what makes thesauruses and many dictionaries so difficult for foreign learners to use. A native speaker would probably not have much difficulty in knowing which of the following words and phrases would be acceptable in different social situations:

> unintelligent, stupid, dense, foolish, ... empty-headed, ... obtuse, ... witless, ... dim-witted, ... thick, thick as two short planks, ... daft, ... soft in the head, not all there, ... two sandwiches short of a picnic, ... out to lunch.
>
> (*Bloomsbury Thesaurus*)

On the other hand, there are situations in which even the most sophisticated user of English has to think very carefully about the exact implications of using one word rather than another. This section of the chapter examines some of the ways in which words have 'more than just a meaning'.

Taboo, slang, and informal

If the list above, extracted from a thesaurus, had been printed more fully, it would have appeared like this:

> See also

• CHAPTER 10
Audience
(p. 117)

unintelligent, stupid, dense, foolish,... empty-headed,... obtuse,... wit-less,... dim-witted (Inf),... thick (Inf), thick as two short planks (Inf),... daft (Inf),... soft in the head (Inf), not all there (Inf),... two sandwiches short of a picnic (Inf),... out to lunch (Sl).

The list could also have included *thick as shit* (Tab Sl).

By using the abbreviations in brackets, the compilers of the thesaurus can give simple guidance about usage:

Inf = informal
Sl= slang
Tab = taboo

Most people have a general idea of the meanings of these three. The dif-ficulty is in applying them.

Taboo

Taboo subjects and the words and expressions associated with them are those which are prohibited for use in general social intercourse, either because they are too holy to be discussed, or, more commonly, because they deal with topics considered to be too vulgar, notably sex and excretion. If you ask, 'Prohibited *by whom?*', the answer is usually 'by most people'. It is not of course a matter of a legal or even a formal religious ban, but rather one of general social agreement. Such agreement is constantly challenged and redefined, and works differently in different social groups.

People respond to it in different ways:

- Some take the topics themselves as taboo and always avoid talking about them.
- Some apply the taboo to the words rather than what they denote and move away from simple 'coarse' words like *shit* and *fuck* to longer, frequently latinate, words like *defecate* and *copulate*.
- Others—often people who still find the topics a little difficult to talk about—go in a different direction and use euphemisms like *do number twos* and *make love*.
- A small number of people, often because of a deliberately adopted social stance, insist on both talking openly about the topics and on using the most explicit language.

Clearly each of these approaches has its drawbacks. What you do and in what social settings depends both on what you feel comfortable with your-self and on your perception of how your audience is likely to respond. How people will respond can be difficult to judge, and never more so than in the area of taboos, because here both language and attitudes are constantly shifting.

Slang

Slang is:

- **language that is less socially acceptable than standard English**

  It is generally less formal and is unsuitable for formal writing and speech. So, from the examples quoted earlier, whereas *dim-witted* is simply an informal usage, *out to lunch* is clearly slang.

- **constantly changing**

  Expressions like *out to lunch*, meaning 'unintelligent', have both a history and a limited lifetime. The phrase probably started life in the 1950s and at some stage in the future will drop out of use (it is already beginning to sound rather dated).

- **often connected with membership of a particular social group**

  The word *slang* was originally used to refer to the language of thieves and other criminals. Now the specialist language of such groups is more correctly referred to as *cant* or *argot*. But particular slang words or expressions are still frequently the preserve of particular groups. As one writer puts it:

> The aim of using slang is seldom the exchange of information. More often, slang serves social purposes: to identify members of a group, to change the level of discourse in the direction of informality, to oppose established authority. Sharing and maintaining a constantly changing slang vocabulary aids group solidarity and serves to include and exclude members.
>
> **Connie C. Eble in the** *Oxford Companion to the English Language*

Informal

Informal language is any language that is casual, familiar, colloquial, 'unofficial'. It is not an absolute; any use of language can be placed on a continuum:

FORMAL ⟵⟶ INFORMAL

Not everyone will necessarily rank different language uses in the same way. For example, these words taken from the thesaurus list quoted earlier could be ranked in more than one way:

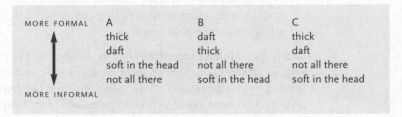

MORE FORMAL	A	B	C
	thick	daft	thick
	daft	thick	daft
	soft in the head	not all there	not all there
MORE INFORMAL	not all there	soft in the head	soft in the head

This kind of judgement is, in any case, difficult to make entirely in the abstract. If possible, it is better to think of the particular audience you have in mind before deciding on a choice of language. It is better to amuse by being over formal than to offend by being too informal.

How would you rank each of these groups of words on a scale of formality/ informality?

1 intellectual, clever clogs, egghead, guru, intellect, boffin, smartarse, highbrow, knowall, pointy-head, culture-vulture

2 insolvent, strapped, short of money, boracic, skint, hard up, in difficulties, cleaned out

3 relax, kip down, rest, take five, have forty winks, snooze, hit the hay, take a nap, take a breather

4 hurry off, scarper, run away, skedaddle, flee, vamoose, decamp, beat it, split

See page 380 for possible answers.

Jargon

Like slang, jargon is connected with group membership. The *Oxford English Dictionary* defines it as:

> See also
- CHAPTER 11
  Subject
  (p. 129)

> Applied contemptuously to any mode of speech abounding in unfamiliar terms, or peculiar to a particular set of persons, as the language of scholars or philosophers, the terminology of a science or art, or the cant of a class, sect, trade, or profession.

(Which some might argue is itself verging on jargon! The OED also defines it as, 'The inarticulate utterance of birds, or a vocal sound resembling it; twittering, chattering', which in the age of Twitter, seems very appropriate.) It is true that the word *jargon* is widely used to indicate disapproval. In fact, as the definition implies, it has two related elements:

1 It is specialist language used by members of a group of people with a common interest.

2 This language is often difficult, off-putting, or incomprehensible to others.

We could add a third feature which is often present:

3 People often use jargon, unthinkingly or deliberately, to confirm their own 'expertise' by one or more of the following:
- showing off
- sounding more knowledgeable or intelligent than they are
- deliberately obscuring the subject matter and confusing others

For example:

> This Spring we persuaded the chief winemaker of the award-winning village cellar of Kientzheim—my old friend from the early days, Jean Petitdemange—to dig deep for a prime example of his art. What a tasting! Despite the tiny volumes available, we couldn't resist *two* of his 'special reserve' offerings.
>
> **1 Gold-medal-winning Alsace classic—a subtle explosion of aroma and flavour**
> Truly excellent Gewürztraminer—the spicy aromatic grape that is Alsace's great speciality. Jean's 1994 'Gewürz' is characteristically dry with intense floral aromas, and a rich spicy flavour.
> 'mid-depth golden-yellow colour. Classic Gewürztraminer aromas of rose petals and lychees. Dry and weighty—beautifully rich and mouthfilling, but with a light minerally hint. Exceptionally long-lasting, rich flavours...'

This is an example of what might broadly be described as 'foodie jargon', that form of over-writing typical of pretentious restaurant menus. (You know the kind of thing: 'Crisp nuggets of chicken with farm-fresh mushrooms, and just a hint of mint'.) It does not achieve incomprehensibility, but in its excessive enthusiasm and desire to sell it will tend to put off all except those who are, or would like to be, wine buffs.

This raises a key feature of jargon. There is nothing wrong with it in its own place. Wine tasting has developed its own vocabulary (jargon)—'long in the nose', 'plenty of tropical fruit on the palate', and so forth. If you are a wine enthusiast speaking to fellow enthusiasts then such language is not just accepted but expected. Others, however, can find it irritating. Civil servants and other state functionaries have developed a variety of jargons which enable them to communicate with each other speedily and, presumably, efficiently. So have doctors, academic sociologists, and a wide range of trades, businesses, and professions. As long as they keep their jargon 'between consenting adults in private', all well and good. It is when they require the rest of us to read or hear their jargon *and respond to it* that the trouble starts.

You try

This extract comes from a notice put up near a minor landslip on the sea front at Lyme Regis.

... Surveys indicated that restabilization schemes could involve either short-term or long-term solutions, although the latter, notwithstanding the inherent costs, was to be preferred.

The funding factor being crucial therefore and the magnitude of the problem beyond the immediate resources of the Town Council, West Dorset's offer of assistance was welcomed and the stabilization project was subsequently included in an application to the Ministry of Agriculture, Fisheries and Food for funding as part of the Coastal Defence Programme.

J. M. Amesby, Town Clerk, June 1996

What do you think it means—in simple English?

See page 380 for a simpler version.

Sometimes jargon results from a desire to define things so precisely that the result is absurd. It is claimed that the US military dreamed up the following technical terms:

Term	Ordinary word
frame supported tension structure	tent
aerodynamic personnel decelerator	parachute
hexiform rotatable surface compressor unit	nut
entry system	doorway
high velocity multipurpose air circulator	fan
interlocking slide fastener	zip

Often jargon is used by people who want to hide the simple truth by using a smoke-screen of words. For example:

Political/bureaucratic jargon	Meaning
incomplete success	failure
poorly buffered precipitation	acid rain
controlled flight into terrain	plane crash
Military jargon	**Meaning**
servicing the target	killing the enemy

Military jargon	Meaning
permanent pre-hostility	peace
We shall not launch the ground offensive until we have attrited the Republican Guard to the point when they no longer have an effective offensive capacity.	We shan't attack until we have killed so many Iraqis that they won't fight back.
The United States and Israel now possess the capability to conduct real-time simulations with men in the loop for full-scale theatre missile defence architectures for the Middle East.	???

Business jargon	Meaning
initiating a career alternative enhancement programme	laying off workers
volume-related production schedule adjustment	closing a factory

How would you define the use and real meaning of each of these jargon terms?

hidden agenda   *ballpark figure*   *cold calling*   *de-skilling*   *hands-on*

and how about these?

core competencies   *disintermediate*   *facetime*   *touch base*   *wetware*

See page 381 for a commentary.

Language and discrimination

Another set of baggage that words carry around with them is that they frequently imply that the user has certain social, personal, or political attitudes. When words are combined into well-known phrases, those attitudes, or prejudices, can become even more apparent. A not-uncommon expression illustrates this well:

> See also

• CHAPTER 10
Audience
(p. 117)

• CHAPTER 12
Time and place
(p. 137)

> Well, you know what Peter's like when faced by a problem—he's a bit of an old woman, isn't he?

Sexism *and* ageism in one short phrase!

Language used to refer to social, physical, or gender groups can display prejudice, bias, thoughtlessness, or neutrality, but what makes words acceptable or unacceptable is not fixed but moves with changing attitudes and even fashion. For example, in the United States at different periods of history and in different social groups, people have referred to:

> niggers, negros, blacks, African Americans

Similarly, people of a particular sexual orientation in Britain have been called:

> poofters, queers, homos, homosexuals, gays

Everyone has to choose their own position on this question, if not word by word, certainly issue by issue. Most people will probably not want to go as far as using 'sobriety-deprived' for 'drunk', or 'involuntarily undomiciled' for 'homeless'. On the other hand you need to be aware that unthinking use of language that some people regard as discriminatory can alienate the very people with whom you wish to communicate. If you want to make a particular point by deliberately flouting these sensibilities, that is a matter of choice, but you should avoid doing it accidentally.

He, she, it, or they?

One problem that will not go away is the lack of a neuter personal pronoun in English. We can refer to animals of either sex, or even babies, as 'it', but not older children and adults. One can avoid gender-specific terms like chairman (chair), foreman (supervisor), and so on. But how do you avoid choosing between 'he' and 'she' in sentences like this?

> Every writer knows that _ should avoid sexist language.

Various possibilities have been explored, including the use of s/he, which is rather ugly and does not solve the problem of him/her and his/hers). Three solutions are now commonly adopted:

1 **Use *he or she, him or her, his or her(s)*.**
   In less formal situations these can be shortened to *he/she, him/her, his/her(s)*. This is an effective way of getting round the problem but can be cumbersome if used excessively.

2 **Recast the sentence so that it is in the plural.**
   All writers know that they should avoid sexist language.
   This is always acceptable, but not always possible. Some sentences do not lend themselves easily to such conversion.

3 **Use 'they' instead of 'him' or 'her', etc.**
   Every writer knows that they should avoid sexist language.
   This is always possible but not always acceptable, especially to those, often older people, who were brought up in the traditions of prescriptive grammar, which teaches that a plural pronoun can only refer back to a plural noun or noun phrase. It is, however, widely used and increasingly accepted.

Other solutions which some writers prefer include:

4 Using *he/him/his* throughout and explaining in a preface that you are not a sexist and that these words refer equally to *she/her/her(s)*.
This is still done but increasingly it is not accepted by large numbers of readers.

5 Doing the same thing, but using the feminine pronouns. Objected to for similar reasons.

6 Using *he/him/his* and *she/her/her(s)* alternately. This can have some rather bizarre effects.

What terms would you use to avoid these gender-specific words?

clergyman   craftsman   layman   man-made   policeman   salesman

See page 382 for possible answers.

Words and connotations

As much of the foregoing material has shown, the meaning of words is not confined to their dictionary meanings. We have seen how they can be acceptable or unacceptable in a wide range of situations, and for many different reasons. More than that, however, very many of the words we use have *connotations*. Imagine, for example, that you wanted to describe a person's physical appearance. If the person is below average height and weight, you could choose between these words and phrases:

> short, diminutive, petite, compact, squat, dwarfish, elfin, dainty, midget, knee-high to a grasshopper, stunted

Of these some are relatively neutral, 'short', for example (although some would argue that this is is 'heightist' and should be replaced by 'of below average height'). Others imply criticism or hostility, such as 'stunted' and 'knee-high to a grasshopper'. Others again are more favourable: 'compact', and 'petite'.

Divide these words to describe personal appearance into three categories:

A those which are favourable to the person described
B those which are unfavourable
C those which are neutral

heavy	well-built	fat
stocky	thickset	burly
brawny	beefy	chunky
hefty	elephantine	obese
gross	comfortable	paunchy
well-endowed	well-upholstered	lumbering

Guidelines

Getting help

1 Make use of a good (and up-to-date) dictionary—the best you can afford. For everyday use a large single-volume dictionary such as the *Oxford Concise* or the *Collins English Dictionary* is practical. Use it regularly, not only to check spellings and meanings, but also to browse in—an excellent way of improving and developing your vocabulary. It is also very valuable to have access to a larger dictionary such as the *Shorter Oxford Dictionary*.

2 Use a thesaurus as an active guide to finding the best word and developing your vocabulary.

3 As you read, and listen to people speaking, be alert for new words, or words that you have heard before but are not sure about. Use a dictionary to check new words you encounter and look for opportunities to use them yourself.

4 Be alert, too, to the contexts in which words are used. Try to grade them in your mind according to the criteria that have been used in this chapter (formal/informal, slang, taboo).

Word structure

5 Develop an awareness of how words are constructed. Use your existing knowledge of stems and affixes to help you 'decode' words that are unfamiliar.
Use the list of prefixes on pages 225–226 to help you in this.

6 Develop an awareness of how words can be changed in their use by the addition of suffixes. Use the list of suffixes on pages 227–228 to help you in this.

7 Use your existing knowledge of words that have been derived from classical Greek and Latin to help you work out the probable meanings of other words similarly derived.

More than just a meaning

8 It is important to be sensitive to other people's responses to taboo language and slang.

9 All of the words and expressions we use in everyday life can be placed on a scale running from formal to informal. You can learn how this works only by being constantly aware of people's attitudes towards language.

10 Jargon is common in many walks of life but it can confuse people or put them off. Again, you need to be aware when you are using jargon and of the effect its use has on others.

11 As readers and listeners we need to recognize when jargon is being used to obscure the truth.

12 Similarly, we need to be aware of the effects discriminatory language can have on others, especially in the areas of gender, race, and disability.

13 It is possible and desirable to avoid gender bias in the use of nouns and pronouns.

14 Many words imply that the user has favourable or unfavourable attitudes towards the subject under discussion. We need to be aware of this when writing and speaking.

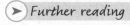 Further reading

John Seely, *Lexis: An Introduction to English Words*
(Oxpecker, 2012), ISBN 9780955345159 (print and e-book versions).

19 Spelling

Why is English spelling so much of a problem for so many people? There are two answers to this question. The first is that actually it is not as much of a problem as many people think. Wrong spelling rarely leads to mistakes of understanding; much more frequently it just annoys sticklers for accuracy. This is not, however, to justify a deliberate policy of letting things slip. It is much easier for everyone if we all spell words in the same way.

The second answer is a matter of linguistic history. Unlike Italian and other so-called 'phonetically spelled' languages, English cannot easily have a direct correspondence between sounds and letters. There are over forty sounds in English, far more than in Italian, and we only have the same twenty-six letters in the alphabet. So we have to combine letters in different ways to represent the 'missing' sounds. To do this we rely on a series of conventions. These developed over a period of history during which the vocabulary of English and its pronunciation were both also developing. Words came into English from many other languages and many retained their original spelling but changed their pronunciation. Other imports came from languages with a different writing system and were written down by travellers and merchants in the best way they could. In all this richness of vocabulary and linguistic vitality there has never been a consistent attempt to reform the whole spelling system and, given the worldwide status of English, probably never will be.

So we are stuck with a spelling system that is far from ideal and the best we can do is to devise workable strategies to help us spell better. There is no doubt that some people find spelling much easier than others. But even so it is possible for even the worst speller to make big strides towards much greater accuracy. There are ways of getting a grip on spelling generally and there are specific rules which can be learned.

Looking for patterns

The key to a generally more positive approach to spelling is to look constantly for *patterns*. There are two kinds of pattern which are helpful:

- patterns of sound/letter relationship
- patterns of letter/letter relationship

Sound/letter patterns

At first sight looking for correspondences between the sounds and letters of English seems a daunting task. The first sound in the name 'George' can be spelled in eight different ways:

j as in *jug*
g as in *gesture*
dg as in *judge*
gg as in *suggest*
dj as in *adjust*
de as in *grandeur*
di as in *soldier*
ch as in *sandwich* (as pronounced by some speakers)

Vowels cause even more difficulty. /i:/ is commonly spelled in seven different ways:

ee as in *beet*
ea as in *beat*
e as in *dene*
ie as in *fief*
ei as in *receive*
ey as in *key*
i as in *routine*

In addition it occurs in these words:

quay   people

Leaving the latter two 'exceptions' on one side, however, it is easy to see patterns of sound/letter correspondence:

beet	beat	fief
feed	heap	thief
feet	leap	piece
feel	real	field
peep	heal	siege etc.

When children are taught to read using by sounding letters (the 'phonic' method), this is how they are taught. *The cat sat on the mat* follows just such an approach.

Letter/letter patterns

The other broad approach to teaching children to read is sometimes called *look-and-say*. This works on the belief that the human brain looks for visual (and other) patterns and that when children are learning to read they often perceive a whole word as a pattern. This accounts for the fact that very early on in the process children will learn to recognize quite long words, provided they have a clearly distinguishable visual pattern, with ascenders and descenders, like *elephant* or *aeroplane*.

As we learn to read we also take on board the combinations of letters that are typical of English. For example, given a small amount of time, most people could think of words that contained these letter combinations:

-IGH-

-UGH-

It is much more difficult to think of words that contain the combination -EGH-. There are some, but they are fairly obscure.

► *See also:*
• CHAPTER 18
Vocabulary
(p.217)

The other way in which we habitually use patterning is in the recognition of word stems, prefixes, and suffixes: once you understand and can spell *psychology* you should not have too much trouble spelling the first part of **psych**iatry and **psycho**-analysis or the endings of geo**logy** and histo**logy**.

Developing a personal strategy

If you wish to develop a positive strategy based on this, you need to begin by analysing the nature of the mistakes you make. It is then necessary to attach your problem words to words that you *can* spell. A typical problem area is the double or single letters that occur in words like *accommodation, imitate,* and *professional.* You *could* try to learn the whole list of problem words by heart. An approach more likely to succeed, however, is to group the words according to a series of patterns and thus relate problem words to others that have the same pattern:

Words with no double letters

pedal
imitate
etc.

Words with one pair of double letters	accelerate assist etc.

Words with two pairs of double letters	accommodation address etc.

You could develop a similar approach to problems of sound/letter correspondence. That is what happens in the most famous spelling rule of all:

> 'I before E except after C, when the sound is long EE'

 See also

• *'Double and single letters'* (p. 250)

This rule works, has very few exceptions (*caffeine, codeine, counterfeit, protein, seize, species*, plus *either, neither, inveigle* if you pronounce them with a long 'ee'). It only causes trouble when people forget the second part of the rule: that the vowels have to make the sound 'ee'.

Finally, and most important, **write it down**. If you wish to remember a visual pattern it is important that you should see it. When you are trying to learn a spelling that causes problems, a well-known method is *look—cover—write—check*:

- **Look** at the correct spelling on the printed page so that you 'print' it on your brain. Spell the word out loud.
- **Cover** it up.
- **Write** it down from memory, spelling it out loud as you do so.
- **Check** against the printed version that you have got it right.

With a problem word this process should be repeated at increasing intervals until you are confident that it is fixed in your mind. Also, when in doubt about a spelling it is always worth trying to write down its various possible forms on scrap paper to see which looks right.

Rules based on patterns

Spelling rules and patterns fall into two broad groups:

- those that cover the spelling of certain sounds which can be written in two or three different ways
- those that explain how adding to a word changes the spelling of the original word

Sounds and letters

-ie- and -ei-

The rules that follow are not exhaustive, but have been chosen because they are useful and fairly easy to remember.

> **i before e except after c when the sound is long 'ee'**
> **examples:** *thief, receive*
> **exceptions:** *caffeine, codeine, counterfeit, protein, seize, species* (**plus** *either, neither, inveigle*)

-c- and -s-

> **c noun s verb**
> (easily remembered because the initial letters are in alphabetical order: C-N-S-V)
>
> | **examples:** | **noun** | **verb** |
> |---|---|---|
> | | *licence* | *license* |
> | | *practice* | *practise* |

but in American English *license* is a noun, and *practice* is used as a verb.

-ise, -ize, -yse

This is an area where an old rule and a new one are in conflict. Traditionally there was a group of words derived from Greek which reflected the Greek spelling by ending *-ize*. Examples include *organize* and *realize*. Today it is permissible to spell almost any word with this sound at the end with *-ise*, except for *capsize* which must be spelled with a -z-. As ever, the important thing is to be consistent. This book, for example, follows the house style of Oxford University Press, using *-ize* where the author would normally use *-ise*. In American English these words are always spelled *-ize*. In addition, a small number of words of Greek origin end *-yse* and must be spelled that way (unless you are American and prefer to spell them -yze). They include *analyse*, and *paralyse*.

-able, -ible

There *is* a rule, but it requires a fair amount of linguistic knowledge to apply it!

-ible is reserved for words borrowed from Latin and the list of 180 or so words spelled in this way is 'closed'—no new words spelled in this way are being created. More common words spelled in this way are:

accessible	admissible	audible
collapsible	combustible	compatible
comprehensible	contemptible	credible
defensible	destructible	digestible

divisible	edible	fallible
flexible	forcible	gullible
horrible	illegible	implausible
inaccessible	incontrovertible	incredible
indefensible	indelible	inedible
insensible	intelligible	invincible
invisible	irresistible	irreversible
ostensible	permissible	plausible
possible	responsible	reversible
sensible	susceptible	suggestible
tangible	terrible	visible

Words derived from Old English words and all new words now created with this ending are spelled -able. So the list includes old words like:

affordable	laughable	washable

and new words (often ugly!) like:

networkable	unclubbable	windsurfable

A quick check, which works most of the time, is that if you remove -able from a word, you are usually still left with a complete word. If you do the same with -ible, generally you are not.

-ar, -er, -or

Tricky, because there is some overlap. In most cases, when a verb is turned into a noun (meaning 'the person who does this') we add -er (or just -r to words ending in -e):

designer	maker	miner

All new nouns made from verbs work in this way. But verbs that end in -ate make nouns ending in -ator. There are a number of other nouns derived from verbs which also end in -or, of which the commonest are:

actor	contractor	contributor	defector
distributor	governor	inheritor	inspector
inventor	investor	persecutor	prosecutor
prospector	reflector	resistor	sailor
supervisor	surveyor	survivor	visitor

There are also a few that add -*ar*, of which the commonest are:

beggar	burglar	liar

Note that in American English words that in British English end in -*our* (e.g. *labour*) are spelled -*or* (e.g. *labor*). Many words that end in -*re* in British English (e.g. *theatre*) are spelled -*er* in American English (e.g. *theater*), but not all (e.g. *massacre, mediocre*).

Rules for changing words

The other group of rules or patterns covers how we spell words when we add bits to them.

Adding -*s*

We add -*s* to words for two reasons:

- to make nouns plural
- to form the she/he form of the present tense of verbs

The rules for both are the same, so the plural -*s* rules are given here, with a few additional rules which apply only to plurals.

1 Normally just add -*s*:
   papers, hopes
2 Words that end with any of the following, add -*es*
   -*ch, -s, -sh, -x, -z*:
   branches, masses, bushes, boxes, chintzes
3 Words that end in -*f* or -*fe*, change the ending to *ves*:
   wives, calves
   Exceptions to this:
   beliefs, chiefs, dwarfs, griefs, gulfs, proofs, roofs
4 Words that end in *vowel* + *y*, add -*s*:
   days, boys
5 Words that end in *consonant* + *y*, change the -*y* to -*ies*:
   babies, spies
6 Words that end in -*o* normally just add -*s*:
   pianos, radios
   There is however a group of common words which add -*es*:

buffaloes	*cargoes* (can be *cargos*)	*dominoes*
echoes	*goes*	*grottoes*
haloes	*heroes*	*mangoes*
mosquitoes	*mottoes* (can be *mottos*)	*potatoes*
tomatoes	*tornadoes*	*torpedoes*
vetoes	*volcanoes*	

Adding -*ing* and -*ed*

When using verbs we often need to add the grammatical suffixes -*ing* and -*ed* to the stem of the verb:

> As I was *walking* along the High Street I *bumped* into an old friend.

Unless the verb is covered by one of the rules that follow, you simply add the suffix. Before adding the suffix:

1 Words ending in *consonant + y;* change the *y* to *i* before -*ed*
  Cry → crying → cried
2 Words ending in *vowel + y;* just add the suffix:
  played
  Exceptions:
  said, paid, laid

Words of one syllable

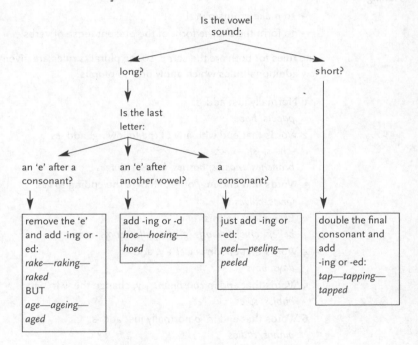

Is the vowel sound:

long?   short?

Is the last letter:

an 'e' after a consonant?   an 'e' after another vowel?   a consonant?

remove the 'e' and add -ing or -ed:
rake—raking—raked
BUT
age—ageing—aged

add -ing or -d
hoe—hoeing—hoed

just add -ing or -ed:
peel—peeling—peeled

double the final consonant and add -ing or -ed:
tap—tapping—tapped

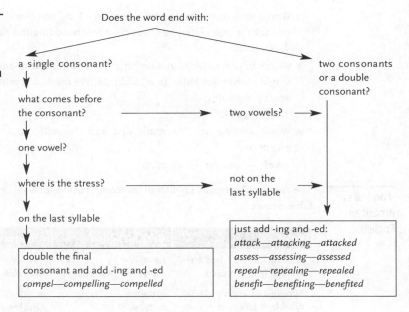

Words of more than one syllable, ending with a consonant

Does the word end with:

a single consonant?

two consonants or a double consonant?

what comes before the consonant? → two vowels? →

one vowel?

where is the stress? → not on the last syllable →

on the last syllable

double the final consonant and add -ing and -ed
compel—compelling—compelled

just add -ing and -ed:
attack—attacking—attacked
assess—assessing—assessed
repeal—repealing—repealed
benefit—benefiting—benefited

Adding -*ly*

Many adjectives can be turned into adverbs by the addition of the suffix -*ly*. Normally this is simply added to the adjective. There are a few exceptions:

1 If the word ends in -*ll*, simply add -*y*:
   fully
2 Words of more than one syllable ending in -*y*, remove the -*y* and add -*ily*:
   happily
3 Words ending with a consonant followed by -*le*, remove the final -*e* and add -*y*:
   terribly
4 Most single-syllable words ending in -*y* are regular, except for:
   daily, gaily

Adding -*er* and -*est*

The comparative and superlative forms of many adjectives are formed by adding the suffixes -*er* and -*est*:

The suffixes are normally added without further change. There are four

   great, greater, greatest

groups of exceptions:

1 Words that end in a consonant followed by -*y*, change the -*y* to an -*i* before adding the suffix:
   happier, happiest

2 Words with one syllable which contain a long vowel sound and which end with *-e* (e.g., *late*); remove the *-e* before adding the suffix:

later, latest

3 Words of one syllable containing a short vowel sound and ending in a single consonant letter (e.g., *sad*); double the final consonant before adding the suffix:

sadder, saddest

4 Words ending in *-l* normally just add the suffix, but there is one exception:

cruel → *crueller* → *cruellest*

-l and -ll in American English

The rules in American English differ from those in British English, as this table shows:

Rule	British English	American English
Adding suffixes when final syllable is unstressed	*traveller* *marvelled, marvelling*	*traveler* *marveled, marveling*
Adding suffixes when final syllable is stressed	*installed* *instalment*	*installed* *Installment*

Awkward customers

Double and single letters

Some words just cause problems which cannot be solved by learning rules. The only thing to do then is to learn them by heart. These are longer versions of the lists suggested earlier in this chapter (on p. 243).

No double letters

fulfil (fulfill in AmE)		
imitate	marvel	omit
patrol	pedal	transmit

One pair of double letters

abbreviate	accelerate	accident	accomplish
accurate	allergy	appropriate	approximate
assist	beginning	brilliant	caterpillar
collapse	collect	commemorate	commit
corridor	desiccated	disappear	disappoint
dissatisfied	discuss	exaggerate	excellent
gorilla	happen(ed)	harass	hallelujah

illustrate	immediate	millenary	millionaire
necessary	occasion	occur	paraffin
parallel	proceed	procession	professional
questionnaire	scissors	sheriff	succeed
sufficient	terrible	tomorrow	tranquillity

Two pairs of double letters

accommodation	accidentally	address	commission
committed	embarrass	guerrilla	happiness
mattress	millennium	possess	successful
unnecessary	woollen		

Words sometimes confused

accept/except

I **accept** everything you say **except** your claim that you are telling the truth.

access/excess

I could not gain **access** to the building because of an **excess** of security **precautions**.

affect/effect

- as nouns

  affect is a relatively uncommon word and means 'mood, mental state, emotion'

  effect means 'the result of an action', or 'belonging' as in personal effects

- as verbs

  affect means 'to alter the state of something, to have an effect on it'

  effect means 'to bring something about', as in effect a change

aisle/isle

An aisle is part of a building such as a church; an isle is a piece of land surrounded by water.

all ready/already

'Now are we **all ready**?' she asked, **already** beginning to get flustered.

all together/altogether

If you put his mistakes **all together**, his reputation looks **altogether** different.

altar/alter

You find an altar in a church. To alter is to change.

apiary/aviary

Both are containers for creatures: an apiary for bees, and an aviary for birds.

ascent/assent

*After John's **ascent** of the Matterhorn, Mary gave her **assent** to his proposal and they were married.*

auger/augur

*The student's inability to use a simple **auger** to bore a hole did not **augur** well for his career as a boatbuilder.*

aural/oral

*In the French examination we had to do a dictation, which tested our **aural** ability, and also give a five-minute talk to demonstrate our **oral** skills.*

awhile/a while

awhile is an adverb; *a while* is a noun phrase. So:

'Let's rest **awhile**', she said after **a while**.

bail/bale

*After being let out of prison on **bail** he went on a parachuting course and learned to **bale** out of an aircraft. On his first descent he broke his leg landing on a **bale** of straw.*

base/bass

*In some operas the **bass** singer plays a villain or other **base** character.*

beach/beech

A *beach* is at the seaside. A *beech* is a tree.

beat/beet

To *beat* something is to strike it (and a police officer patrols a *beat*). *Beet* is a root vegetable.

berth/birth

A ship is tied up in its *berth*. *Birth* is what happens when a baby is born.

biannual/biennial

*If you're lucky you get **biannual** holidays (every six months); if you're unlucky they are **biennial** (every two years).*

boar/boer/boor/bore

A *boar* is a wild pig (or a male domestic pig). A *Boer* is a white South African of Dutch descent. A *boor* is a person (usually a man) who doesn't know how to behave. A *bore* is the opposite of an interesting person.

born/bome

*The couple's problems seemed too great to be **borne**, especially after their sixth child was **born**.*

boy/buoy

A *boy* is a young male person; a *buoy* is a floating marker used by sailors.

brake/break

To *brake* is to slow down (e.g., in a car); if you *break* something it will need mending.

bridal/bridle

A bride may wear a *bridal* veil. A horse wears a *bridle*.

broach/brooch

If you *broach* something you open it and start to use it. A *brooch* is a personal ornament.

buy/by/bye

by is a preposition with a range of meanings; *bye* is a noun with meanings in cricket and other games; either spelling can be used in *by the by(e)* and *by(e)-law*

calendar/colander

*I must put a note on the **calendar** in the kitchen to remind me to buy a new **colander** for the vegetables.*

callous/callus

'*Is that a wart on your finger or just a **callus**?*' *she asked **callously**.*

cannon/canon

*The cathedral **canon** wanted to fire a small **cannon** from the tower to scare the pigeons but he was told it was against the **canons** of the church.*

canvas/canvass

*When he went round the area to **canvass** votes, he carried his election literature in a **canvas** holdall.*

carat/carrot

A *carat* is a unit of weight used by jewellers; a *carrot* is a root vegetable.

cast/caste

The *cast* of a play is composed of actors and if you *cast* something you throw it. *Caste* is a system of hereditary classes in India.

caster/castor

Caster sugar is a very fine form of sugar; a *castor* is a small wheel on a piece of furniture (and there is also *castor* oil).

censer/censor/censure

A *censer* is a container in which incense is burned.

A *censor* is someone who controls the content of books, newspapers, films, and other media.

If you *censure* someone, you criticize or condemn them.

cereal/serial

*As he ate his breakfast **cereal** he read the comic-strip **serial** in his daily paper.*

chord/cord
Chord is a musical term; a *cord* is a string.

coarse/course
Coarse is the opposite of fine; a *course* is something you follow.

complement/compliment
A *compliment* is paid to someone you admire. The *complement* is what completes something: the ship's *complement* is its crew, without which it would be incomplete.

complaisant/complacent
Someone who is *complaisant* is accommodating and wishes to please others.

A *complacent* person is certainly easily pleased and probably pleased with himself.

confidant(e)/confident
As with all words ending with -*ant*/-*ent*, the former is a noun and the latter an adjective:

*He was so **confident**, he did not need a **confidant** in whom to confide his fears.*

council/counsel
*At the meeting of the royal **council** the king asked his senior ministers for their **counsel** about what he should do.*

councillor/counsellor
A *councillor* is a member of a council; a *counsellor* is an advisor (and in the US a *counselor* is a lawyer).

credible/credulous
*Although the story was so far-fetched as to be hardly **credible**, my friend was so **credulous** he believed every word of it.*

crevasse/crevice
*From a great height the huge **crevasses** in the ice looked like tiny **crevices** in a sheet of crumpled paper.*

crochet/crotchet
Crochet is a type of thread work used for making small garments and other objects; a *crotchet* is a note in music.

curb/kerb
A *curb* is something that restrains someone or something (or curbs them).

A *kerbs* is the edge of a pavement.

currant/current
A *currant* is a piece of dried fruit.

A *current* is a moving stream of water in the sea.

Current also means 'happening now'.

defuse/diffuse

If you *defuse* something you literally remove its fuse, so more generally it means 'neutralize, remove the danger from'.

If you *diffuse* something you spread it around.

dependant/dependent

*His father was not **dependent** on the state, although he had nineteen **dependants**.* (In American English *dependent* is used for both.)

deprecate/depreciate

*The cricket authorities **deprecated** the batsman's bad behaviour, arguing that it would only cause the reputation of cricket as a sport to **depreciate**.*

desert/deserts/dessert

*The arrogant explorer refused to take any advice so when he perished in the **desert** he got his just **deserts**. They served baked Alaska for **dessert** at his wake!*

detract/distract

*When politicians seek to **detract** from the merits of their opponents it is usually to **distract** attention from their own shortcomings.*

dinghy/dingy

A dirty little sailing boat could be described as a *dingy dinghy*.

discreet/discrete

Someone who is *discreet* can be relied on not to give away secrets. *Discrete* means 'separate'.

elicit/illicit

You *elicit* information from someone. If something is *illicit* it is against the law.

eligible/illegible

If you are entitled to something, you are *eligible* for it. *Illegible* means 'unreadable'.

emigrate/immigrate

*As a rule, those who **immigrate** into one country must first have **emigrated** from another.*

eminent/immanent/imminent

Things or people that are eminent stand out in some way.

If something is *imminent* it is just about to happen.

Some philosophers have believed that God is *immanent* (all-pervading) in the universe.

ensure/insure

*Before they went on holiday he **ensured** that the house and contents were fully **insured**.*

exalt/exult

If you *exalt* something you raise it up, literally or figuratively.

If you *exult*, you rejoice.

extant/extent

*I do not know to what **extent** belief in miracles is still **extant** in our society.*

faint/feint

Faint means 'feeble'. To *feint* is to pretend.

fatal/fateful

*On that **fateful** day, just as the soothsayer had predicted, Caesar received a **fatal** injury.*

faze/phase

*I was completely **fazed** by her behaviour, which seemed to mark a new **phase** in our relationship.*

flaunt/flout

*The streaker **flouted** all the conventions of cricketing society by **flaunting** his body in front of the Test Match crowd.*

forbear/forebear

If you *forbear* you refrain from doing something. A *forebear* is an ancestor.

foreword/forward

*In her **foreword** to the book she put **forward** some new arguments.*

gild/guild/gilt/guilt

*At courses run by the **Guild** of Cake Decorators you can learn how to put gold icing, or **gilt**, on a cake; they call the lesson '**Gilding** the gingerbread'. The slogan 'Naughty but nice' suggests that if you eat cream cakes you should feel a pleasurable **guilt**.*

grill/grille

A *grill* is something you cook on.

A *grille* is a barred opening in a wall.

hoard/horde

It is a *hoard* of treasure, but a *horde* of invaders.

human/humane

Most *human* beings who eat meat expect the treatment of the animals they consume to be *humane*; they do not want them to suffer.

impractical/impracticable

An *impractical* person, who does not have much idea of how things should be done, is likely to suggest *impracticable* (unworkable) solutions to problems.

inapt/inept

An *inapt* solution is one which is not suitable for that particular problem. It may well be suggested by someone who isn't very good at such things, who is, in fact, *inept*.

ingenious/ingenuous

Ingenuous means 'Honourably straightforward; open, frank, candid' (*OED*)—often innocently so.
Ingenious means clever.
Disingenuous means deviously clever but pretending to be honourably straightforward, etc.

interment/internment

Interment means burial.
Internment means imprisonment.

lightening/lightning

*During a long and very dull lecture about the effects of thunder and **lightning** on pregnant moles, the only thing that was **lightening** my boredom was the thought that it could not go on for ever.*

liqueur/liquor

A *liqueur* is a strong and usually sweet *liquor* (alcoholic drink) such as Cointreau or Bénédictine. A *liquor* can also be a more general term for a liquid.

loathe/loath/loth

If you *loathe* something, you hate it and are *loath* (unwilling) to have anything to do with it. *Loth* is an alternative spelling for *loath*.

lose/loose

These two are sometimes confused (because *lose* rhymes with *choose?*). You might, for example, *lose* a pet dog if you left it *loose* rather than tied up.

meter/metre

A *meter* is used to measure things. A *metre* is a distance and also the regular pattern of strong and weak syllables in *metrical* poetry.

militate/mitigate

To *mitigate* is to lessen the harmful effects of something or someone.
To *militate* is to conflict with or work against someone or something.

miner/minor

A *miner* digs underground.
A *minor* is under-age.

moral/morale

*The **moral** of the story was that when an army's **morale** is low it loses battles.*

naval/navel

Naval means concerning the navy.

A *navel* is a belly button, or a kind of orange.

pain/pane

If you are in *pain* you suffer. Windows contain *panes* of glass.

palate/palette/pallet

The *palate* is part of the mouth.

A *palette* is the range of colours used by an artist or the small tray they are placed on.

A *pallet* is a wooden platform on which goods are stacked for storage or carriage. It is also a straw bed or mattress.

passed/past

These two are sometimes confused.

Passed is the past tense and past participle of the verb *to pass*:

I have **passed** my exam; all the students in our year **passed**.

Past is an adjective or a preposition:

I have **passed** all my examinations so the time for worrying is **past**.

He walked **past** the house.

pastel/pastille

A *pastel* is a kind of crayon or a pale shade of a colour. A *pastille* is a sweet or something you suck.

pedal/peddle

You will find a *pedal* in a car or on a bicycle. To *peddle* something is to sell it.

peninsula/peninsular

Peninsula is a noun:

Devon and Cornwall form a **peninsula**.

Peninsular is the adjective derived from it:

The **Peninsular** War was fought in Spain against the French.

precede/proceed

As the procession **proceeded** along the Mall, the royal carriage **preceded** that of the prime minister.

prescribe/proscribe

Prescribe means recommend or advise.

Proscribe means ban or forbid.

principle/principal

Principle is a noun and means what is central to something, a fundamental truth:

Whenever we argued he always insisted on taking things back to first **principles**. *Principal* can be either an adjective or a noun. As an adjective it means 'main, or chief'; as a noun it means 'the head or leader of a group or organization':

The **principal** rule, or **principle**, on which the college was run was that the **Principal** was always right.

rain/reign/rein

Rain refers to weather; *reign* to kings and queens; and *rein* to horses.

resister/resistor

A *resister* is someone who resists.

A *resistor* is an electronic device which reduces the flow of an electric current.

sceptic/septic

He was always a **sceptic**, so he did not believe me when I told him that the wound had gone **septic**.

sensual/sensuous

Sensual refers to pleasures experienced through the body, often sexual. *Sensuous* refers to pleasures experienced through the mind, often artistic.

shear/sheer

To *shear* is to cut (e.g., the wool off a sheep). *Sheer* means 'perpendicular'. It can also mean 'absolute'.

sight/site/cite

He argued that tourism was bad for the Developing World and **cited** one example where a popular **site** had become an eyesore rather than a **sight** for sore eyes.

stationary/stationery

Stationary is an adjective and means not moving.

Stationery is usually a noun referring to paper and other office consumables, but it can be a modifier, as in *the stationery shop*.

taught/taut

Subjects are *taught* in schools.

Taut is the opposite of loose or slack.

teeth/teethe

Teeth is a noun and *teethe* a verb.

urban/urbane

Urban means relating to a city or cities in general.

Urbane means cultured and smooth-mannered.

waiver/waver

*She never **wavered** in her determination to get the bank to renounce their legal right to repossess her house. In the end she got the **waiver** she was requesting.*

who's/whose

Who's means 'who is'; *whose* means 'of/belonging to whom'.

Guidelines

1 It is important to realize that because of the complexity of English the number of people who have no problems with spelling is tiny.

2 So most people need to develop strategies for dealing with spelling problems: strategies that work for them.

3 Always look for patterns and remember that spelling is a visual matter.

4 Learn difficult spellings by the *Look—Cover—Write—Check* method.

5 Test doubtful spellings by writing down possible versions and seeing which one looks right.

6 Use the sound/letter rules listed in this chapter.

7 Use the rules for adding endings listed in this chapter.

8 Try to place problem spellings in a group of similar spellings which also includes words you *can* spell.

9 A lot of 'spelling' mistakes are actually the confusion of two words with slightly different spellings but very different meanings. These have to be learned.

10 Use a good dictionary.

20 Punctuation

Punctuation marks

- Full stop
- Question mark
- Exclamation mark
- Colon
- Semicolon
- Comma
- Apostrophe
- Inverted commas
- Capital letter
- Hyphen
- Dash

Using punctuation

- Direct speech and other quotations
- Abbreviations
- Lists
- Enclosing text, including non-defining relative clauses

Punctuation is a set of conventions that make it easier to read written English. It is important to stress that the so-called 'rules' of punctuation are simply conventions—agreed ways of separating a text into sections that the reader's eye and brain can assimilate. Like any other set of conventions (table manners, for example), punctuation changes over time. There are fashions; people experiment, and as a result the 'rules' change.

Some areas of punctuation are clear-cut and straightforward. For example, no one would disagree that a sentence should begin with a capital letter. Other points are much more a matter of opinion and style: commas and semicolons, for example. So punctuating well is a combination of knowing a number of fixed 'rules', and applying a series of rather looser conventions to your own writing style.

No two people, however experienced they may be as writers, will punctuate in exactly the same way. All this guide to punctuation can do is to set out the principles and leave you to choose how heavily or lightly you wish to punctuate your own writing.

In this chapter, punctuation is looked at from two points of view:

- the punctuation marks and their functions
- the different ways in which we can use punctuation to achieve the effects we wish in our writing

Punctuation marks

In this section of the chapter, the marks are listed and the main uses for each one are set out. Examples are given where these will help understanding, otherwise not.

Full stop

Full stops (US *periods*) are used:

1 To mark the end of a sentence.
2 At the end of 'minor' (verbless) sentences:
   *Liverpool now head the Premier League. **But not for long**.*
3 After some abbreviations. This is a complicated matter and is covered in detail in the 'Abbreviations' section of this chapter on pages 270–1.
4 To show that something has been omitted.
   I suggest we delete the sentence, 'If this is not done…will be reduced.'
   These are sometimes referred to as ellipsis dots, or points. There are normally three of them. They are also used to show that a sentence is left unfinished:
   'It was just one of those awkward…' she finished lamely.
5 As a decimal point.
6 In email and web site addresses: <www.oup.com> <www.askoxford.com>

Question mark

A question mark ends a sentence, as a full stop does, and is used to indicate that the sentence is a question.

1 The sentence often takes the correct grammatical form for a question:
   Have you seen the latest Bola Agbaje play?
2 If a statement sentence is intended as a question, this is indicated by a question mark:
   'You've seen the latest Bola Agbaje play?' she asked.

3 Some sentences end with what is called a tag question:
*'You've seen the latest Bola Agbaje play, **have you**?' she said.*
If the tag question is *really* asking a question, then it should be followed by a question mark. In many cases, however, the speaker is just requesting confirmation, and then there is no need for a question mark: *'You've seen the latest Bola Agbaje play, **haven't you**,' she said.*
If you are not sure whether you need a question mark, read the sentence aloud. If your voice falls at the end of the tag question, then it doesn't need a question mark. If it rises, then it does.

4 You can also place a question mark in brackets after a word or phrase in a sentence that seems to you questionable:
He said he was absolutely delighted (?) that you were coming for Christmas.

Exclamation mark

The exclamation mark is very similar to the question mark, except that, as its name suggests, it marks exclamations rather than questions.

1 It indicates that a sentence is exclamatory:
'Get out of my way!' she shouted.

2 It does the same thing in minor (verbless) sentences:
Danger! Keep out!

3 You can also place an exclamation mark in brackets after a word or phrase in a sentence that seems to you amusing, ridiculous, or otherwise causes you to exclaim:
He said he was absolutely delighted (!) that you were coming for Christmas.

The full stop (and the associated question and exclamation marks) are the strongest punctuation marks, used to divide clauses into separate sentences. If we do not want to go as far as this in separating elements, we can use a colon or a semicolon. These two punctuation marks do similar but distinct jobs.

Colon

⊳ See also
· *Lists*
(p. 271)

The colon has a small number of related and clearly defined functions.

1 It introduces a list:
When the secret door was opened, it revealed an amazing treasure trove of unlikely items: old clothing, broken picture frames, tarnished silver cutlery, a stuffed elephant's foot, and dozens of old football-match programmes.

2 It introduces a piece of speech:

At last the old explorer spoke: 'This is the most unhappy day of my life.'

3 It introduces another section of text that the preceding words have led up to:

If I have learned one thing in life, it's this: never trust someone who says, 'I must be honest with you.'

Semicolon

The semicolon is midway between a full stop and a comma in strength.

1 It is used to separate two clauses that are related:

Sometimes it is right to forgive; sometimes it is wrong to forget.

If these two clauses were separated into independent sentences by the use of a full stop, the relationship between them would be weakened:

Sometimes it is right to forgive. Sometimes it is wrong to forget.

2 It can separate a clause and a related phrase:

To err is human; to forgive divine.

3 It can separate items in a list, when these are either clauses or extended phrases:

a *Young people today lack all reverence for the old; they live only in the present; they do not expect to reach old age themselves.*

b *There were several important reasons why the initiative was a failure: a serious lack of funds; the unwillingness of many groups to participate; and a general lack of confidence in the leadership.*

In the second example, some writers would use a comma instead of the second semicolon.

It is worth observing that when the semicolon separates two balanced or related clauses it can be replaced by a full stop. When it separates the items in a list it can be replaced by a comma. Problems can occur when the writer gets these two functions confused. The example in (1) above should not be punctuated:

Sometimes it is right to forgive, sometimes it is wrong to forget.

This 'comma splice', joining two independent clauses, is frequently confusing for the reader, who expects the comma to be doing a different job, and so should be avoided.

Comma

The comma is the most difficult punctuation mark to use well. It is essential for clear writing, but there are few hard-and-fast rules. It has been said that the person who has learned how to use commas has learned how to write.

The traditional advice used to be that you should read a text aloud and where it was necessary to make a short pause, there you should put a comma. While there is some truth in this, it does not always work. It is important to remember that most reading is silent, and the comma is as much an instruction to the eye as to the voice. It helps the reader see speedily which items in a sentence are linked and which are separated.

1 We use commas to separate items in a list:
In her diary she itemized all the foods she most disliked: popcorn, fish and chips, anchovies, white bread, and margarine.

It is sometimes argued that you should not place a comma before *and* in a list. As the example shows, sometimes it is essential to put a comma before *and*, to indicate the sense. If the last comma were removed, the final item on the list would be *white bread and margarine*, whereas the writer means that she disliked both white bread and margarine separately, not as a combination.

2 We use a comma to indicate a break between clauses, where this increases clarity and helps the reader:
Although I don't like coffee, milk shakes are one of my favourite drinks.
Remove the comma, and the reader cannot easily see how the sentence works. The eye passes over the grammatical break, to read:
Although I don't like coffee milk shakes…
and then slows down, as the reader realises that it is not clear whether the writer is referring to one kind of drink or two.

See also
• *Parentheses*
(p. 272)

3 Commas also serve to enclose sections of a sentence. This often indicates that the enclosed section adds extra information, but is not essential to the structure and meaning of the main sentence:
Lord Plonkett, for many years our man in Havana, is now on the board of several tobacco companies.
The phrase *for many years our man in Havana* could be omitted and the sentence would still work effectively.

4 They are used to introduce a piece of direct speech:
She said, 'I don't have to do it, you know.'

Apostrophe

The apostrophe is the most abused punctuation mark in English. Everywhere—on posters, chalked up on greengrocers' slates, even in broadsheet newspapers—we see it wrongly used. So it is not surprising that many children, and adults too, have just given up. What makes it worse is the fact that, if we abandoned it completely and never used another apostrophe, it would cause almost no problems of confusion in our writing. But, for the moment at least, we are stuck with it.

Apostrophes have only two purposes:

1 To show that one or more letters have been left out. This happens most often with commonly contracted forms:

it is	→	it's
did n̶o̶t̶	→	didn't
can n̶o̶t̶	→	can't

There is only one additional point to note. In these contractions you only ever use **one** apostrophe, between the *n* and the *t*, even when letters are omitted in more than one place. So

s̶h̶a̶l̶l̶ n̶o̶t̶	→	shan't (not sha'n't)

2 To show possession. The rule is this:
- for singular nouns, add **'s**:
  Harry's hat   the budgie's cage
- for plurals that end in **s**, just add the apostrophe:
  her parents' advice
- for plurals that do not end with **s**, add **'s**:
  children's games

The only problem area is proper nouns that end in *s*, such as *James*: should it be *James'* or *James's*? Either is correct.

It is also worth pointing out that possessive *its* meaning *of it* has no apostrophe: *The cat hurt **its** paw*.

If you add to these rules a third:

Apostrophe + s should never be used to indicate a plural

you have a complete 'Apostrophe kit'.

Inverted commas

 See also

• *Direct speech*
  (p. 269)

Inverted commas are used:

1 To mark off the words spoken in a passage of direct speech:
'There's no need to look at me like that!' he snarled.

2 To show that the words enclosed are a quotation:
It is not clear what is meant when the contract refers to 'other authorized persons'.

3 To indicate a book or other title:
'Gone with the Wind'
'The Oxford Guide to Effective Writing and Speaking'
In printed matter, however, it is the convention to miss out the inverted commas and set such book, film, play, radio, and TV titles in italics.

4 To show that an expression is not one that you would choose:

He converted his large rambling 19th-century house into a number of 'apartments'.

It is also necessary to decide whether to use single or double inverted commas. This is partly a matter of individual style (although single inverted commas are now widely used), but it is important to be consistent: choose which you are going to use and then stick to it throughout a text. If a quotation contains a second quotation, or a title, within it, then this should use the form of inverted commas not so far used:

'I really don't understand,' he replied, 'why you say, "No one is to blame," when it is quite clear whose fault it was.'

Capital letter

Capital letters are used as follows:

1 For the first letters of people's names:
Virginia Woolf

2 In other proper names. (A proper name is usually the name of a place or institution, or the title of a person, play, book, film, or other work of art.) The convention is that all the main words are capitalized, while the less important words are not. So nouns, verbs, adjectives, and adverbs should have initial capital letters:
The Bishop of Bath and Wells
All's Well that Ends Well
If the proper name begins with an article, then that too should have a capital letter, but only if it is an essential part:
Have you ever been to The Hague?
but
I have never visited the United States of America.

3 In abbreviations, where the capital is the first letter of the word abbreviated and stands for the whole word:
BBC USA

 See also

• *Abbreviations*
(p. 270–1)

Hyphen

Hyphens have three main uses:

1 Sentence construction
If you need to show that certain words are meant to be taken together you hyphenate them:
They were showing their latest ready-to-wear collection.
If you intend the words to be read separately, you don't hyphenate them:

His new suit was ready to wear.

(This has a different meaning from *His new suit was ready-to-wear.*)

2 Printing

In printing (and with many word processors and similar programs) when a word is too long to fit onto the end of a line it is split into two parts. The part on the end of the line ends with a hyphen. Computers will do this automatically (although not necessarily very well), and it can also be done manually.

3 Spelling

Hyphens are frequently used to link the words that make up a compound. Practice varies and it is difficult to make hard-and-fast rules. But these guidelines generally apply:

- If you are forming a verb from a compound noun use hyphens:
  a booby trap
  The road was booby-trapped.
- If you are forming a noun from a phrasal verb or prepositional verb, hyphenate the noun:
  This led her to build up her hopes unduly.
  There was a build-up of carbon monoxide in the room.
- If you are forming a new (or relatively new) word with a prefix you often need to use a hyphen. Compare these versions with and without hyphens:
  anti-government   antigovernment
  pro-abortion   proabortion

Dash

A dash is longer than a hyphen and is used for different purposes. It comes in two sizes, an em dash (—) and an en dash (–). An em dash is used:

- in a pair to mark parentheses:
  She was helpless—almost to the point of faintness—when he was around.
- instead of a colon to introduce an example or something the rest of the sentence leads up to:
  They were all there—Daisy, old Trevor, Martin, and even Hilary.
- to introduce an aside:
  I just told him to go away and leave me in peace—the way you do.
- in direct speech to indicate that a speaker breaks off in mid-sentence or is interrupted:
  'I'm not sure what you mean. You want me to—' She hesitated.

Increasingly, however, the em dash is being replaced by an en dash with a space on either side of it. For example:

She was helpless – almost to the point of faintness – when he was around.

The use of the em dash for the purposes listed above is beginning to look very old-fashioned.

An en dash is used to indicate sequences:

> *2003–2005, A–Z*

Using punctuation

Some aspects of punctuation are best described by starting with what the writer wants to do. In this section, this functional approach is followed.

Direct speech

It is sometimes necessary to quote what someone has said or written, word for word. To do this, we use a combination of inverted commas and other punctuation marks and conventions. As is often the case, there is no one 'correct' way of doing this. What follows is a description of the commonest method. It assumes throughout that it is spoken words that are being quoted, but the same approach applies to the quotation of written texts.

1 The actual words spoken are enclosed in single or double inverted commas.
2 The words spoken follow the normal rules of punctuation for sentences—**within the inverted commas**. In other words, each sentence begins with a capital letter and ends with a full stop, question mark, or exclamation mark; all other punctuation marks are used as normal:
He said, 'I don't believe a word of it. Do you?'
3 If the words, 'he said' or some similar expression precede the words quoted, then they are followed by a comma or colon, before the opening inverted comma(s).
4 If the words, 'he said' or some similar expression follow the words quoted, then there should be a comma, question mark, or exclamation mark at the end of the quoted speech and before the inverted commas. (See 5)
5 Every group of words quoted that is enclosed between inverted commas must end with a punctuation mark immediately before the closing inverted comma(s). If such a mark does not naturally occur (e.g. a full stop or question mark), then a comma should be placed in this position.
6 If there is more than one speaker then each time a new person speaks you should begin a new paragraph.

This approach is illustrated in the following text.

> *On the green I saw a white man coming with a cassock on, by which and by the*
> *face of him I knew he was a priest. He was a goodnatured old soul to look at,*
> *gone a little grizzled, and so dirty you could have written with him on a piece of*
> *paper.*
> *'Good-day, sir,' said I.*
> *He answered me eagerly in native.*
> *'Don't you speak any English?' said I.*
> *'French,' says he.*
> *'Well,' said I, 'I'm sorry, but I can't do anything there.'*

It is important to remember that inverted commas should enclose only the actual words used. It is not uncommon to see incorrectly punctuated sentences like this:

> *He said that 'he was delighted with the outcome of the talks.'*

What he actually said was, 'I am delighted with the outcome of the talks.' So the sentence should be either:

> *He said, 'I am delighted with the outcome of the talks.'*

or:

> *He said that he was 'delighted with the outcome of the talks'.*

Notice that because this is not true direct speech, but simply a quotation within a sentence, the final punctuation of the sentence comes **outside** the inverted commas. (Contrast it with: *He said, 'I am delighted with the outcome of the talks.'*)

Abbreviations

There is a certain amount of confusion about how abbreviations should be punctuated; some writers are not clear whether, or when, they should use a full stop. This is partly because the convention itself is in a process of change. What follows is one explanation of how it works, but it is easy to find texts that do not follow this set of 'rules'.

1 If an abbreviation is made up of individual capital letters, each one of which stands for a whole word, then each should be followed by a full stop:
Bachelor of Arts → *B.A.*

2 Abbreviations composed of initial lower-case letters should follow the same rule:

exempla gratia (for example) → *e.g.*

In fact *e.g.* often appears as *eg*.

3 If an abbreviation forms an **acronym**, that is to say a common name by which an organization is known, composed of initial letters, then full stops are not required:

British Broadcasting Corporation → BBC

4 Increasingly in British English abbreviations consisting of capital letters are written without full stops even when they are not acronyms. In American English this does not happen to the same degree.

5 If the abbreviation consists of the first part of a word then it should end with a full stop:

August → Aug.

6 If an abbreviation begins with the first letter of a word and ends with its last letter, then a full stop is not required:

Monsignor → Mgr

Lists

► *See also*

• *Colon,
Semicolon*
(p. 263–5)

Lists have already been touched on. If a list forms part of continuous text, then the items are normally separated by commas, or—if each is more complex, especially if it already contains commas—by semicolons.

The list can be preceded by a colon:

> *He quickly reviewed the options open to him: owning up to what he had done; trying to bluff his way out of it; or simply walking away before anyone noticed.*

In many documents, however, we may wish to use the layout of the text to clarify the items in the list. This is something which is done frequently in this book. If you have a number of points which you wish to stand out, they can be presented like this:

> *Our family Christmas package offers*:
> • *luxury accommodation;*
> • *all meals;*
> • *free welcome hamper on arrival;*
> • *presents under the tree.*

Here the list has been punctuated as if it were continuous prose; the items have been separated by semicolons and the last is followed by a full stop. If you find this is rather formal, then there is no reason why you should not remove the semicolons; the items are already perfectly clearly separated by the layout and the use of bullet points. It is even possible to remove the semicolons and final full stop, since the layout will make clear what is intended.

If each of the items forms a complete sentence, then they should be punctuated as such, as in the following example.

> *An unexpected rise in tax revenues means that the chancellor has three options available to him:*
> * *He can act prudently and use the extra money to reduce the PSBR.*
> * *He can mix prudence and political benefit by reducing the PSBR appreciably* **and** *cutting income tax by 2p in the £.*
> * *He can bow to the demands of backbenchers and cut tax by up to 4p in the £.*

Purists might protest that this misuses the colon, arguing that you cannot follow a colon with a complete sentence that starts with a capital letter. On the other hand each of the bullet points introduces a complete sentence, which would look strange if it did not begin with a capital and end with a full stop. Most people would find the punctuation as printed acceptable, but for those who do not the best solution is probably to conclude the introductory sentence with a full stop rather than a colon.

Parentheses

It is often necessary to enclose a section of text between two punctuation marks, so that it is separated from the rest of the sentence. This is called placing the enclosed text **in parenthesis**. The punctuation marks used are:

* commas: ,xxx xxxx xxx,
* dashes: —xxx xxxx xxx—
* brackets (or parentheses): (xxx xxxx xxx)

The important thing to remember is that points marking a parenthesis always come in twos:

> *My maternal grandfather,* **a well-known traveller and early photographer,** *died in Venice and was buried there. My grandmother—***who was understandably vexed at this arrangement***—fought to have his body exhumed and returned to Britain. The arrangements were made by Messrs Brownlow and Kemp (***a local firm of builders and funeral directors***), who happened to have an employee who was fluent in the Venetian dialect.*

It is normally the case that if a section of text is enclosed in this way, the sentence would still work perfectly well if the 'bracketed' section were removed. The commonest way of enclosing text for this purpose is to use commas. Dashes have a slightly relaxed, casual feel about them, while parentheses can seem stiffer and more 'scientific'.

Relative clauses

There is one specialist use of pairs of commas which needs to be mentioned, although it is probably missed by many readers. Frequently a relative clause **defines** the noun or noun phrase to which it refers:

> *The person **who was standing by the window** turned out to be a visiting professor from Australia.*

➤ *See also*

• CHAPTER 17
More about grammar
(p. 209)

Such clauses should not be enclosed by commas or any other punctuation. Sometimes, however, a relative clause is used not to define, but just to provide additional information:

> *All the people at the meeting were women except one. This man**, who seemed ill at ease in such company,** said nothing for several minutes.*

Here the relative clause is **non-defining**, and so is separated by commas. It could be omitted from the sentence without destroying its grammar or meaning.

Guidelines

1 Always remember that the primary purpose of punctuation is to aid the reader. Too many punctuation marks make a text confusing; too few make it ambiguous and difficult to follow.

2 A number of punctuation marks have fairly clearly defined rules for their use, about which there is little disagreement. These are referred to below (numbers 3–6).

3 Every sentence has to begin with a **capital letter** and end with a **full stop, question mark**, or **exclamation mark**. Problems only occur if you are not sure whether what you have written is a complete sentence or not.

4 The rules for using **apostrophes** are not difficult and can be learned.

5 The same applies to **colons** and **hyphens**.

6 The punctuation of direct speech and other quoted matter, using **inverted commas** and other punctuation marks, is also largely defined by a number of simple rules which can be learned.

7 Other punctuation marks and situations are more complicated and depend on experience and judgement.

8 The use of **semicolons** and **commas** is complex and needs thought. Essentially they serve to **separate** items that need to be kept apart or

to **enclose** sections of text—often because these contain additional, non-essential information.

9 Abbreviations can also cause problems, but a simple rule is that if you are in any doubt it is better to omit a full stop than insert one.

> **Further reading**

John Seely, *Oxford A–Z of Grammar and Punctuation*
(Oxford University Press, 2013) ISBN 9780199669189

㉑ Speech

---

1 Speech sounds

- Vocal sound is shaped by the 'organs of articulation' to make speech.
- Vowels are sounds produced with an open mouth.
- Consonants involve blocking the flow of breath in the mouth.
- Clarity of speech requires clear articulation, especially of consonants.
- The sounds of English can be transcribed using a phonemic transcription.

2 Stress and intonation

- Intonation is the 'tune' of sentences and carries an important part of the meaning.
- Words consist of one or more syllables.
- Polysyllabic words have one syllable that is stressed more than the others.
- Sentences also carry stressed and unstressed syllables and this pattern of sentence stress helps convey meaning.

3 Accent and pronunciation

- Different regions have distinctive ways of pronouncing English: regional accents.
- Received pronunciation, a social rather than a regional accent, is the socially dominant accent in Britain.

The human voice works on the same principle as any musical wind instrument. A column of air is forced over a 'reed', the vocal cords, which are caused to vibrate. This vibration is amplified in a hollow space, primarily the mouth, and sound is produced. The vocal cords can be tightened or slackened and this alters the musical pitch of the sound produced.

Essentially if you open your mouth wide and sing a musical note, this is what happens. The tone you produce is the raw material of speech. In order to speak we have to shape it and cut it up into small segments to construct the speech sounds, or *phonemes*, out of which words are built. This process is called *articulation* and the parts of the body we use for it are sometimes referred to as the *organs of articulation*.

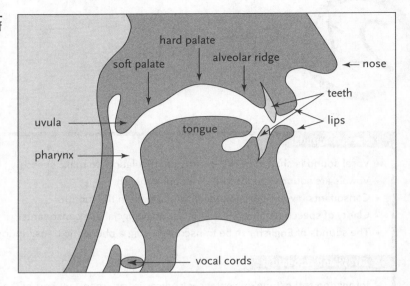

The organs of articulation diagram with labels: soft palate, hard palate, alveolar ridge, nose, teeth, lips, uvula, tongue, pharynx, vocal cords

Breathing and speech

The supply of air is essential to the production of vocal sound, so there is an important connection between breathing and voice production. At the simplest level, if you don't coordinate breathing and speech properly you will find that you run out of breath in mid-sentence. Most commonly this happens when people are nervous or when they have to say a lot very quickly. More prepared and extended sections of speech, such as a public reading or an after-dinner speech, allow opportunities for pre-planning. Actors often plot precisely where in a major speech they will take breath, and radio performers have to be careful about not taking noisy breaths close to the microphone.

It is also important, when speaking to large numbers of people without the benefit of a public-address system, to make sure that breath is used efficiently. Speakers who try to produce vocal sound in the same way as is done in conversation end up shouting and will, eventually, lose their voices. In such situations it is necessary to 'project' the voice by proper use of the diaphragm, the sheet of muscle and tendon which lies immediately beneath the lungs. If the diaphragm is used to push air up (i.e. from the 'bottom' of the lungs) greater volume can be produced without straining the vocal cords. This technique can be learned and developed by practice.

You can learn how to use the diaphragm quite simply.

Locating the diaphragm:

1 Stand comfortably, feet slightly apart, and rest the backs of your fingertips on the lowest ribs, so that the upper parts of your fingers are resting lightly on the upper abdomen.

2 Breathe normally and then stop partway through breathing out.

3 Now pant in and out without taking further breath in the normal way. Feel the movement of the diaphragm as it pushes the lungs up and down.

Using the diaphragm:

4 Now take a good breath and, opening the mouth comfortably, make a continuous and fairly quiet 'er' sound.

5 Partway through the breathing-out cycle, while you are still sounding the voice, use the diaphragm to suddenly push the sound out harder—the effort involved is exactly the same as that for panting. This should produce a sudden increase in volume.

There is a range of similar exercises which can be used to develop understanding and use of the diaphragm further and which are of particular value to those involved in regular public speaking.

Speech sounds

The phonemes of English can be divided into two main groups: vowels and consonants. (It is important to remember that we are considering *sounds* here and not letters. The first sound of the word *thin*, for example, is spelled using two letters, t-h, but it is only one sound.)

Vowels

This sound/letter discrepancy becomes painfully clear when we look at vowels, for while there are five vowel letters, a-e-i-o-u, there are twenty or so vowel sounds, depending on regional accent.

Vowels are speech sounds produced with an open mouth. The sound is formed using the shape of the mouth and the position of the tongue, which does not, however, block the passage of the air.

Say the following sequence of vowels. As you do so, observe the shape of your mouth and the position of your tongue. Try to observe where in the mouth the vowel appears to be shaped.

1 *ee* as in *teeth*

2 *oo* as in *soon*

3 *ar* as in *far*

4 *u* as in *hut*

Vowels can be pure, like those listed above, or they can be combined into *diphthongs*, in which one pure vowel glides into another. The vowels in these words are diphthongs:

hate—height—soil—foul

Consonants

When we make consonant sounds, the passage of air through the mouth is blocked or impeded in some way. Different consonants require the use of different organs of articulation. For example, the first consonant of *pin* is produced using the lips, while the first consonant of *goat* uses the middle of the tongue and the hard palate.

The quality of the consonant sound depends on the way in which the blockage of air is achieved. For example:

- **nasal**

  the mouth itself is blocked off in some way and the sound is made in the nasal cavity. For example, all the consonants of *mining*.

- **plosive**

  the air is blocked and then released with a small 'explosion'—as in the first sound of *pat*

- **fricative**

  air is forced through a narrow gap between two parts of the mouth. Examples are the first sounds of *first* and *shirt*.

Pronounce the first consonant of each of these words several times. In each case work out which of the organs of articulation are used and what type of sound is produced.

1 nice	**3** sing	**5** vase	**7** kick	**9** dance
2 butter	**4** tap	**6** zoo	**8** the	**10** heart

Clarity and articulation

When speech is indistinct and difficult to hear or follow it is often because the speaker is not articulating the consonants clearly enough. The quality of the vowels will tell us a lot about where a speaker comes from (both regionally and socially). Without clearly pronounced consonants, however, we may not be able to understand what is said. For this reason, particularly when speaking in public, it is important to work at the clear articulation of consonants, especially those which fall at the end of words.

Writing speech sounds down

It is easy to forget that written English is a transcription of speech; speech is not a pronunciation of writing. You sometimes hear people say words to the effect of 'You aren't pronouncing it right. It's written with a "c", and you aren't pronouncing the "c".' English spelling—chaotic and confusing as it may appear at times—is an attempt to put down on paper the words we say. Like the language, it has evolved over a period of time and was further confused by the efforts of 'reformers' who attempted to introduce some system into it at different points in the past. All have failed, with the result that, if we were 'logical', the word we normally spell f-i-s-h could also be spelled **ghoti**:

> **gh** as in cou**gh**
> **o** as in w**o**men
> **ti** as in commo**ti**on

Faced with such a difficulty, students of language have devised different ways of transcribing speech sounds accurately. There is an *International Phonetic Alphabet* which can be used to transcribe *any* speech sounds. As might be expected, however, this contains a vast number of symbols and is not particularly useful if all one wants to do is focus on the sound system of a single language. For this we need to look not at *phonetics*, the study of speech sounds generally, but at *phonology*, the study of the sound system of a language—how sounds are used to communicate meaning. We need a way of writing down the *phonemes*, or significant sounds of the language—a *phonemic transcription*.

The most widely used phonemic transcription system for British English is that developed by A. C. Gimson. The list that follows is based on Gimson's. Note that phonemic symbols are usually enclosed by two obliques: //.

Consonants					
/p/	as in	pin	/s/	as in	sin
/b/		bin	/z/		zeal
/t/		tin	/ʃ/		shin
/d/		din	/ʒ/		leisure
/k/		kin	/h/		hot
/g/		goat	/m/		mine
/tʃ/		chin	/n/		nine
/dʒ/		gin	/ŋ/		sing
/f/		fin	/l/		line
/v/		vineyard	/r/		right
/θ/		thin	/j/		yet
/ð/		this	/w/		wet

Vowels					
/iː/	as in	beat	/əː/	as in	hurt
/ɪ/		bit	/ə/		the
/e/		bet	/eɪ/		rain
/æ/		bat	/aɪ/		die
/ʌ/		but	/ɔɪ/		boy
/aː/		hart	/ou/		toe
/ɔ/		hot	/au/		out
/ɔː/		fort	/ɪə/		dear
/u/		put	/ɛə/		air
/uː/		boot	/uə/		tou

Stress and intonation

Individual speech sounds are not, of course, the only way in which we use our voices to communicate meaning. This is easily seen if you look at the different ways in which the same sequence of words can be said. The sentence, *You're going out* can, for example, be spoken in these ways:

1 as a flat statement of fact, with the voice falling at the end

2 as a question, with the voice rising at the end

3 as a question which asks in effect whether 'you' or someone else is going out, with emphasis on 'you' and the voice rising at the end

4 as an emphatic statement of fact, almost an order, with the words strongly stressed and a short pause between each

In normal writing the only way in which we can show these variations is by the use of punctuation, underlining, or other typographic conventions:

1 You're going out.

2 You're going out?

3 **You're** going out?

4 (Very difficult!) You're ... *going* ... **out!**

Here we have used two different types of sound signal: intonation and stress.

Intonation

Intonation is the 'tune' of the language. If you listen to people speaking and pay attention to the way in which the pitch of their voices rises and falls, rather than to the individual sounds and words, you will see that this is not just a matter of statements and questions, but is essential for the communication of meaning.

See how many different ways you can think of to say the single word *really*—imagining that it comes in the middle of a conversation and stands on its own. For example:

• showing casual interest in what has been said

• showing eager interest in what has been said

• making it clear that you are not the slightest bit interested

• showing that you don't believe a word of what you are being told

• showing incredulity

You can probably think of more!

Stress

There are two different kinds of stress in English, word stress and sentence stress. Both are essential to communicate meaning satisfactorily (and both cause many foreign learners of the language severe problems).

Syllables

English words consist of one or more syllables. Each syllable must contain a vowel. This may have one or more consonants before and/or after it. In the examples that follow the letter V represents a vowel *sound* and C a consonant *sound*. Notice that sometimes one consonant sound may be represented by more than one letter ('sh' is one sound) and vice versa (the single letter 'x' requires two sounds—*ks* or *gz*—depending on where it comes in the word).

Words of one syllable

or	V
my	CV
aim	VC
bit	CVC
scratched	CCCVCC

Words of two syllables

tapers	CVCVC
matchbox	CVCCVC

Words of more than two syllables

examination	VCCVCVCVCVC (5 syllables)

Word stress

The syllables of a word can be spoken with more or less force or emphasis. Where a syllable is spoken with emphasis it is said to be stressed. Syllables that are not spoken with emphasis are unstressed. Each of these two-syllable words has one stressed and one unstressed syllable:

motor
de**tach**

In longer words there may also be a lesser, secondary stress—here marked by italics:

ex*am*ination
exem*plified*

Sentence stress

The situation is complicated by the fact that sentences, too, are stressed to underline their meaning. A sentence can carry a normal stress:

We're going to **Spain** for a *holiday*.

   ↑   ↑

  MAIN STRESS SECONDARY STRESS

Sometimes, however, we may wish to change this normal pattern to provide extra information. We may, for example, want to emphasize that we are travelling to Spain for a holiday and not on business:

We're going to *Spain* for a **holiday**.

   ↑   ↑

  SECONDARY STRESS MAIN STRESS

Sentence stress is very important. We use it to communicate part of the meaning of the sentence and it also determines the rhythm of our speech. However quickly or slowly you speak, the stresses in your sentences will be fairly evenly spaced in time. Since the pattern of stresses in the sentence is pre-determined (by meaning), this means that longer groups of words without any stress are apparently 'gabbled' and shorter ones appear to pass more slowly and deliberately. This **stress-timing** of English can cause serious problems for foreign learners. To the French learner, for example, it can seem that the English speak with a mixture of excessive force (stress) and a slovenly swallowing of whole words and phrases (because of stress-timing). By the same token the English learner of French finds it difficult to unlearn stress-timing and use a more measured and regular *syllable timing* when speaking French. While the French have word stress, they use sentence stress much less, preferring to rephrase a sentence or to add words to indicate special emphasis.

Accent and pronunciation

In different countries of the world, and in different regions of those countries, English words are pronounced differently. The most obvious differences appear in vowel sounds: compare, for example, the way in which a Londoner, someone from North Yorkshire, and a New Yorker pronounce the vowel in *bath*. But consonants, too, vary as we travel from place to place. Many Londoners, for example, would say the last consonant of *bath* as /f/. Many Scots do not use the typical 'tapped' /r/ of Southern English (in which the tongue just taps the ridge above the top teeth) preferring a longer 'trilled' sound.

Received pronunciation

In many countries regional accents are common at all levels of society, but in Britain there has grown up over a period of time one non-regional accent which is widely considered to be 'better' than others. Based on the accents of Southern England, and used by many educated and influential people throughout society, it is known technically as *received pronunciation* (or *RP*) and sometimes called 'BBC English' or 'educated English'. It is also sometimes confused with standard English. There is, however, no direct connection between the two—although many people who regularly use standard English also speak using RP. While it is possible to speak standard English with a regional accent, it would sound very strange to speak a regional dialect using RP.

It has to be said that while the use of a standard dialect makes very good sense, the 'superiority' of RP has more to do with class consciousness than clarity of communication. Unfortunately, however, it remains true that if people with strong regional accents wish to succeed in the company of people to whom these things are important they may well have to learn to play the game according to the RP rules.

Word pronunciation

Speakers are sometimes judged by the way in which they pronounce (or 'mispronounce') words. Some people even have a few key words by which they judge others. For example, do you pronounce the first vowel of *either* to rhyme with *eye* or *me*? Do you talk about a **con**troversy or a con**tro**versy? None of this should matter very much—the purpose of a standardized pronunciation is that people understand each other—but again social judgements can and will be made. Any good-sized dictionary will provide information about both the phonemes of a word and how it should be stressed, but some use a phonetic transcription, which you need to be able to follow. (It is usually explained in the introduction to the dictionary.)

An easier way of finding out how a word is pronounced is provided by some online dictionaries and smartphone and tablet apps. Clicking on an icon produces a spoken pronunciation of the word. Examples can be found at:

<http://www.howjsay.com/>
<http://www.macmillandictionary.com/>

Another, analogue, approach is to consult a 'guide to usage':

> **controversy** This word is now very often pronounced in Britain with the stress on the second syllable, but this pronunciation attracts criticism from some people. The traditional British pronunciation with the stress on the first syllable is normal in American English.
>
> Sidney Greenbaum and Janet Whitcut:
> *Longman Guide to English Usage*

Of course, as with other controversial matters of usage, different authorities may not necessarily agree. (And it is interesting to note that the two online dictionaries referred to above offer both pronunciations without comment.)

Guidelines

1 Remember that good breathing is essential to good speech. If you are reading aloud or making a speech, prepare carefully so that you do not find yourself running out of breath at key points.

2 When you need to speak loudly, use your diaphragm to produce the extra force required, and so avoid shouting and straining the vocal cords.

3 Regional and social accents are largely carried through the vowels. Be aware of the social dimension of speech: many people give received pronunciation greater prestige than regional accents. If you have a strong regional accent you may have to choose between remaining 'true to your origins' and compromising by using a regional version of RP (RP with 'quieter' regional vowels).

4 Clarity of speech is greatly affected by the quality of the consonants. It is important to articulate these clearly, which requires awareness, effort, and, sometimes, practice.

5 Be aware of the impact of intonation and sentence stress on the communication of meaning. Listen to experienced speakers (for example, good broadcasters) to hear how they use these features of speech. Faulty stress and intonation, and the wrong use of pauses, are common causes of poor communication. Listen to bad broadcasters (of whom there are plenty) to hear how irritating this can be.

6 The correct pronunciation of words involves both the separate sounds of which they are composed and word stress. Some people are very aware of small variations of pronunciation. If it is important to impress such people, then be aware of the 'pitfalls' and avoid them.

D The process of writing

This section of the book looks in more detail at the production of extended pieces of writing, beginning with the initial idea and going right through to the use of modern technology to produce the final document.

22 Getting ready to write

Time spent on preparation before you write is rarely wasted. This chapter describes how to write a statement of intent, setting out the subject matter, audience, and purpose of your writing, the timeframe within which it must be completed, and its format.

23 Making notes and summaries

As you prepare to write, and even while you draft your text, you will probably find that you move between brainstorming ideas, researching information, and organizing your material. Making effective notes is the key to linking these activities and keeping the whole process under control. This chapter examines the many different ways in which you can make notes, using old-fashioned pencil and paper or on a computer. It concludes with an explanation of how to write an effective summary of a longer text.

24 Research

Research is an essential part of many extended writing tasks. This chapter sets out the important principles that underlie effective research and examines how to use libraries and work online. The chapter concludes with a case study showing how these ideas work in practice.

25 Planning and drafting

Some writers like to prepare a detailed plan before they begin to write; others prefer to work out their ideas as they write. In this chapter the merits of each approach are analysed and detailed guidelines are provided for each.

26 Editing and revising

Almost every text benefits from some form of editing; the longer the text, the more important editing becomes. Writers need to understand the principles of editing and to be able to edit their own work. This chapter describes how a text is edited and at what stages this work can be done. It concludes with an analysis of the stages a sample text went through in the course of drafting and revising.

27 Presentation

The layout and appearance of a piece of writing are an important part of the way in which it communicates to the reader. Elements such as headings, spacing, typefaces and their size and spacing all contribute to this, as does the appropriate use of visuals such as diagrams and charts. Writing for the web and e-books presents new challenges that can be exploited, if you understand how HTML affects the way in which texts are read.

22 Getting ready to write

The first stage in preparing to write

The brief

- externally imposed
- personal project

Statement of intent

- What?
- Who?
- Why?
- When?
- How?

A worked example

Whatever kind of writing you do, there are four stages you usually have to go through before you begin:

- statement of intent
- generating ideas
- research
- planning the order

For simple pieces of writing this process may just take place in your head. For longer projects, on the other hand, it will almost always need to be written down.

The brief

The statement of intent is a short document you write for your own use setting out the essential features of your writing project. Even if you think you have a very clear idea of what you are going to write, it is still useful to take time to clarify your objectives.

How you go about this depends on how the project originated:

- as an externally imposed brief, for example:
  - a report requested by your line manager
  - an article commissioned for a newsletter
  - an essay set as part of a college course
- as a personal project

Externally imposed

An externally imposed brief may be as simple as a short conversation or email. Sometimes the brief will be rather more detailed. For example:

Even when a brief is as detailed as this, you should still interrogate it in order to produce a more precise and usable version. In the next section we shall look at how this can be done.

Personal project

In the case of a personal project it is still more important to write a brief before you do anything else. If not, you may well find yourself floundering as you work through your first draft.

Statement of intent

A statement of intent should contain answers to all the following questions:

- **What?**

  A definition of the subject matter

- **Who?**

  The target audience for your writing

- **Why?**

  Your purpose(s) in writing

- **When?**

  There is often a deadline for writing tasks and you need to schedule all aspects of a writing project with this in mind

- **How?**

  The format of your writing

We'll examine these one by one.

What?

To answer this question, you should isolate the most important features only. The more detailed points can be picked up later. One way of starting this process is to highlight key words:

> We need to think about changes in truancy over the past three years and the possible causes. I'd also like you to have a look at how well you think the current policy is working and how we could change it to improve things.

Here the subject matter consists of four elements:

- Changes in attendance rates over the past three years
- Causes for these changes
- Weaknesses in policy
- Possible remedies

Who?

The brief also gives a fairly clear idea of who will read this piece of writing:

> The Governors want to discuss this at their next meeting in March. We need to talk about it at the Senior Management Team meeting the week before. Can you prepare a paper for that meeting?

- The report will be read by the Principal.
- It will then be read by the members of the Senior Management Team.
- It may very well form the basis of a paper that is taken to the next meeting of the Board of Governors.

Each of these three scenarios has important implications for the way in which the report is framed. If you are writing for a small group of colleagues whom you meet every day, and who share a common language and experience, you are likely to write in a different way than if you are addressing a group of people who are not necessarily experts and whom you may only know on a more formal basis. (So if the paper has to be re-written for the Governors, you will need to bear this in mind.)

Why?

Pinning down the purpose of a piece of writing is often the most difficult part of the brief. The commonest general purposes for any kind of writing can be summed up in this list:

▶ There is more about purpose in Chapter 13: *Purpose* (p. 143)

- to inform
- to persuade
- to make a record
- to entertain
- to interact
- to find out
- to regulate

However, as soon as you start to look at our sample writing project, you see that there isn't just one purpose behind it, but several. The first three in the list above are all likely candidates:

- **to inform**

  The report will provide detailed information about truancy rates: are they rising or falling? And by how much? Is the trend accelerating or slowing down?

- **to persuade**

  You are being asked to suggest changes of policy, so you need to give good reasons why these are better than other possible changes, or no changes at all.

- **to make a record**

  Your report will no doubt be filed as part of the record of how the school has tackled truancy in the recent past and how it proposes to deal with it in the future (and why).

The first two may seem to be the most important, and it is certainly true that they need to be carried out efficiently. But this report is very probably going to form the basis of some change of policy. If so, when that policy is reviewed, people will reread the report and judge it against how well the revised policy has worked. A shrewd writer will bear that in mind when expressing facts and opinions—especially opinions—about the previous policy.

This leads on to minor purposes which you might not otherwise think of. The writer of any document always has his or her own agenda. While your main purpose may be to inform, you probably also want to show yourself in a particular light, whether to the Governors, to the Head teacher, or to your colleagues, and this too will tend to influence the way you write.

When?

In the original email you have a clear indication of the timetable:

> The Governors want to discuss this at their next meeting in March. We need to talk about it at the Senior Management Team meeting the week before. Can you prepare a paper for that meeting?

This can be developed into a writing schedule, which should include dates for:

- Completion of first draft
- Circulation for comments
- Editing and redrafting
- Final delivery

How?

The final element in a brief describes the format(s) in which your writing will be presented. It is important to pin these down, because different formats require different structures. In the email, the writer has been asked to 'prepare a paper', which is slightly vague. In this case the best model is the report format: this text may form the basis of a more formal presentation to the Governors, and that will almost certainly need to be a formal report.

Normally a report consists of the following parts:

> There is more about writing reports in Chapter 7: *Reports* (p. 81)

- Executive summary
- Body
- Introduction
- Main text, possibly divided into sections or chapters
- Conclusion(s)
- Appendices

Shorter reports may omit the executive summary and appendices. However, in this case both are probably needed:

- The primary audience is composed of busy people who may only have time to skim-read paperwork before a meeting. The executive summary enables them to get a quick grasp of the report's main points and conclusions. It will also direct their attention to those sections in the body of the report they need to spend more time on. For those who read the report more carefully, it provides a rapid reference to refresh their memories.
- It will also be useful to have an appendix containing the statistics on which the factual part of the report is based.

You should also work out roughly how long the finished text should be: its extent. When you get to the editing stage, this will enable you to work out how much cutting and compression are required.

A worked example

So for this particular writing project, your writing brief might look something like this:

```
Paper for Senior Management Team on Truancy Policy

Subject matter:
  • Changes in attendance rates over the last
    three years
  • Causes for these changes
  • How well the current policy is working
  • How we could change it to improve things

Readership

  • Suzanne McFarland
  • Senior Management Team
```

- (Governors)

Purposes

- Provide all necessary data for new policy
- Suggest new policy options
- Recommend best options

Schedule

- To Suzanne McFarland by 15 February
- Ready for SMT meeting by 22 February
- Governors' Meeting 15 March

Format

- Standard report format, including executive summary
- Appendix with truancy data set against dates and significant events

Extent: about 3000 words

Read the writing brief below and then produce a statement of intent following the pattern described above.

Brief

A group of business people from Hangzhou, near Shanghai in China, are due to visit your area as guests of the Chamber of Commerce. They will be taken on a three-hour trip to local places of historical and cultural interest. You have been asked to write a short guide describing the places they will visit and providing background information.

(You will find a model answer on page 383.)

Guidelines

1. Consider writing a statement of intent, whether your starting point is:
   a. externally imposed
   b. a personal project

2. Any statement of intent should contain answers to these questions:
   a. What?
   b. Who?
   c. Why?
   d. When?
   e. How?

3. What?
Make a list of the main content to include.

4. Who?
List *all* those who will read the document (i.e. not just the final audience).

5. Why?
Think carefully about the purpose of your document, and list both major and minor objectives.

6. When?
Make a schedule for the stages of the writing project, to include:
   a. delivery of first draft
   b. consultation with others involved
   c. redrafting and editing
   d. final delivery

7. How?
Give careful thought to the format and extent of your document.

23 Making notes and summaries

Making notes is central to the process of preparing to write. It links:

- generating ideas
- research
- planning

Why make notes?

- to remember
- to generate ideas
- to understand
- to organize
- to plan

Note-making formats

- freeform
- list
- table
- flowchart
- concept map

These can be:

- digital: using computer software, or online
- analogue: using pencil and paper

The last chapter suggested that the process of preparing to write consisted of a sequence:

Brief —> Generating ideas —> Research —> Planning

In the real world the process isn't quite so straightforward. The brief should certainly come first, but the other stages tend to interact with each other.

You start off generating ideas, then do a bit of research; perhaps you begin to make a plan, which then suggests other research and ideas, and so on. The problem is: how do you keep track of what is going on? If you work in this non-linear way, there is a danger that everything goes spinning round in your mind so that you simply get confused, or bogged down in detail and never get to the writing stage.

The solution is to make notes: the notes you make as you go through the idea-generation/research/planning process will help to hold things together, and will provide an invaluable resource when you need to review the progress of your project.

Why make notes?

Like other kinds of writing, making notes can have a variety of purposes. Among these are:

- to remember
- to generate ideas
- to understand
- to organize
- to plan

To remember

Notes are an essential way of recording your ideas, things that are said, and things that you read. While you are thinking about a piece of writing, ideas can come and go with remarkable rapidity. It is all too easy to have what seems like a brilliant idea only to find later that it has disappeared and that you cannot bring it back into your mind. If you cultivate the habit of 'thinking on paper', this is much less likely to happen.

The same consideration applies when you are reading a text or listening to a lecture or presentation. While you may remember the broad outline of what you have read or heard, the detail may well escape you.

The skill of making notes lies in being able to see at the time which details are likely to be useful and which are not.

To generate ideas

We can use notes as a means of generating ideas. This is often done using a concept or mind map, a process that is described later in this chapter, and which can be described as 'brainstorming on paper'.

Brainstorming is sometimes thought of as a purely group activity. A small or large group work together to generate ideas for a project, generally with one member of the group nominated to record the ideas as they are thrown up. Often the 'rule' is made that all ideas should be given equal value, that no judgements should be made about the value of any idea. (Although this is a rule that groups find it as easy to break as to make.)

There is, however, a contrary view that solo brainstorming is of equal or greater value than the group version. The social situation of a group can be a distraction, and for many writing projects you are more likely to be working on your own. Even when working on your own, though, it is worth trying to follow the rule of inclusiveness: however odd an idea may seem at the time, when you return to it later you may see that in fact it has unsuspected merits.

To understand

You can also use notes to help you understand an idea, or a text. Sometimes it is difficult to see your way through complicated information. Jotting down what seem to be the main ideas, searching for links, similarities, and differences, and then indicating them graphically, is a helpful aid to understanding.

For example, you might begin by jotting down a few basic ideas, and then use each one as a hub from which new, more detailed ideas can be developed. Looking back at the notes later you may see new connections, which can be indicated by drawing linking lines on your notes.

To plan

Making notes is also an essential part of planning longer texts. The material in a brainstorming diagram almost certainly does not form a coherent plan for writing. It will need to be reordered into a hierarchy, or outline. This, too, is described in detail later in this chapter.

Note-making formats

There are no hard-and-fast rules about how to make notes—indeed, there are almost as many note-making systems as there are note-makers. What's more, individual note-makers employ a variety of styles within a single page of notes, as can be seen in the illustration on page 300.

On the other hand, there are a number of well-known formats for notes, of which the commonest are:

- freeform
- list
- table
- flowchart
- concept map

To these we need to add the choice between:

- pencil and paper
- computer-based

The simplest form of note-making is simply to jot down items with no regard for pattern. While this 'back-of-an-envelope' approach may seem messy and undisciplined, it has its advantages. Most obviously, if you do not know what the pattern is, then a freeform approach can help you discover it. The following example illustrates this in action.

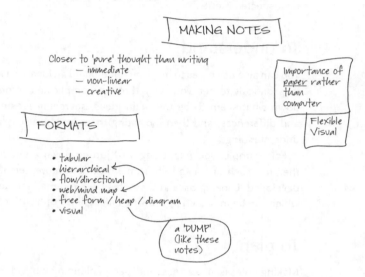

It shows some organization—in the use of bulleted lists, for example. But other ideas are just jotted more or less at random. Lines, arrows, and circles are added to show connections and emphasis.

List

A list is a common form of note-making, and often that is all that is needed. There are two in the illustration above. But you can make lists as complicated as you like. It is often useful to develop a list into a hierarchy. There is more about lists and hierarchies later in the chapter.

Table

Another development of the list idea is to tabulate information, as in the following example:

SOURCES OF INFORMATION

MEDIUM	IN-HOUSE	RESTRICTED	PUBLIC
Human	Colleagues, friends	Contacts in other organizations	Consultants
Analogue	Files, internal memos and reports	Academic research	Books, journals, newspapers
Digital	Company intranet	Subscription websites	Websites

Flowchart

If you are making notes on a sequence or process, then a flowchart is a useful format. The following example shows part of a simple set of notes about planning a new garden.

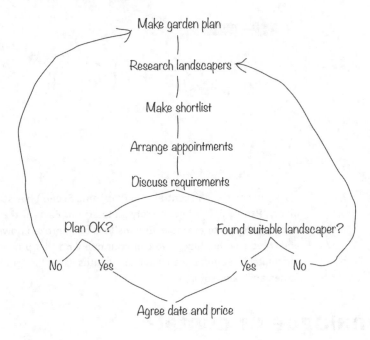

Concept map or mind map

One of the commonest and most recommended formats is a concept map or mind map. Mind maps generally only have one central starting point, while concept maps can have more than one, and allow easier 'cross-referencing' between different parts of the map. For practical purposes, however, the two are very similar and we are free to use whichever approach suits the job in hand. The example below shows the beginnings of a mind map analysing the opening scene of Shakespeare's *The Comedy of Errors*.

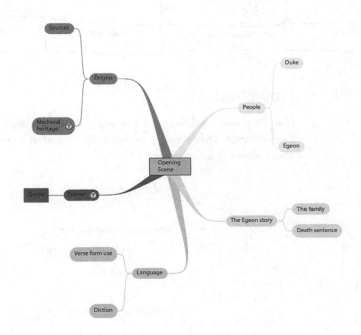

As you can see, the central idea ('Opening Scene') has spun off five main ideas, 'People', 'The Egeon story', and so on. Each of these has then led to other ideas. For example 'Origins' has been broken down into 'Sources' and 'Medieval heritage'. We can continue with this process more or less indefinitely. 'Sources' can lead to 'Plautus' and 'St Paul's Letter to the Ephesians', and so on.

Analogue or digital?

Whatever your reason for making notes, and whatever format you adopt, you have the choice between:

- digital (computer-based)
- analogue (or pencil and paper)

Digital

There is a wide range of software available for note-making. The programmes available can be roughly categorized like this:

- hierarchical
- concept-mapping
- database
- hybrid

What follows is not a survey of all the available software, but a brief analysis of what each approach to note-taking offers.

Hierarchical

Many word-processing programmes now include an outlining feature, which allows the user to order ideas in a hierarchy. This is usually promoted as an initial step in a writing project, but it can equally well be used for making notes. There are also standalone outliners which offer the user a much bigger set of features, so that they can be used for managing large-scale individual or collaborative projects.

Generally speaking, outliners are not well suited to the collection of large amounts of data, although they may offer the ability to attach text, images, and other files to a note. What they are good at is enabling the user to have a simple overview of a large subject and then to drill down into the details. So if, for example, we are planning to write about Morbihan in Southern Brittany, our notes can be collapsed to this:

- Towns
- Coast
- Tourist attractions
- Activities

At the click of a mouse they can be expanded to this:

- Towns
    - Major ports
        - Lorient
        - Vannes
    - Other coastal towns
        - Port-Louis
        - Carnac
        - Locmariaquer
    - Inland
        - Le Faouët
        - Pontivy
        - Josselin
        - Ploërmel

and so on.

Outlining applications are available for use on desktop computers, mobile devices, and online.

Concept maps and mind maps

Again, there is a large choice of software, with a wide range of features (and prices—from freeware to packages costing hundreds of pounds). All allow the user different degrees of freedom to format a mind map to reflect the thinking process behind it. The diagram below shows an example made using the application Novamind.

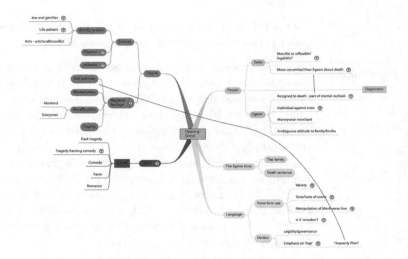

As you can see, it is an expansion of the previous mind map: many more ideas have been developed and the links between different ideas are being drawn in.

Database

Outliners and mind mapping programmes are highly suited to recording and generating ideas. What they are not so good at is storing quantities of material. When you are researching you need some way of collecting and storing a range of material: pages from the web, PDFs, images, text files, and so on. Having collected it, you then need to be able to organize, sort, and search this material. In addition, you need to keep track of the sources of all this material, so that it can be cited correctly when you refer to it.

There are a number of programmes available to cater for this group of needs. For Apple Mac users the best known is probably DevonThink, but this is not available on other platforms. Probably the most popular alternative is the web-based Evernote. Alternatively it is possible to use a bibliographic programme that allows you to attach files to individual references. Examples are EndNote and Bookends.

Hybrid

In addition to these three main types of software there are also hybrids, which combine two or more of the types, and some which approach note-making in a more individualistic way. Like many things which claim to be multifunctional, this 'Swiss Army Knife' approach fulfills no single function as well as the more specialist programmes. On the other hand, it is convenient to contain and control all your material inside one package. Two of the more interesting hybrids are Scrivener (Windows and Mac) and Curio (Mac only), and a highly complex one with a steep learning curve is Tinderbox (Mac only).

Scrivener is first and foremost a tool for writers. It enables the writer to draft non-fiction and fiction quickly and easily, keeping separate segments of a draft, and separate drafts ... separate. It then allows you to work visually, arranging and rearranging your material as much or as little as you like, before compiling it into a finished draft. It includes an outliner and the ability to work in full screen, thus avoiding distractions. Alongside this writing space, there is a research space into which you can import and arrange material from the web, movies, sound files, PDFs, text files, and images.

Curio is more obviously a storage, organization, and note-making environment. In a single 'idea space' you can combine text, outlines, tables, images, and mind maps and arrange them as you wish. Such a world of possibilities will intrigue some writers, while others will simply find it distracting.

Paper-based

Computer-based note-making is attractive to many and has these advantages:

- It makes it easy to store and organize large quantities of information in diverse formats.
- It facilitates quick searches of stored information and enables the user to perceive links and relationships that might otherwise go unnoticed.

However, it also has serious disadvantages:

- It inevitably limits freedom: you have to use it within the constraints set down by the programmer.
- The limitations of a particular piece of software can act as a set of blinkers, preventing the user from seeing other possibilities.
- It can be expensive.

By contrast, paper-based note-making and information storage is cheap and unconstricted. With just a sheet of paper and something to write and draw with, you are free to explore the working of your own mind (or that of the writer or speaker you are focusing on) in whatever way you like. You can write, draw doodle, and link disparate ideas, as you feel the need. Sheets of paper can be reordered, cut up and stuck together in different ways, fixed to the wall, or filed away in a ring binder. Hand-made notes have a personality and an immediacy that can never be matched by their digital counterparts. Admittedly it may take longer to sort them and to find what you are looking for, but in the very act of searching and sorting, you may well come across something unexpected and see connections that had not occurred to you before.

Use one of the note-making formats to make notes of the text below. As you work, observe how the process of making notes affects the way you read the text.

Crime

People want to live in an orderly society in which they can go about their public and private lives without fear of being injured or having their property damaged or stolen by others. We wish to be free to do as we like without harming others and without interference from others. We also allow the state to stop us from doing things that harm ourselves. In addition we empower the state to protect us from threats from outside the country and to protect our security. Individual citizens have to be prevented from acting in a way that threatens national security. In order to achieve this we empower the state to pass and enforce laws and to punish those who break them. This is the foundation on which the criminal law is built: to prevent individuals from behaving in ways which harm others or society as a whole.

How do we define a crime?

Lawyers use two Latin phrases when they are defining crimes: *actus reus* and *mens rea*. *Actus reus* means literally 'guilty act'. To find someone guilty of a crime it has to be proved that they committed an action defined by the law as a crime. So, for example, the law distinguishes between the crimes of assault and battery. Assault means acting in such a way towards someone that they are put in fear of personal injury. In other words you can assault someone without touching them. Battery, on the other hand, means deliberately making physical contact with someone without their consent.

The last sentence contained the word 'deliberately'. *Mens rea* is the second component of a crime and means 'guilty mind'. A crime is a criminal act done with a 'guilty mind'. The law distinguishes different degrees in this. For some crimes, like murder, it has to be proved that there was specific intent: when X raised the axe he specifically intended to kill Y. For other crimes, it is necessary to prove recklessness or negligence by the perpetrator. There is a fourth group of crimes in which the perpetrator's state of mind is of no importance. If you are caught by a police speed trap breaking the speed limit it makes no difference at all whether you intended to or not; the simple fact of exceeding the limit is sufficient. Crimes of this kind are referred to as absolute or strict liability offences.

Making a summary

When you are referring in some detail to a book or other source, you can either quote directly from it, or summarize what it says. The ability to write a clear and accurate summary is a valuable skill, useful not only when referring to a text produced by someone else, but also when you have to reduce the length of your own writing. This is one way of approaching it.

1 List the main points made in the text.
2 Make sure that they are in the most logical order (rearrange them if necessary), and under each one make a brief list of supporting arguments and data.
3 Without referring to the original text, make a first draft of the summary.
4 Check your draft for length and cut it if necessary.
5 Now check it against the original. Look for two things:
   a important points you have missed out (if there are any, make sure they are included).
   b any accidental direct quotations from the original (if there are any, reword them).
6 Write a final draft, keeping an eye on length.

Stages 1, 2, and 6 are illustrated in the example that follows.

Refugees & the Dispossessed

Kenya, being a relatively stable country with opportunities to make a living or at least work the tourists for hand-outs, is a natural magnet for refugees from strife-torn neighbouring countries. Nairobi and Mombasa and, to a lesser degree, the coastal resort towns, are the favoured destinations. You'll come across plenty of these people on your travels and it's relatively easy for them to remain anonymous if they can make enough money to stay off the streets.

There's nothing remarkable about this—it happens all over the world. What is remarkable in Kenya is the number of unattached teenage and early-20s mothers—many of them Kenyan but also quite a lot from Uganda, Sudan, Ethiopia, and even Rwanda. With the break-up of many traditional communities as a result of colonial policies that were designed to bring people into the money economy, and the continuation of this system under post-colonial regimes, there has been large-scale movement of people to urban areas. Most arrive with nothing and are forced to live in overcrowded shanty towns (some 60% of Nairobi's population lives in these places) with little hope of anything resembling a steady job with reasonable pay.

As a result, all the facets of urban alienation can be found in these places with drunkenness, theft, and rape (particularly of schoolgirls) being fairly commonplace. But this isn't confined to the major urban areas. It appears to be fairly widespread everywhere outside of traditional tribal areas.

As far as the girls are concerned, once they become pregnant they're expelled from school (in other words, it's the end of their educational prospects) and, as likely as not, rejected by their families, too. In 1986, the number of young girls who found themselves in this position (according to official figures) was 11,000, and it's been rising steadily ever since. The options for those to whom this happens are extremely limited. A few shelters do exist (usually run by Christian organizations), but it's only the lucky few who get in. For the rest, it's very poorly paid domestic work or the flesh market.

Main points

1. a lot of refugees in Kenya
2. many are young mothers
3. the poor gravitate to cities
4. leads to crime and degradation
5. the girls become outcasts
6. they can only become servants or prostitutes

Main points plus key details

1. a lot of refugees live in Kenya
   a. surrounded by countries where there are problems
   b. Kenya prosperous and it's easy to get a job or beg
2. the poor gravitate to cities
   a. breakdown of old communities
   b. development of cash economy
   c. not enough jobs
   d. development of shanty towns
   e. leads to crime and degradation
3. many of the poor are young mothers
   a. Kenyans, but also refugees from surrounding countries
4. the girls become outcasts
   a. pregnancy leads to expulsion from school and rejection by family
   b. increasing problem—numbered in 10,000s
5. they can only become servants or prostitutes
   a. no qualifications
   b. lack of work

Kenya's relative prosperity means that it attracts refugees from the troubled states that surround it. They find it quite easy to get employment or to beg in the popular tourist resorts. The breakdown of old, tribal society and the growth of a cash economy have led many of the poor to move to the cities, but there are not enough jobs, so shanty towns have sprung up. Here people live surrounded by poverty, degradation, and crime. Many of the poor Kenyans and refugees are young mothers who have found that pregnancy has made them outcasts. Unable to continue their schooling, and often rejected by their families, they are left with little choice; they can either become servants or prostitutes.

Guidelines

Notes as a link

1 Use note-making as a link between
   a generating ideas
   b research
   c planning

Purposes

2 Note-making is an important way of remembering
   a ideas you have
   b things you read
   c what you hear at lectures and presentations
3 Use note-making to generate ideas.
4 It is also a useful way of helping to understand complex texts.
5 Make notes when planning a piece of writing.

Formats

6 Freeform notes allow you to
   a collect ideas and information quickly
   b see the links between ideas
7 Hierarchical lists are particularly useful when generating a plan for a piece of writing.
8 Certain types of information are best recorded using a table.
9 Processes can be recorded using a flowchart.
10 Concept or mind maps are highly flexible and particularly valuable when brainstorming ideas.
11 Notes can be set down using computer software or old-fashioned pencil-and-paper methods.

Computer-based

12 Hierarchical lists can be compiled using a word processor or a special-ist outlining programme.

13 A variety of mind-mapping programmes are available. Most allow you to generate hierarchical lists from your mind map.

14 If you have a lot of information to record, then you probably need a database programme.

15 There are also hybrid programmes that combine a number of these features.

16 Computer-based note-making has several advantages, especially in its ability to store and locate large quantities of information.

Pencil-and-paper

17 Paper-based note-making is cheap and has the advantage of allowing complete freedom.

Writing a summary

18 When you are referring to a text in detail, consider writing a summary rather than quoting at length.

19 When summarizing, it is better to use your own notes as an intermedi-ate stage rather than working directly from the original text.

20 Check your final version against the original for errors and omissions.

(24) Research

Research essentials

- relevance
- integrity
- availability
- detail
- storage
- access
- referencing

Searching

- library catalogues
- internet search engines

Case study

- print media
  - Amazon
  - Google Books
  - National Archives
  - newspapers
- internet research
  - Wikipedia
  - Google

Research essentials

How much research you do depends on the situation. If you are writing about a subject on which you are very knowledgeable, 'research' is probably a question of sorting through information which is already in your head and making sure that there are no details that you need to look up.

Other subjects may require detailed research lasting several weeks or even months. In this section we will look at the process of research from the viewpoint of a writer who has to start from scratch.

To begin with, some principles underlying all research. All these will be dealt with in more detail in the rest of the section.

Basic principles

Relevance

Any material you select for your research must be relevant to your subject. This might seem so obvious as to be hardly worth saying, but it is sometimes tempting to use a text or internet site simply because it is quick and easy, and to try to bend your writing to include it, when you would be better off spending longer searching for something that is truly relevant to your chosen subject.

Integrity

You need to be assured that any material you choose has integrity. In academic writing this generally means that books and articles have undergone some form of peer review. In the world of business you need to feel confident that the source speaks with demonstrable authority. This principle is all the more important now that a vast amount of 'information' is readily available on the internet. Not all information is good information: not all 'information' is true.

Availability

It must be possible to access material you have discovered within the time available and at a cost you can afford. If you are working on a limited (or non-existent) budget and have only a little time, then there is no point in hoping to rely on a journal article that only exists in Korean (unless that is a language you speak), or a book for which there is a three-month waiting list at the library.

Detail

Any text you locate must offer an appropriate level of detail for your chosen topic. At one extreme, there is little value in working through a high-powered academic journal article if you are writing a brief introduction to the subject, and at the other you need something more than an entry in an encyclopedia if you are writing a PhD thesis.

Storage

Right from the start, you must develop an appropriate storage system for the information and ideas you discover, whether you prefer a pen-and-paper approach, or a computer-based system—or a combination of the two. Your storage system needs to be straightforward, consistent, and logical.

Access

Linked to this, you need to organize things in such a way that having stored information, you can find it again when you need it. Once more, this seems obvious, but there are few researchers who have not, from time to time, spent precious hours trying to locate an item of information that were sure they had 'somewhere'.

Referencing   Along with accessing information comes the need to be able to provide accurate information about provenance. No one should ever have to trust you as the sole authority for the reliability of a piece of information.

Searching

How you go about finding the material you need depends, of course, on your starting point. Often you will have a certain amount of material upon which to base your search; a college reading list, your own notes, or an earlier document that you have been asked to revise, for example. Occasionally you have to start from ground zero. If so, you will probably need to begin with one or more of the following:

- specialist bibliographies and other listings
- library catalogues
- internet search engines

If you are researching highly specialized topics, you may be fortunate enough to have access to a bibliography dedicated to your area of study. Shakespeare scholars, for example, can refer to the World Shakespeare Bibliography, run by the Folger Shakespeare Library in Washington. This sophisticated online search engine enables students to locate books, articles, and films relating to all aspects of Shakespeare's life and work published anywhere in the world. (But it isn't free.)

Library catalogues

More often, you will need to turn to a library catalogue. Again this will involve an online search, the precise form of which will depend on the library. In Britain the largest library with the largest catalogue is the British Library. Anyone can search this by going to http://explore.bl.uk. An Advanced Search page then allows the user to search under a large number of headings, including author, title, subject, and date of publication.

Even if you do not have a reader's ticket for the British Library, you can request (and pay for) copies of relevant material to be sent to you.

Other countries' national library catalogues that can be searched include:

- **USA**
  <http://catalog.loc.gov/>
- **India**
  <http://www.nationallibrary.gov.in/>
- **Australia**
  The National Library of Australia catalogue is also now available as a smartphone app.

- **Canada**
  <http://www.collectionscanada.gc.ca/lac-bac/search-recherche/lib-bib.php?Language=eng>

University
libraries

University libraries also have online catalogues. These are, of course, available to students and staff of the university, but they can also often be accessed by outsiders. The Bodleian Library at Oxford, for example, offers a number of publicly accessible catalogues at <http://www.bodleian.ox.ac.uk/bodley/finding-resources>.

If have a reader's ticket for a university library, such facilities are invaluable; if you do not, then you have to fall back on publicly available major libraries, each of which will have its own arrangements for the issuing of readers' tickets.

Even if you cannot get to use one of these major libraries, their catalogues are still a very valuable resource, enabling you to locate the details of books and articles which can then often be borrowed using the public library service and inter-library loans, or the British Library Document Supply Service.

Internet search engines

For many, however, the first port of call will be an internet search engine. By far the most widely used is Google, which, at the time of writing, is used by about two-thirds of all web searchers. Second and third places are taken by Bing and Yahoo. There are also sites which offer to combine a number of search engines in one.

The world of internet searching is too big to be covered in any detail in a book of this scope. An excellent starting point if you wish to explore the topic in more detail is Internet Tutorials (<http://www.internettutorials.net/>), where you will find a mass of information about how and where to search for information, both general and subject-related.

There are a number of things to bear in mind when using web search engines. The first and most obvious is that the results lists are composed by machines not human beings. This affects not just what items you are offered, but also the order in which they appear. Search engines use complex algorithms to list hits in the way that their makers consider will be most useful to the searcher. Website owners who want their sites to be on the first page of results engage in a variety of Search Engine Optimization (SEO) strategies in order to achieve this.

A second point that differentiates websites from books is that a very large number of them are commercially orientated. While it is true that some authors of non-fiction expect to make a lot of money from their books, most do not. In general, the money they do make comes from book sales. The monetization of information on the internet is more complicated. Many sites that offer information do so as part of a broader strategy of making money by selling things: physical objects, downloads, and advertising. They may also sell indirectly via affiliation: when you click on a link, you are taken to another site. If you then purchase from that site, the owner of the first site receives a fee. This is sometimes far from clear. So while a website may apparently offer a considerable amount of information for nothing, there is often a catch.

Thirdly, there are far fewer constraints on the publication of information on the internet than there are on the publication of a book. Traditional publishing involves a number of built-in quality controls, so that readers can expect a certain level of consistency and reliability from books. Even when a book is self-published—as is increasingly the case today—the process is quite long-winded, and books have a greater degree of permanence. This still influences authors (or at least the more responsible ones) to go through at least a basic level of quality control. With a website or blog, publication can be almost instantaneous and quality control is often slight or non-existent. Responsibility for monitoring quality is thus transferred from the maker to the user. Let the reader beware!

Case study

In this section we'll apply some of the principles set out so far to a hypothetical writing project: an extended article to mark the fiftieth anniversary of the attack on the British Embassy in Jakarta on 16th September 1963, and its destruction two days later. It is to be written for a general readership, and sets out to explain exactly what happened and why.

Print media

If you are beginning your research from scratch it is a useful strategy to choose a small number of books that can be used as a base: one or two titles that are sufficiently detailed and that contain a bibliography and, ideally, footnotes. From this starting point you can build up a suitable reading list. The two best places to start are Amazon and Google Books.

Searching on Amazon

If you go to the Books section of Amazon and click on Advanced Search, the first field is headed 'Keywords'. Keying in 'Jakarta 1963' and clicking on 'Search now' produces 49 results. Clicking on a title takes you to a detailed page for that book. Here you are given:

- picture of the cover
- bibliographical details
- different formats in which the book is available, and the Amazon price for each
- a publisher's blurb
- often, but not always, readers' reviews (to be treated with a certain amount of caution)

If you are lucky, the publisher will also have enabled the 'Look inside' feature. This enables you to see:

- the title page
- the imprint page (containing the publisher's version of the bibliographical data: not necessarily the same as those Amazon gives)
- the table of contents
- the index
- sample pages from the book

This feature makes it possible to gain a very good idea of the book's usefulness. In addition, lower down in the left-hand column, you will see a list of pages in which your chosen keywords appear. If you click on these, it will take you to the relevant page in the book.

Google Books   Google Books is an ongoing (and controversial) project to digitize the world's books. In a search like this, its usefulness depends to a degree on what rights Google has managed to acquire. Since it covers a much wider range of printed material than Amazon, a simple search on 'Jakarta 1963' produces rather more hits than is useful: over 100,000. To narrow it down, you need to go to the Advanced Search page. This offers you further choices:

Find results

- **with all of the words:** ....
- **with the exact phrase:** ....
- **with at least one of the words:** ....
- **without the words:** ....

We can narrow the search down by filling these fields in like this:

Find results

- **with all of the words:** *Jakarta 1963*
- **with the exact phrase:** *British Embassy*
- **with at least one of the words:** *attack mob riot*

This reduces the number of hits to about 200. For each of these hits we get the book's title with a link to a more detailed page and a sample excerpt containing the keywords. This in turn leads to a full page or pages with the keywords highlighted. Again, this should give a clear idea of whether the book is likely to advance our research. Google Books also provides information about where the book can be found in libraries and bookshops. This is fairly rudimentary, but it is a start.

National archives

It is important to remember that books are far from being the only print medium of use to a project like this. Official records and newspapers are also very useful. Official records are stored in national archives collections, which can be accessed in person and also online:

- **Britain**
- **USA**
- **India**
  <http://nationalarchives.nic.in/>
- **Australia**
- **Canada**
  <www.collectionscanada.gc.ca/index-e.html>

Each has its own search system, of course. A search of the British National Archives offered an interesting starting point:

> Prime Minister's Office: Correspondence and Papers…PREM 11/4310
>
> **Attacks on British embassy in Djakarta following creation of Greater Malaysia. Attacks on British embassy in Djakarta following creation of Greater Malaysia INDONESIA Prime Minister's Office: Correspondence and Papers, 1951–1964**
>
> Date: 1963

Another hit, an entry for more general diplomatic documents, notes that, 'The records for 1949 to 1963 were…lost when the embassy was looted and burned by rioters in September 1963.'

Newspapers

Newspapers are an invaluable source for historical researchers. In Britain the national collection is held by the British Library and, again, can be searched online using the catalogue listed earlier. The main collection of newspapers is housed at Colindale, and can be consulted there. More information is available at: <http://www.bl.uk/reshelp/inrrooms/blnewspapers/newsrr.html#>. Local and regional newspapers can be searched separately at: <http://www.britishnewspaperarchive.co.uk/>, but it should be noted this is a premium, not a free service.

If you are looking for freely available national newspaper archives anywhere in the world, then a good place to start is Wikipedia: <http://en.wikipedia.org/wiki/Wikipedia:List_of_online_newspaper_archives>

Most of the British newspaper archives listed here require payment, but if you belong to a UK public library that has a subscription, some of them can be accessed free. The most widely available are:

- **The Times**
  Covers the period from 1785 to 1985
- **Newsbank**
  Covers national and regional newspapers from 1985

Internet research

While many people naturally turn first to Google when researching online, you can often save time by beginning with Wikipedia, the online collaborative encyclopedia.

A search using the keywords 'British Embassy', 'Jakarta', and '1963' produces 19 hits. Each of these indicates a section of a larger article on a broader subject, but the listing details the relevance of the hit to your search:

> **September 1963**
> The following events occurred in September, 1963 . . . Rioters burn down the British Embassy in Jakarta , in protest at the formation of . . .
> 9 KB (1,057 words) - 20:19, 27 January 2012
> **Indonesia–Malaysia confrontation (section 1963)**
> (collectively known as British Borneo, now East Malaysia) in September 1963 . . . Two days later, rioters burned the British embassy in Jakarta . . .
> 97 KB (13,959 words) - 11:35, 22 April 2012

and so on. Each of these is a link that can be explored further.

On Google, the same keywords produce about a million hits. If you were to go through them all, at ten hits to a page, that would involve examining 100,000 pages. So we need to narrow down the search. Adding '16th September' so that the contents of the search box read 'Jakarta 1963 "British Embassy" "16th September"' reduces the number of hits to a more manageable 143, or 15 pages. However, when you go through these hits, they don't seem to offer much that is relevant and new.

By now, however, we have a range of information that we can use to inform further web searches. For example, from the books and newspaper articles already located, we know that the British Ambassador to Indonesia at that time was Andrew Gilchrist. Keying in 'Andrew Gilchrist Jakarta ambassador 1963' produces over two million hits, of which the early pages contain a range of very promising-looking links to pages of information about this unusual and controversial figure.

Specialist archives

Sir Andrew Gilchrist died in 1993. Many diplomats leave their personal papers to a university archive, and, sure enough, a search on Google for 'Sir

Andrew Gilchrist archive' reveals that his papers are held by the Churchill Archives Centre at Cambridge. You can search their catalogue online (at http://janus.lib.cam.ac.uk/) to see that it contains, among other things:

> Papers relating to Gilchrist's diplomatic posting in Jakarta, Indonesia, 1963–66. Includes his diaries and material relating to the riots and destruction of the Embassy (1963).

Summing up

This sample search has ranged over a number of different sources of information. While all of it has been internet-based, relatively little of the actual information located is to be found on websites. Instead, we have been pointed to books, newspapers, and archives that can be accessed by using the internet. Of themselves, Google and Wikipedia provided relatively little. This is not to say that they never do—far from it—but rather to emphasize that serious researchers will cast their nets rather more widely.

Guidelines

Principles

1 There are a number of broad principles that should guide your research:
  a Material must be relevant.
  b You need to be confident that it is accurate and reliable.
  c Material should be accessible within the time and budget available.
  d It should carry the level of detail that you need.
  e You should establish an efficient storage system for material you collect.
  f You need to be able to access information quickly and easily.
  g You also need to be able to reference it accurately and fully.

2 It is important to be cautious when approaching information published on the internet: there is a lot of unreliable 'information' out there.

Searching

3 Sometimes it is possible to use a specialist bibliography to start off your search for information.
4 A major source is library catalogues, which can be accessed online:
  a For researchers in the UK, the best starting points are the British Library Catalogue and the national libraries of Scotland and Wales.

    b Others to consider include the Library of Congress in the USA and the national libraries of Australia, Canada, and India.

    c University library catalogues can also often be consulted online by the public.

  5 The most famous (and widely used) search engine for the internet is, of course, Google, but there are many others, including Bing and Yahoo.

  6 It is worth taking time to plan a major internet search. A good starting point for the inexperienced web researcher is the Internet Tutorials website.

Print media

  7 When searching, it is a useful idea to begin with one or two core texts to serve as a basis for your research.

  8 A good place to start is the 'Advanced Search' feature on Amazon.

  9 This is especially useful if a title has 'Search inside' enabled, because it means that you will be able to look for keywords inside the book's text.

  10 The second important search location is Google Books, which covers magazines and pamphlets as well as books.

  11 An important source of official documents is collections of national archives.

  12 There are also specialist archives, which can be located by using an internet search engine.

  13 Newspaper archives are also a valuable source of information, especially to the historian and biographer.

Websites

  14 It is often a good idea to begin an internet search by looking at what Wikipedia has to offer.

  15 You can then move on to a more generalized search using one of the major search engines.

25 Planning and drafting

Planning your writing

When preparing to write, you should use the notes you have made earlier when

- setting out your statement of intent
- brainstorming
- doing research

The planning process includes

- preparing a list of main points
- developing a satisfactory pattern

Paragraphing

Effective use of paragraphing is at the heart of good writing:

- as a means of structuring a whole text
- as a way of shaping the argument as you write
- as a technique for ensuring that the argument flows through the text and so is easy to read

So the writer should use paragraphing:

- when planning
- when writing
- when revising

Planning your writing

The traditional advice is that if you are tackling an extended piece of writing you should begin by making a plan and then use that as the basis for your writing. However, many writers either pay lip service to this advice or ignore it completely. They prefer instead to work out their ideas through a process of drafting and redrafting. On the other hand, outside the world of creative fiction, it is relatively rare for writers to sit down to face an empty screen or blank sheet of paper with no idea at all of what they are going to write. They may not have written their plan down, but they probably have a list of the main points in their heads and use this as the backbone for their writing.

Chapters 22–24 cover the main elements of preparation for writing. They suggest that there is an interaction between:

- Defining the writing brief
- Generating ideas
- Doing research

They also suggest that if you are going to keep track of these interactive processes you need to make notes. These can then form the basis of your writing plan, but they are *not* the same as a coherent plan for the writing itself.

At this point, therefore, you have to make a choice:

- Shall I make a detailed writing plan?
- Shall I use the drafting method to work out how to order my material?

Frequently writers find that they do a bit of both. They start with an outline and then fill in the detail and change the ordering of things as they go along. The advice that follows assumes that you want to make at least a basic plan before you begin to write.

Deciding the main points

Begin by looking at the ideas and material you have collected, and pick out a small number of key points which will form a framework to which arguments, ideas, and information can be attached. This process may seem rather time-consuming, but it will almost certainly save much more time later. If this planning stage is faulty, you may find that your writing slows down and eventually stops as you discover that your original plan doesn't work; alternatively, when you finish, you may realize that the text just isn't coherent and needs to be rewritten.

As an example of how this planning stage works, we'll imagine that you have been asked to prepare a report for a holiday company that is seeking to promote up-market holidays in less well-known areas of Kenya. Your have brainstormed the subject and have produced a mind map, part of which looks like this:

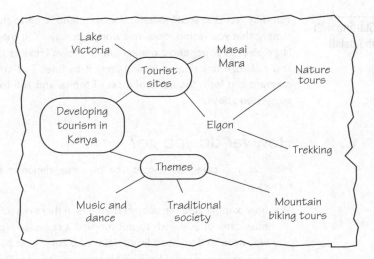

This could yield this list of main topics:

- new tourist sites that could be developed
- new themes for tourism
- the facilities that exist and new facilities that may be needed

If your main topics are well chosen, each will lead to a number of subtopics which explore it:

- new tourist sites that could be developed
    Mount Elgon
    Lake Victoria

These in turn will subdivide again and so on, to produce a hierarchy:

- new tourist sites that could be developed
    Mount Elgon
        walking and climbing
        wildlife safaris
            on foot
            by 4×4
            camping
    Lake Victoria

and so on.

You may feel that your material does not lend itself to this approach—or,
simply, that your mind 'does not work that way'. You may prefer to take a
large piece of paper and a marker and jot down ideas as they occur to you.
You can then link related ideas together by lines and arrows. This rough
diagram can form the basis of a set of topics and sub-topics like the one
suggested above.

How far do you go?

How far you take this process of planning depends on a number of
factors:

- how complicated the subject matter is: if there is a lot of detail to communicate, or you wish to put forward a complex argument, you may
  well need to do quite a lot of detailed planning on paper
- how good you are at holding ideas in your head as you write
- how spontaneous you want to be

Some would argue that if you make a very detailed plan, with the hierarchy
of ideas fully worked out, you become constricted by the rigidity of the plan
and are not free to change it as you go along.

Developing a satisfactory pattern

A successful text is one where the reader is taken along by the flow of the
writing, doesn't get lost or confused, and comes away with the feeling that
the ideas it contains could not have been expressed in any other way. So
it is important to develop a pattern in which ideas are developed logically
and necessary information is introduced at exactly the right point. Where it
is necessary to use ideas or information that have not been referred to for
some time, the reader needs a gentle reminder of what these are. If the flow
of ideas needs to take a sudden new turn, this may need preparation or
explanation. At every point the reader's needs, expectations, and possible
difficulties must be considered.

The introduction is often the most difficult section to write. That first sentence can often prove exasperatingly elusive. Novelists sometimes agonize
for weeks over the first sentence of a new novel; it sets the tone of what is
to come and fixes the reader's expectations.

These are the openings of three extended texts. What thoughts and expectations does each arouse in you as reader?

A The 'average Frenchman' is often known today as Monsieur Dupont or Monsieur Durand. Durand means obstinate. John Bull, according to the Larousse Encyclopaedia, is 'the nickname given to the English people to indicate their obstinacy'.

B The French government has introduced new measures aimed at reducing the taxes and financial costs of running a small business or being self-employed in France.

C The sheer physical diversity of France would be hard to exhaust in a lifetime of visits. The landscapes range from the fretted rocky coasts of Brittany to the limestone hills of Provence, the canyons of the Pyrenees to the Germanic picturesqueness of Alsace, the volcanic uplands of the Massif Central to the wide grain fields of Touraine, the wooded valleys of the Dordogne to the glacier-capped peaks of the Alps.

You will find a possible response on page 383.

However important the first sentence or two may be, the introduction to a text will normally consist of one or more paragraphs and may be a complete chapter or even section of a book. It has to perform these functions:

- It gives the reader an indication of what the subject matter will be.
- It persuades the reader that reading this text is going to be at least worthwhile and—if possible—enjoyable.
- It establishes a relationship with the reader by the language and tone adopted.

The conclusion

Second only to the introduction in difficulty and importance is the conclusion to a piece of writing. If the introduction hopes to entice readers to sample the mouth-watering delights that are in store, the conclusion should aim to send them away with a nice taste in their mouths, rather than feeling unsatisfied or dyspeptic. It should remind readers of what they have been reading, by:

- summing up key points without being unduly repetitive
- if action is required, highlighting what it is
- rounding off the text neatly and—if possible, and appropriate—in an entertaining way

Planning, drafting, editing, revising

The process by which thought is translated into written sentences is not easy to analyse or explain. The four words which head this section all describe aspects of that process, and the fact that there are four of them underlines the point that it is not a simple one. Sometimes, it is true, I write a sequence of sentences and then deliver them to their intended audience without looking through them and making changes. But such occasions are rare. As soon as I read through what I have written and even begin to consider altering it, I have moved from writing to editing. If I decide to make a second version of my text, then I am beginning to redraft. Simple texts may receive only minor alterations, to ensure that the sense is clear; longer and more complex ones, like this book, go through several drafts before they are made public.

It could be argued that writing consists of no more and no less than adding one sentence to another, but that would be a misleading over-simplification. It is easy enough to write one sentence and then to write another. The problem is how to judge whether the two sentences you have written fit together properly, or whether you need to adjust one or both of them—or even add a third to help them out. What is missing is a guiding principle, and that guiding principle is the paragraph.

Paragraphing

To adapt the proverb: 'Look after the paragraphs and the sentences will look after themselves.' If you have a clear sense of how your text should break down into paragraphs and if you understand how to write paragraphs through which the argument of the text flows clearly and unobtrusively, then the individual sentences should cause you few problems. On the other hand, if you haven't given any thought to paragraphing, then you can write the most beautiful sentences in the English language but your text will still be difficult and displeasing to the reader. Writing a text of any length requires the writer to keep an eye on both the particular sentence being written at the moment and the whole text of which that sentence forms a small part. Paragraphing is the means by which this is done.

The best way to see how this works in practice is to examine a short text. The extract that follows comes from an introduction to geomorphology, the study of how the formation and development of rocks creates landscape.

Paragraph 1	Most of the spectacular landscapes of England and Wales are found within the rugged, higher lands of the north, west and south–west. Why is there such a striking difference between the areas of mountains and moorlands, and the gently undulating lowlands characteristic of the south and east? The answer lies in the nature of the rocks and of their susceptibility to being worn away by the elements.	The introductory paragraph not only introduces the subject matter, but indicates how it will be tackled. The words 'the nature of the rocks' tell us how the following paragraphs will be arranged.
Paragraph 2	There are three major types of rock. Igneous rocks are formed by the cooling of molten material ('magma') that escapes to the surface layers of the Earth from the interior. Metamorphic rocks are formed by baking and deformation at high temperatures and pressures. Sedimentary rocks are formed under much quieter conditions, by the accumulation of material on the sea floor or land surface. Most of the igneous and metamorphic rocks are hard and compact, and are therefore more resistant to attack at the Earth's surface than the weaker sedimentary rocks. And so it is hardly surprising to discover that many of the upstanding areas in England and Wales are composed of igneous and metamorphic rocks, the moorlands of the South-West Peninsula (except Exmoor), the highlands of North Wales, and the Lake District.	The lead sentence follows this up and tells us what the paragraph will contain: a brief explanation of igneous, metamorphic, and sedimentary rocks. This is then linked to the original question posed in the first paragraph: why is there such a contrast between the landscapes of the north and west and those of the south and east?
Paragraph 3	Let's now fill in some of the details by looking at the different rock types to see how they are formed, how resistant they are and what sort of landscapes they give rise to in England and Wales.	This short paragraph stands as a signpost to show how the next part of the text will develop.
Paragraph 4	When the Earth came into being nearly 5000 million years ago it was made up of molten magma. This gradually cooled and solidified at the surface, forming a crust, but the interior of the Earth remained hot and molten. Today, when this molten material is pushed up under great pressure through cracks in the crust, volcanoes are formed. On reaching the air, the magma cools rapidly to	This paragraph introduces the first main section in which igneous rocks are described in more detail. The lead sentence makes clear that the approach will be historical: how igneous rocks were originally formed. This topic is developed in the rest of the paragraph, ending with a reference to volcanoes...

Paragraph 5	form hard, compact rocks such as basalt. The exact type of volcanic rock formed depends on the chemistry of the magma. Some volcanic eruptions also produce much softer ash, which is nothing more than the shattered rock fragments that originally blocked the volcanic pipe.	
Paragraph 5	Although there are no active volcanoes in Britain today, some of our older rocks were formed in this way. Particularly well known are …	…which is neatly picked up in the lead sentence of the next paragraph.

Building the argument

If we look at the way in which the paragraphs of this text are constructed and used, we can pick out a number of general points about paragraphing:

Developing the pattern

The paragraphs form a pattern which helps the writers develop their argument. Paragraphs 1-3 form an introduction to the subject:

1 leads into the subject and its two main interrelated aspects: landscape and geology
2 introduces the three main types of rock and gives a brief explanation of how each was formed
3 points forward to the main subject matter of the text and explains how it will be tackled

Paragraphs 4 onwards then go through the three main rock types in much more detail.

4 introduces the topic of igneous rocks by going right back to the formation of planet Earth
5 moves this discussion to the geographical region we are concerned with: the British Isles

The shape of a paragraph

A typical paragraph has three sections:

- **an introduction**

  Each paragraph in the quoted text has a sentence at or very near the beginning which introduces the subject matter of the paragraph:
  There are three major types of rock. (para. 2)
  When the Earth came into being nearly 5000 million years ago it was made up of molten magma. (para. 4)

- **a conclusion**

  At or near the end of the paragraph is a sentence which rounds it off:

And so it is hardly surprising to discover that many of the upstanding areas in England and Wales are composed of igneous and metamorphic rocks, the moorlands of the South-West Peninsula (except Exmoor), the highlands of North Wales, and the Lake District. (para. 2)

- **the body of the paragraph**

The body of the paragraph leads in an orderly and convincing way from the introduction to the conclusion. The body of paragraph 2, for example, consists of four sentences:

- *Igneous rocks…interior.*
- *Metamorphic rocks…pressures.*
- *Sedimentary rocks…surface.*
- *Most of the igneous and metamorphic rocks…sedimentary rocks.*

The introductory sentence offered us three different types of rock. The body of the sentence delivers them, so that the concluding sentence can say, in effect: 'There you are—*that*'s why the north and west are different from the south and east.'

Hooks

If the thought is to flow comfortably from paragraph to paragraph, there need to be hooks which link the paragraphs together:

> *Some volcanic eruptions also produce much softer ash, which is nothing more than the shattered rock fragments that originally blocked the volcanic pipe.*
>
> *Although there are no active volcanoes in Britain today, some of our older rocks were formed in this way.*

The final sentence of paragraph 4 rounds this part of the topic off by dealing with softer volcanic rocks and the reason for them. It uses the word 'volcanic' twice, which draws it to the reader's attention. The writer then makes the link to Britain by using 'volcanoes' in the first sentence—even though the statement is a negative one. A less skilful writer might have missed this opportunity. See how much weaker the link would be:

> *Some volcanic eruptions also produce much softer ash, which is nothing more than the shattered rock fragments that originally blocked the volcanic pipe.*
>
> *Many of the older rocks in Britain are igneous.*

There are many different ways in which the link between one paragraph and the next can be made. The main ones are:

- **subject matter and vocabulary**

as in the case of volcanic activity in the example just given.

> See also

· CHAPTER 17
  *More about
  grammar*
  (p. 203)

- **the use of conjunctions:**

  ... It seemed as though the attempt on the summit could not fail. All was in place for a successful assault.

  But we had reckoned without the weather...

- **the use of pronouns:**

  ... and it was while leading a tour round the Uffizi Gallery that she first met Berenson.

  He had, of course, been a famous figure in Florence for many years...

- **the use of sentence adverbials**

  These work in a similar way to conjunctions, but whereas conjunctions are used to join sentences and parts of sentences, sentence adverbials are also used to show the links between paragraphs:

  o **Adding and listing**

  In narratives, explanations, and arguments we often want to place items in a particular order. We indicate this fact and show the order by using words like 'first':

  There were several reasons why the new marketing campaign was unsuccessful. **First** *the advertising agency had misunderstood the brief.* **Then** *the weather was quite unseasonally hot, which made sales of woolly hats extremely difficult.* **Finally** *our competitors slashed their prices.*

  Sometimes the sequence is less important, but we still wish to make it clear that items are linked:

  The child had a succession of bad school reports. **Furthermore** *she was caught shoplifting...*

  Sentence adverbials used in this way include: *at the same time, finally, first, last, meanwhile, next, soon, then, also, as well, at the same time, besides, furthermore, in addition, moreover, too.*

  o **Giving examples**

  Sometimes we wish to introduce an example or list of material which exemplifies part of the argument:

  He had written several popular books about astrology, **for example***: 'What your stars foretell'.*

  Other words used in this way are *namely, as follows.*

  o **Saying things another way**

  We may also wish to restate something using different words:

  Even when he was Managing Director, Sam was first and foremost a salesman. **In other words** *he had little interest in production problems.*

  o **Cause and result**

  In texts that contain an argument, one sentence is often the logical development of what has gone before:

They were rather slow to produce a prototype and this proved much more expensive than had been expected. **As a result** the time and money available for development work were limited.

Other sentence adverbials of this type are: *accordingly, as a result, consequently, hence, so, therefore, thus.*

o **Contrasts and alternatives**

A sentence can be contrasted with what has gone before:

The team has been remarkably unsuccessful this year, which is a cause for some concern. **On the other hand** *they are still young and have a lot of latent talent.*

Other sentence adverbials of this type are: *all the same, alternatively, anyway, by contrast, conversely, even so, however, instead, nevertheless, on the other hand, rather, yet.*

o **Concession**

Another type of contrast is similar to that used in adverbial clauses of concession: despite this fact, the following is true. For example:

The teacher was sure that she had counted all the children. **Nevertheless** *when the coach got back to the school Liam was missing.*

Other sentence adverbials of this type are: *however, yet, even so.*

The following paragraph comes from the beginning of an account of the life and psychology of a Frenchwoman. The sentences have been numbered for ease of reference. What is the subject matter of the paragraph? Which sentences form the introduction and conclusion? How do the other sentences develop the argument of the paragraph? How might the ending of the paragraph lead on to what is to follow?

1 *What is Thérèse thinking, as she shows you to your table in La Vieille Alsace in Strasbourg, and helps you order your meal?*

2 *She gives the impression that she knows exactly what to say, what to do, all energy, a brisk walk, a direct look, friendly solicitude.*

3 *If you have been there before, she can remember more about you than you ever told her.*

4 *How are you to know that she is not a waitress waiting for better times, that she is not calculating the size of the tip you can afford to give, that she has a master's degree in the history of art?*

5 *Thérèse has been doing this job for fifteen years because she has a purpose in life.*

You will find a commentary on this on p. 384.

Think paragraphs!

There are three stages in writing, at each of which you need to keep the principles of paragraphing clearly in mind.

1 Planning

When you make a written plan, you should remember that the paragraphs you are going to write are the way in which you will execute that plan. Each point in your plan should represent either one paragraph or a small group of paragraphs. If your argument is at all complicated it is very useful to make a separate point in the plan for each paragraph you are going to write.

2 Writing

As you write, you have to carry in your mind:

- the structure of the individual paragraph (beginning, middle, and end)
- its hooks to the preceding and succeeding paragraphs
- its position in the plan of the whole text

3 Revising

Fortunately it doesn't all have to be done at the moment of writing. When you revise you can check the structure of each paragraph, its links to the paragraphs before and after, and its placing in the overall structure of the text.

Guidelines

Planning your writing

1 The notes you have made as you define the task, brainstorm, and research form the basis of your planning.

2 Begin by deciding the main points you wish to make in your text.

3 You can then develop each of these with more detailed subsidiary points to flesh out your plan.

4 Alternatively you may prefer to develop the list of main points by a process of drafting and redrafting.

5 Whichever route you follow, you should ensure that your writing follows a pattern that is clear to the reader.

6 It is particularly important to have an effective introduction and conclusion.

Paragraphing

7 Use paragraphing as a planning tool. Remember, as you make your plan, that each point in it represents either one paragraph or a small group of linked paragraphs.

8 As you write, form your thought into paragraphs.

9 Begin each paragraph with one or two sentences that introduce the topic of the paragraph.

10 The beginning of the paragraph should also have some kind of 'hook' to the previous paragraph. There is a list of these in the section on 'Building the argument' in this chapter (p. 328).

11 Make sure that the paragraph ends with one or two sentences that round it off and lead on to the next paragraph.

12 The body of the paragraph should lead smoothly from the introduction to the conclusion.

26 Editing and revising

Editing

Editing is an integral part of the writing process and is best done by both:

- the writer
- an external editor

Editing consists of

- selecting and ordering material
- amending and cutting the text
- checking for accuracy

Revising

Writers can edit their own text:

- as they write
- after they have finished the first draft

Most do both.

Revision includes

- changes to the structure of the text
- alterations to the choice of words and the way in which sentences are constructed
- corrections to spelling, punctuation, and grammar

Editing

It may seem strange to place 'editing' before 'revising', but there is a reason for this. We normally think of editing as a process that is performed on a text by someone other than the writer: the writer writes the text and then the editor edits it. In fact, as we shall see, most of the elements that are involved in editing are also done by the writer *before* the text is submitted to the editor. Or they should be.

The word 'edit' is used in a number of different ways in everyday speech. They are well summed up by the definitions offered in the online *Oxford Dictionaries Pro*[1]:

- prepare (written material) for publication by correcting, condensing, or otherwise modifying it
- choose material for (a film or radio or television programme) and arrange it to form a coherent whole
- change (text) on a computer
- (edit something out) remove unnecessary or inappropriate material from a text, film, or radio or television programme

To understand what is involved in the editing process, you need to look at some of the verbs used in these definitions:

- choose
- arrange
- remove
- change
- modify
- condense
- correct

From a writer's point of view these can be arranged in three groups:

1. **Selecting and ordering material**
   'choose' and 'arrange'
2. **Amending and cutting the text**
   'remove', 'condense', 'change', and 'modify'
3. **Checking for accuracy**
   'correct'

1. Selecting and ordering material

It is an essential part of writing to select the best material and then arrange it in the best possible order. What makes this task difficult is that when you have written something, you are often too close to it to be able to see it as others see it. This is why it is always advisable, when you have completed a text, to ask someone else to read and comment on it. Failing that, you should leave it for as long as possible and return later to re-read it.

2. Amending and cutting the text

One of the most difficult aspects of writing is cutting your own words. You have spent time and effort working out how to say something in the best possible way. To come back and decide that those precious sentences must be removed can seem almost impossible. Yet, as Sir Arthur Quiller-Couch wrote a century ago, it must be done:

[1] This is available at <http://english.oxforddictionaries.com/>. Readers in Britain may well find that they have free access to this via their public library membership.

> *Whenever you feel an impulse to perpetrate a piece of exceptionally fine writing, obey it—wholeheartedly—and delete it before sending your manuscript to press. Murder your darlings.*
>
> Arthur Quiller-Couch: *The Art of Writing*, 1916

> See also
- CHAPTER 22,
  (p. 289)

Similarly, you have to beware of occasions when you have indulged yourself in your writing, and look for opportunities to condense your text, changing it until it fulfills the requirements of your writing brief.

3. Checking for accuracy

This is the activity that is most often associated with editing: the editor goes through the text looking for errors of fact, grammar, spelling, and punctuation. It is, of course, very important, but it generally comes quite late on in the preparation of a text. All writers correct errors as they spot them, but there is no point in going through your writing word by word to correct it until you have made the bigger changes described above. Otherwise you will waste time correcting something that is later trashed.

Who does what when?

The writer

Ultimately the best editor you can have is yourself. This is not to say that you don't need the services of an external editor; it is a very remarkable writer indeed whose work cannot be improved by a sympathetic and experienced professional editor. However, the ultimate responsibility for your work rests with you—and 'sympathetic and experienced professional editors' can be difficult to find.

Most writers find that as they write they insert new material, re-order items, cut and change the text. The extent to which editing is done 'on the hoof' varies from writer to writer and according to circumstances. For some it can become an obsession getting in the way of completing the text. However, only you can decide the extent to which you edit and how much of this essential work you allocate to a separate working stage.

The editor

If you are writing for publication, or working as a member of a work group of some kind, then your finished draft will generally be submitted to another person for editing. In the world of professional publishing this is a specialist role with clearly defined responsibilities, but many of these apply equally well to less specialist editors. They can be summed up like this:

1 **Checking that the text complies with the brief**
2 **Checking that it is factually accurate**
3 **Making sure that it is suitable for its intended purpose and audience**
4 **Assessing its readability for the intended audience**

For each of these, the editor will make a list of recommended changes that are then sent back to the writer for discussion and negotiation, before a revised draft is produced.

At this stage there are three more editorial tasks:

5 Checking grammar, spelling, and punctuation

6 Making sure that the text is consistent and complies with house style

There are often two or more ways of spelling a word or referring to the same thing. For example, do you write 'organise' or 'organize'? Both are possible, but once you have made your choice, you should use it consistently throughout your text. Publishers and large organizations generally have a policy for all these choices, their 'house style', often issued to editors and writers in the form of a printed book, or booklet. If not, it is always possible to adopt a published style guide. So, for example, the *New Oxford Style Manual* tells us that the preferred spelling is 'organize', with 'organise' as a British English alternative.

7 Marking up for typesetting

The design of books or other extended documents generally contains a number of different styles for text and headings. (This is discussed in the next chapter.) It is the editor's job to indicate to the designer how these styles should be applied to the text.

The proofreader

Once the text has been typeset, it must be checked for errors that have crept in (or that may have been present all along). This important and time-consuming work generally needs to be done by at least two people:

- the writer
- someone else, ideally an experienced proofreader

The writer will in fact be looking for two things:

- mistakes that have been introduced
- places where the editor and designer have, between them, misinterpreted his or her intentions

The external editor will also search for errors. In addition, he or she will be on the lookout for places where the design does not work to support the text: perhaps the headings are wrong, or an illustration does not appear in the right place.

All the corrections and changes that are requested have to be marked up on a printout of the designed text, or on the digital file. There are standardized symbols for this purpose: in Britain they are listed in a British Standard (*BS 5261C: 2005—Marks for copy preparation and proof correction*), the relevant sections of which are widely available, for example in the *Writers' & Artists' Yearbook* or online. It is not essential to stick slavishly to the standard marks, but you do need to be sure that those you are working with understand your mark-up.

Revisions to the text

To illustrate how a text takes shape, here are extracts from two drafts of the previous edition of this book.

Like many writers, I usually write direct on to a word processor, which is very convenient, but obscures the process of revising and re-drafting. Knowing that I would need examples of revision, I wrote the first draft of this chapter by hand:

First draft manuscript

Writing is a process of refinement. We begin with a fairly rough version and gradually, by a process of cutting, adding altering and so - we hope - improving, we

~~can be divided~~

work towards a finished product. The changes that we make ~~fall into two groups.~~ happen at different stages

- ~~those we make~~ as we go along

- ~~those we make~~ when we have finished the first draft.

placed in three categories

They can also be ~~categorised in a different way.~~

- *'correcting'* - putting right errors of spelling, grammar, and, to some extent, puntuation

  although punctuation is also a matter of style

- *'editing'* - changing the way in which one or more sentences are written.

  This can be to improve their style - make them sound better - or, if they do not convey the meaning we intend, to clarify them.

  changes'

- *'structural* We may realise that, even ~~if~~ after careful planning, the shape of the whole section is wrong and the ordering of the paragraphs, for example, needs to be modified drastically. ~~Normally this~~

Normally this third kind of change should only be done when a first draft has been completed. If you find yourself ~~chang~~ making major changes to the structure before you finish the first draft, it suggests that your initial planning was seriously faulty.

Compare the original handwritten version (i.e., before alterations were made to it) and the corrected word-processed version below.

1 What are the main changes that have been made?
2 Why do you think they were made?
3 In what other ways could the extract be improved?

You will find a commentary on these and subsequent questions on p. 384.

First draft word-processed

When this was keyed in and printed off; further changes were made:

Writing is a process of refinement. We begin with a fairly rough version and gradually, by cutting, adding, re-ordering we work towards a finished product. The changes that we make happen at two different stages:

- as we go along,
- when we have completed the first and subsequent drafts.

~~Changes~~ are of three main types: *The changes themselves*

- **Editing:**
  changing the way in which one or more sentences are written, in order to clarify the meaning or improve the style.
- **~~Making structural changes~~:**   *Altering the structure*
  we may decide that even after the planning stage has been worked through, the shape of a whole section is wrong and the ordering of paragraphs need drastic modification. Normally this kind of change should only be done when a draft of the whole text has been completed. If you find yourself making major changes before you finish the first draft, it suggests that your initial planning was seriously faulty.
- **Proof-reading:**
  putting right errors of spelling and grammar. We may also amend punctuation, although this is only ~~partly~~ a matter of   *Sometimes*
  'correctness'~~, it is frequently~~ a question of style.   *and can often be*

1 What are the main changes that have been made between the first and second drafts?
2 Why do you think they were made?

You will find a commentary on this on p. 384.

Second draft

When the first draft was revised, further changes were made:

What kind of changes?	Writing is a process of refinement. We begin with a fairly rough version and gradually, by cutting, adding, and re-ordering we work towards a finished product. The changes that can be made happen at two different stages: • as you go along • when you have completed the first and subsequent drafts The changes themselves are of three main types.
Changes to the structure	You may decide that even after the planning stage has been worked through, the shape of a whole section is wrong and the ordering of paragraphs needs drastic modification. Normally this kind of change should only be done when a draft of the whole text has been completed. If you find yourself making major changes before you finish the first draft, then probably your initial planning was faulty.
Revisions to the text	The commonest type of revision is to change the way in which one or more sentences are written, in order to clarify the meaning or improve the style.
Corrections	At some stage you have to put right errors of spelling and grammar. You may also amend punctuation, which is sometimes a matter of correctness and sometimes a question of style.

Approaches to drafting

The purpose of all the changes you make in a text is to improve communication and increase its effectiveness. Weakness of vocabulary and of sentence and paragraph construction, and uncertainty of tone, will damage the impact of your text. As you work through successive versions of a text, your aim is to remove such weaknesses. Unfortunately they are your weaknesses; as a result you may well not be the best person to find and eradicate them.

The trusted reader

The advice of other readers is invaluable as you build and improve your text. If possible, therefore, show it to one or more people whose judgement you respect. If you cannot do this, then your second-best ally is time. If you can leave a piece of writing for a while, go away and do something entirely unconnected with it, and then return, you stand a much better chance of seeing it with fresh eyes. What seemed clear fluent prose may still read well ... or it may be revealed as flawed and unsatisfactory.

Drafting strategies

Structure, approach, and tone

Ultimately the responsibility for your text lies with you, the writer. You have to judge whether it successfully achieves what you set out to do. The following list of questions is designed to help you focus on this.

➤ *See also*
- CHAPTER 10
  Audience
  (p. 117)
- CHAPTER 11
  Subject
  (p. 129)
- CHAPTER 13
  Purpose
  (p. 143)

1 Does it cover all the required aspects of my selected subject?

2 Does it contain material that is not relevant to the subject and which can be cut out?

3 Does it fulfil the original purpose(s) I had when I started writing?

4 Do I address the audience in a way that is suitable for their knowledge of the subject and ability to understand what they read?

5 Is the tone of my writing suitable for this audience?

6 Is the text organized so that it is as easy as possible for readers to make their way through it and be able to find material easily later?

7 Does the paragraphing present the argument in a clear and logical way?

8 Are the paragraphs linked so that the text flows easily?

Sentence construction

9 Are my sentences clear and easy to read?

10 Are there a large number of long sentences? (Sentences of over 40 words are generally considered 'long'.)

11 Are the sentences that are long still easy to follow?

12 Are there too many short sentences, making the text choppy and uncomfortable to read?

Vocabulary

➤ *See also:*
- CHAPTER 10
  Audience
  (p. 117)
- CHAPTER 18
  Vocabulary
  (p. 217)

13 Is the technical vocabulary I have chosen appropriate for my audience?

14 Is the language suitable in other ways, avoiding jargon, euphemism, and cliché whenever possible?

15 Have I avoided excessive repetition of words and phrases?

16 Are there any other quirks of style that readers may find irritating?

One good way of testing your writing is to read it aloud. Very often this will highlight sentences and phrases that are unsatisfactory. They just sound 'wrong' when read aloud.

It should not be necessary to add that in addition to testing your text in the ways suggested above, you also have to check it carefully for accuracy of grammar, spelling, and punctuation.

Guidelines

Editing

1 Remember that editing isn't just a matter of checking for accuracy. It consists of:

    a selecting and ordering material

    b amending and cutting the text

    c checking for accuracy

2 Initial editing is done by the writer. You can do this:

    a as you write

    b as a separate stage when you have completed the first draft

3 In major writing projects there will often be an external editor who will work on your completed draft.

4 If not, it is always a good idea to get someone else to check your text.

5 Failing that, set the draft aside and check it after a reasonable interval of time. This will enable you to see it 'with new eyes'.

Revising

6 Begin by thinking about the structure of the whole text. It may need reordering.

7 Revising the text *can* be done while you are writing and *should* be done after you have completed a draft.

8 Use the checklists provided on page 341 and above.

9 Check the whole text against your intentions when you started writing. In particular think about audience and purpose.

10 Check the wording of each sentence carefully for:

- clarity
- style

11 Look at your vocabulary, checking it for suitability, accuracy, and avoidance of jargon and cliché.

12 When you have completed structural and other editorial changes, check your work carefully for errors in:

- spelling
- grammar
- punctuation

➤ *Further reading*

The best short guide to editing, now sadly out of print, but available in libraries and second hand (at a price) is:

Jo Billingham, *One Step Ahead: Editing and Revising Text*
(Oxford University Press, 2002), ISBN 9780198604136.

New Oxford Style Manual
(Oxford University Press, 2012), ISBN 9780199657223 is an authoritative editing manual, combined with a comprehensive style guide.

$\widehat{27}$ Presentation

However good your text may be, if it is not presented to the reader with care, it will not have the impact it should. This text, for example, is so badly presented that it puts the reader off straight away:

How we view the relationship can affect: choice of vocabulary, use of short forms in writing, choice of pronouns, choice of standard or non-standard grammar. Some words are considered by many people to be informal, colloquial, slang, or even obscene. Dictionaries often indicate this by abbreviations, for example: colloq. -colloquial; inf. -informal; sl. -slang. Such definitions can be misleading, however. It is very difficult to draw a clear line between what is 'formal' and what is 'informal' language.

Presented with care and thought, however, it becomes accessible and even welcoming:

Effects on language

How we view the relationship can affect:

- choice of vocabulary
- use of short forms in writing
- choice of pronouns
- choice of standard or non-standard grammar

Vocabulary

Some words are considered by many people to be informal, colloquial, slang, or even obscene. Dictionaries often indicate this by abbreviations, for example:

colloq.	colloquial
inf.	informal
sl.	slang

Such definitions can be misleading, however. It is very difficult to draw a clear line between what is 'formal' and what is 'informal' language.

With the widespread use of computers and word-processing and other software, a huge range of options is available to the writer who wishes to present a text effectively and attractively. The technology and software are discussed in the next chapter. Here we are concerned with the ideas behind effective presentation.

Layout

Major word processing and page layout applications make it possible for anyone to design their text in the best possible way. Most applications offer templates that mean you do not have to start from scratch when designing a newsletter or brochure, for example. However, for major projects you may well want to present your text in a specific and individual way.

The main features of the design of this book are illustrated in the following diagram. Not all of them are required in all documents, of course, and they can be adapted to suit particular circumstances.

Type

You can select the typeface you wish to use and its size. Many programs now even display the names of the typefaces in a pull-down menu as they will appear, which is very useful if you are not familiar with the names of typefaces, or have a considerable number on your computer.

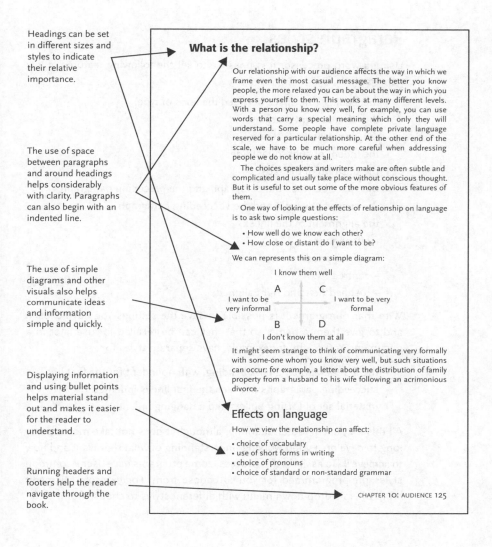

The computer also allows you to style the typeface you are using. For example:

plain

bold

italic

shadow

<u>underline</u>

SMALL CAPITALS

You can also select the colour and shade in which your text is displayed and printed.

Paragraph styles

Using a word processor it is possible to set the following features of any paragraph:

- the leading (the space between the lines of type)
- the left and right margins
- the indent of the first line
- the indent of subsequent lines
- the position of the tabs
- the space between the paragraph and the preceding paragraph
- the space between it and the succeeding paragraph
- the alignment of the lines:
  - left aligned
  - right aligned
  - centred
  - justified (left and right aligned)

With many programs it is possible to save the settings you have chosen and to give them a name, so that they can be recalled for use later in a document. You might, for example, have separate styles for:

- the first paragraph after a heading, with no indent for the first line
- succeeding paragraphs in which the first line is indented
- material set out using bullets and a hanging indent

All this may seem rather daunting, although it does not take most people long to develop a good working understanding of what they want and how to achieve it. To assist in this process, some programs have useful common styles pre-programmed for you to choose from. For example Microsoft Word offers a drop-down menu with different styles to choose from:

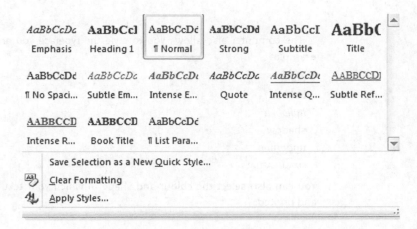

The program then allows you to specify exactly how you want each feature of the paragraph to appear:

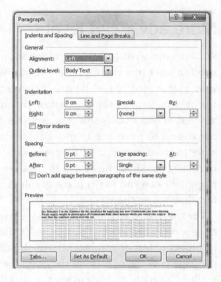

Other layout features

It is also possible to achieve a range of other effects involving typefaces, backgrounds, and graphic elements.

- **headings**

  These can be set in a contrasting typeface, size, and colour and may be accompanied by a rule (line) above or below, or both.

- **boxes and tints**

  If you wish to mark off a section of text it can be surrounded by a rectangle (box), be set against a tint, or a combination of the two.

- **bullet points**

  You can use a range of bullet points to mark the beginning of each of a number of listed features. For example:
  ○
  ●
  ◆

- **flags**

  You can draw the reader's attention to an important section or sections within the text by the use of graphic symbols:
  ☛
  ✎
  ✔

These symbols are all taken from a typeface called Zapf Dingbats, which is widely available.

More advanced layout

Writers who wish to achieve more sophisticated layouts will probably need to work in a slightly different way. Word processors normally work with a standard 'page' which is defined when you start work on the document. Some programs allow you to have several different pages defined in one document. It is possible to indent the text as described above and to have one or more columns on each page. It is even possible to have columns of different widths on the same page. It is not normally possible, however, to arrange blocks of text 'freely' on the page. Nor can you easily place graphics wherever you like and have the text flow round them.

For these effects you need to use a page layout program in which the page is more like a layout pad on which the user places objects. These may be blocks of text or graphics. These objects can then be moved around on the page until the user is satisfied with the arrangement. Text can be made to 'flow' from one text box to another and flow round graphics. In the larger programs, you can also create master pages with text blocks and graphic spaces predetermined.

While the more complicated effects are the preserve of large software packages, word-processing programs like Microsoft™ Word and Apple Pages™ incorporate increasingly sophisticated page layout elements.

Readability

Newcomers faced with such a range of typefaces, sizes, and leading are sometimes fascinated by the effects they can achieve. It is important to remember that above all a document must be readable. Any of the following can interfere with readability:

- **making lines of text too long**

  12–14 words to a line is as much as most readers can cope with.

- **making the typeface too large or too small**

  Normally this should be in the range 9pt to 12pt.

- **getting the leading wrong**

Visuals

Visual images are a powerful way of communicating complex ideas.

Tables, charts, and diagrams

Business people are accustomed to the use of charts and diagrams to present numerical information in a way that makes it easier to understand and assimilate. These methods are not always so familiar to those outside the world of business and finance. The simpler types of numerical chart are, however, very useful in a wide range of applications.

Suppose, for example, a school has the following data about one year's examination entries and the grades achieved:

Subject	Total	A	B	C	D	E	F
English	173	15	27	42	35	33	21
Maths	164	10	23	56	43	29	3
Science	153	22	34	31	33	21	12
French	108	11	24	46	13	9	5
Geography	116	3	9	47	39	14	4
History	119	1	7	29	22	45	15
Total	833	62	124	251	185	151	60

There are various ways in which the head teacher could present this information to the public.

Column chart

As the name suggests, this presents data as a series of columns. The higher the column, the bigger the number. So the English exam grades could be presented like this:

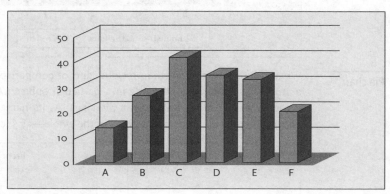

We can also use a column chart to compare sets of data. The table below shows the actual numbers of passes at each level in three subjects:

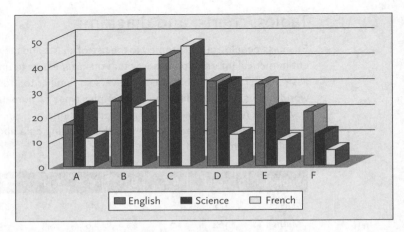

A comparison of raw data like this is not as helpful, however, as one in which we express the numbers for each grade as a percentage of the total entry:

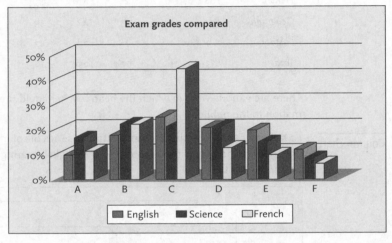

Pie chart

What is interesting about the previous kind of comparison is how likely a student is to get a good grade in a particular subject. Another way of presenting this kind of data is in a pie chart. As its name suggests, this shows different values as proportions of the whole—as slices of the pie:

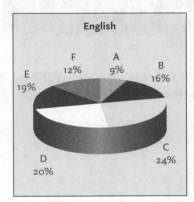

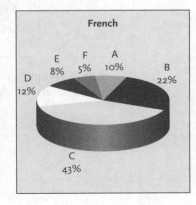

Line chart

You only have to compare the A, B, and C segments of the two diagrams to see how much more successful French has been than English.

A line chart is useful if you want to show how things have progressed over a period of time:

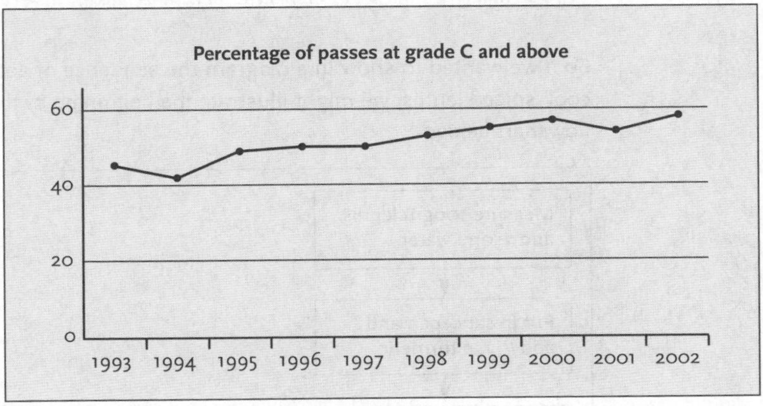
Percentage of passes at grade C and above
60
40
20
0
1993
1994
1995
1996
1997
1998
1999
2000
2001
2002

Other data

We can present information that is not numerical (or a combination of numerical and non-numerical information) visually.

Gantt chart

Gantt charts (named after their inventor) are concerned with progress across time, and are used for scheduling. Their best known (and loved, perhaps!) application is for blocking out periods when staff will be away from the office on holiday:

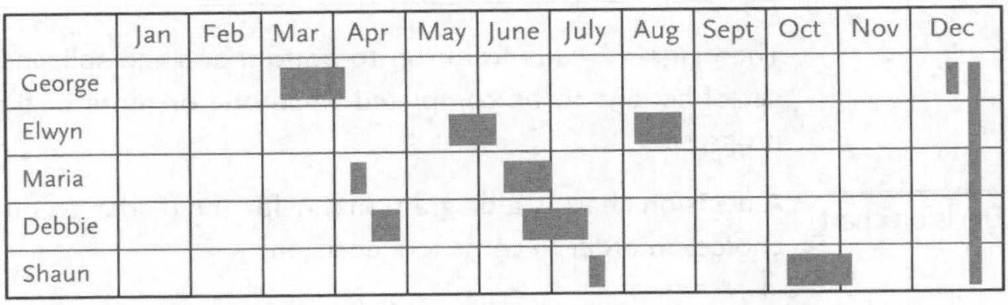
Jan
Feb
Mar
Apr
May
June
July
Aug
Sept
Oct
Nov
Dec
George
Elwyn
Maria
Debbie
Shaun

Gantt charts are also used for project planning, showing the period taken up by a project and the different phases of its execution:

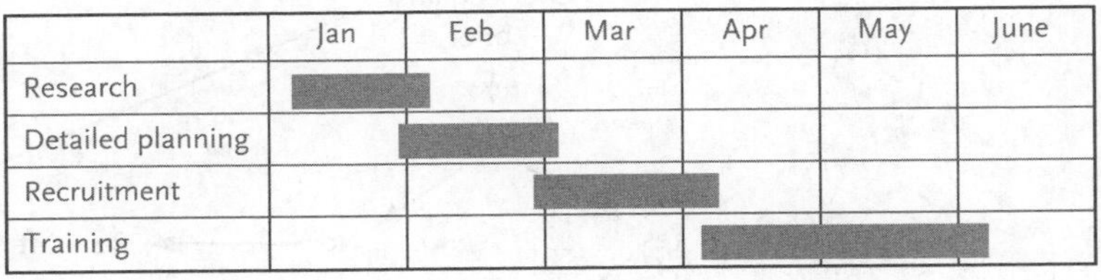
Jan
Feb
Mar
Apr
May
June
Research
Detailed planning
Recruitment
Training

Flowchart

If you want to show a process diagrammatically, you can use a flowchart. This term is used to cover a range of different diagrams. The one we are concerned with here is defined by the *Concise Oxford Dictionary* as:

> *a diagram of a sequence of movements or actions making up a complex system.*

So if we wanted to show in a diagram the sequence of actions required to cook spiced lentils, we might illustrate the beginning of the process in the flowchart below.

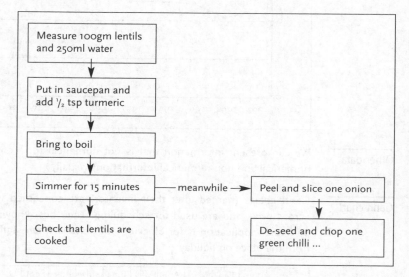

The diagram reads from top to bottom and the split indicates a second set of actions to be completed while one or more of the first set are in progress.

Decision chart

A decision chart is a diagram that helps the reader go through a series of choices in order to come to a decision:

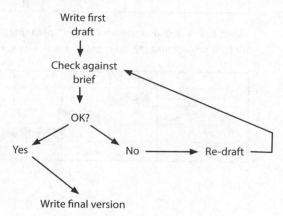

The simple example at the bottom of page 354 comes from a workflow for drafting a document based on a brief. It illustrates the idea that once the first draft of the document has been completed it is necessary to check it against the brief to make sure that all requirements have been carried out ('OK?'). If the answer to this question is 'Yes', then the writer is free to continue to the next stage: 'Write final version'. But if the answer is 'No', then it is necessary to redraft and then go back to 'Check against brief'.

E-writing

When designing a document for print you can control exactly how it looks and be confident that when it is printed, that is what you will get. Indeed, using the portable document format (PDF) developed by Adobe, you can guarantee that if you send the digital file to anyone else—whatever computer system they are using—it will look exactly as you intended.

However, the same does not hold true when writing for the web or for an e-book. This requires a completely different approach. The reason is that e-writing will present differently according to the device on which it is viewed. Whereas you can fix the position of different elements on a printed page, effectively 'nailing them down' so that they do not move, e-text flows to fill up the space allotted to it. A web page will look different in different web browsers and on different computers. It will look different again if you view it on a smartphone or tablet. This is because of the process by which the text is transmitted and interpreted. Web pages are written in a computer language called HTML (**H**yper**T**ext **M**arkup **L**anguage). This encodes the text so that the receiving device can interpret and present it to the reader. For example, I might want to present text to the reader like this:

Forms of the verb

All verbs have five forms, or parts:

1. stem   walk
2. present tense   walk/walks
3. past tense   walked
4. -ing participle walking
5. -ed participle walked

We can can use the stem to form the infinitive: to walk.

Regular and irregular verbs

All verbs do not work in the same way as the example we have used.

In HTML I have to write this:

> **Forms of the verb**
>
> All verbs have five forms, or parts:
>
> <ul>
> <li>stem walk</li>
> <li>present tense walk/walks</li>
> <li>past tense walked</li>
> <li>-ing participle walking</li>
> <li>-ed participle walked</li>
> </ul>
>
> We can can use the stem to form the infinitive: to walk.
>
> <h3>Regular and irregular verbs</h3>
>
> All verbs do not work in the same way as the example we have used.

The effects for the writer

Fortunately, there are plenty of applications that enable us to write for the web or for e-books without having to know how to write HTML. But it is important to understand what is going on 'under the bonnet' and how it affects your approach to writing. In particular, you need to realize that you no longer have full control over what your text looks like. For example:

- The fonts your readers see will depend on what is available on their computer or other device.
- The line length will vary according to the size of the screen (and window) being used.
- Vertical and horizontal spacing will be variable.
- Adding extra tabs and carriage returns will make no difference to the spacing. They will usually just be ignored.
- Features such as bullet points, numbered lists, and tables will probably not display as you expect.

Styles

The example of HTML shown above used a number of style tags. For example '<h2>' means 'open the style called "heading level 2"', and '</h2>' means 'close the style called "heading level 2"'. For the reading device to know what a level 2 heading is meant to look like, it has to refer to a style sheet. This is a list of specifications explaining the size, spacing, and so on, of this heading.

Consequently writers need to think in terms of different styles as they write. A basic list of styles for a web page or e-book would include:

- **body text**

  This governs the way in which the main part of the text is presented.

- **lists of bullet points**

  These are sometimes referred to as 'unordered lists'.

- **numbered lists**

  These are sometimes referred to as 'ordered lists'.

- **block quotes**

  Extended quotations can be marked off from the rest of the text by giving them additional spacing above and below and on the left- and right-hand sides.

- **headings**

  You can have several levels of heading, but three are sufficient for most purposes.

Web navigation Web pages also contain navigation aids:

- **menus**

  A web page may have one or several menus. These often take the form of tabs like filing tabs. Clicking on one will take you to another part of the website. Each menu item may lead to a sub-menu, often appearing as a drop-down menu.

- **hyperlinks**

  Clickable links will take you to:
  ◦ another part of the same page
  ◦ a different page
  ◦ a different website

- **downloads**

  You can also click on a link to download an image, an audio or video file, or a PDF.

E-book navigation E-books have similar navigational features to a website. However, the most important is the table of contents (TOC). It is essential—especially for non-fiction e-books—to include a detailed, clickable table of contents. It is also useful in non-fiction and reference books to include brief clickable contents lists at the start or end of each chapter (or both). In addition, information e-books should make full use of hyperlinks and clickable footnotes. Using an information e-book can seem off-putting to some readers, but with proper navigation, e-books can provide a reading experience that is at least as good as, if not better than, that provided by their print counterparts.

Guidelines

Type
1 Take care that your layout makes the text as clear as possible.
2 Use headings of different weights to indicate how the text is structured.

3 Set out lists and similar data using bullet points and hanging indents.

4 Make generous use of space on the page so that it is easy for the reader to see where different sections are.

5 Use running heads and running feet to help the reader navigate through a long document.

Visuals

6 Choose a suitable and attractive typeface for large blocks of text.

7 Normally use a serif face for large amounts of text and reserve sans serif faces for special text.

8 Only use display typefaces for headings and special effects.

9 Select a typesize between 9.5pt and 12pt for normal text.

10 Make sure that the leading (space between lines of text) is neither too tight nor too generous.

11 Always make sure that your text is readable; in particular make sure that lines are not too long (normally not more than 14 words to a line).

Layout

12 Whenever possible, use visuals to illustrate your text, especially when a visual representation can replace a large amount of text.

13 Use diagrams and drawings to illustrate physical objects and processes.

14 Use flowcharts and other diagrams to represent abstract ideas.

15 Use graphs, bar charts, and pie charts to point up the significance of numerical data.

E-writing

16 Remember that when you write for the web or for an e-book, you relinquish full control over what your text will look like.

17 By contrast with the fixed layout of a printed page, text on websites and in e-books flows to fit the space available. So don't expect your document to look the same to every viewer.

18 Use a standard set of styles to give your text a clear and readable appearance wherever it is viewed.

19 Take the opportunity to insert clickable navigation devices to assist your reader.

➤ *Further reading*

John Seely, *ePublish! From Manuscript to Finished e-Book in 10 Easy Stages*
(Oxpecker, 2012), ISBN 9781908948021 (print and e-book versions).

Robin Williams, *The Non-Designer's Design and Type Books*
(Peachpit Press, 2007), ISBN 9780321534057.

Glossary

Most of the terms explained in this section concern the grammar of English. All are explained in greater detail in the main part of this book.

page 283   **accent**   The ways in which two different people pronounce the same word may differ considerably, especially in the vowel sounds. If so, we say that they have different accents. A person's accent may come from the area where they were brought up, or from their social background, or a mixture of the two.

See: RECEIVED PRONUNCIATION, DIALECT

page 271   **acronym**   A word formed from the first letters of a group of words, for example the name of an organization:

UNICEF

BBC

An acronym is either pronounced as a word (like UNICEF) or as a series of letters (like BBC). In either case it is used as a noun (e.g. 'The clever old BBC's latest ploy …').

adjective   When we go to school we are taught that adjectives are 'describing words', which gives a good idea of how they are used. Grammatically they:

- modify nouns (e.g., 'the *red* house')
- act as the COMPLEMENT of a clause (e.g., 'She is *happy*.')

adverb   Adverbs are a class of words with a wide range of grammatical functions. The commonest are:

- to modify verbs ('She *slowly* came round.')
- to modify adjectives ('I am *really* sorry.')
- to modify other adverbs ('I behaved *very* badly.')

page 197   **adverbial**   Part of a clause which modifies the verb and provides information in answers to questions such as:

WHEN?:   'I met her *this afternoon.*'
WHERE?:   'We went *to the cinema.*'
HOW?:   'We travelled *by bus.*'
WHY?:   'She left her husband *because of her love for another man.*'

Within a clause an adverbial can be a group of words, a phrase, as in these examples, or it can be a single word—an adverb.

A COMPLEX SENTENCE may contain one or more adverbial clauses. These work in a similar way to the adverbial phrases, but contain a FINITE VERB:

'I met her *when we had both finished work*.'

There are also 'sentence adverbials', which provide some kind of comment on the sentence as a whole:

'*Unfortunately* our team lost again.'

affix *see:* WORD STRUCTURE.

page 193

agreement The subject and the verb in a clause must agree:

1 IN NUMBER
'She *was* very sad and her parents *were* supportive.'

2 IN PERSON
'I *am* going, Mary *is* going, and you *are* going.'

article A small class of words consisting of 'a', 'an', and 'the'.

page 192

aspect The form of the verb in a sentence can tell us not only *when* an action occurred (the TENSE), but also *how*. Compare these two sentences:

A
'As I *was walking* to work yesterday, I met Mrs Pepys.'

B
'I *walked* to work yesterday because I wanted to call in on Mrs Pepys.'

In **A** the speaker wants to show that the action of walking was continuing at the moment when something else happened. In **B** the speaker sees the action as a completed, one-off event. English verbs have three aspects. In the present tense they are:

SIMPLE: 'I walk.'
CONTINUOUS OR PROGRESSIVE: 'I am walking.'
PERFECT: 'I have walked.'

auxiliary verb *see:* VERB PHRASE

page 188

clause A group of words (which normally contains a subject and a finite verb) that either forms a whole SIMPLE SENTENCE or part of a MULTIPLE SENTENCE.

cliché In French the word 'cliché' means an engraved plate used in the past by printers. Once you have made such a plate you can use it as many times as you like to print a picture. Of course, if you pretend that each picture is an 'original', you will soon be found out. The same is true of language. Expressions such as, 'I will leave no stone unturned' were once new, but they have been used so many times that today they seem tired and stale. On the other hand, many common idiomatic expressions are clichés—'leading light', 'let sleeping dogs lie', and 'end of the road', for example. No one would try to avoid such expressions altogether; it is a matter of balance.

pages 126, 232 **colloquial** A term usually used to refer to everyday (often spoken) language as opposed to the more formal, polite, or 'posh' language that many people feel they ought to use. The word is sometimes used as a term of criticism: 'Her language was rather colloquial for a headteacher.' But this ignores the fact that we all use a range of different forms of language according to the situation we are in.

page 196 **complement** A clause component. One of the seven basic clause patterns is:

My wife + became + a district councillor
SUBJECT + VERB   + COMPLEMENT

where the subject and the complement both refer to the same person or thing and are joined by a LINKING VERB. Another clause pattern is:

The company + made + me   + Head of Security
SUBJECT   + VERB + OBJECT + COMPLEMENT

Here the object and the complement both refer to the same person or thing.

page 205 **complex sentence** A MULTIPLE SENTENCE which contains a main clause and one or more subordinate clauses. A main clause is one that can with little or no alteration stand alone, whereas a subordinate clause cannot, as in this complex sentence:

'We have decided + that we should close the plant.'
—MAIN CLAUSE — + —SUBORDINATE CLAUSE—

page 204 **compound sentence** A MULTIPLE SENTENCE which contains two or more main clauses joined by COORDINATING CONJUNCTIONS. For example:

'First she went to Woolworths, then she visited the bank, and finally she had a coffee in Fuller's.'

Here the three clauses are of equal status and are joined by the coordinating conjunctions 'then' and 'and'.

page 206 **conditional** A conditional sentence is one containing an 'if'. For example: 'If you don't stop making that noise, I shall go mad!' Conditionals come in different forms, according to how 'open' the condition is. Compare these four sentences:

A
If you heat water to 100°C at sea level, it boils.

B
If Martha comes, we'll open a new pot of jam.

C

If you thought about it even for a moment, you'd see that he's wrong.

D

If I were you, I'd think again.

Sentence A describes a fact that will never change—a law of nature. The event described has happened many times before and will doubtless happen many times more. Sentence B concerns something that has not yet happened, but the speaker believes that it is perfectly possible that it will. In sentence C, on the other hand, although the event described is possible, the speaker thinks it rather unlikely. Sentence D sets up an impossible condition—'I' can never be 'you'.

Although the large majority of conditionals use 'if', there are other words which can be used: 'although' and 'provided that', for example.

pages 211–15 **conjunctions** As their name suggests, these are the 'joining words' of grammar, used to combine two or more clauses into one MULTIPLE SENTENCE. They may be COORDINATING CONJUNCTIONS, like 'and' and 'but', OT SUBORDINATING CONJUNCTIONS, like 'when', 'although', and 'because'.

conjuncts These are adverbials which help to relate one part of a text to another through a relationship of meaning. For example: 'Peter and I had planned to go into business. When it came to the crunch, *however*, he lacked the necessary capital.' Here the word 'however' shows the relationship between the second sentence and the first; in this case, there is a contrast—the first sentence sets up an expectation and the second one knocks it down. Conjuncts are a useful way of making the link between two paragraphs.

pages 277 **consonant** The alphabet contains 21 consonant letters:

bcdfghjldmnpqrstvwxyz

RECEIVED PRONUNCIATION has 24 consonant sounds (although some linguists classify two of them as 'semi-vowels'—the sounds at the beginning of these two words: 'wet' and 'yet'). In some cases a consonant letter is almost always pronounced in the same way and is represented by one consonant sound symbol—for example, the first sound in the word 'bet'. In other cases there are sounds for which there is no single letter equivalent. Examples are the first sound in 'this' and the last sound in 'bath'—which are spelled the same but pronounced differently!

contraction In speech we sometimes miss sounds out and squash words together, producing contracted versions of words. In writing, the omission of letters in contracted forms is partly shown by the use of apostrophes:

'I shall not' becomes 'I shan't' (not 'I sha'n't')

pages 204

coordinating conjunction A CONJUNCTION used to join two CLAUSES in a COMPOUND SENTENCE. Examples are:

and, or, but, then

defining relative clause *see:* RELATIVE CLAUSE

page 184

descriptive grammar The type of grammar which is based on the analysis of a body of carefully selected spoken and written texts and leads to a set of statements which describe how language actually works, rather than how the writer thinks it should. It is commonly contrasted with PRESCRIPTIVE GRAMMAR.

page 181

dialect English exists in a wide number of different versions, or *dialects*, spoken by different social and geographical groups. For example, the natives of Glasgow use a number of words and grammatical constructions that are not used by those of Penzance. Of course there is a large amount of overlap between these different dialects, but the question still arises: 'What is English?' Most regional dialects have an associated form of pronunciation, or ACCENT. There is one dialect of English which has more prestige than any other, STANDARD ENGLISH. It is widely used in speech in education, the professions, government, and business, and is the normal form in written texts. In this book, unless otherwise stated, comments about English are always about the standard form.

page 190

directive Sentences which instruct, command, or request are frequently constructed in a special way that is different from STATEMENTS. For example:

'Keep off the grass.'
'Just leave me alone!'

The most obvious difference between a statement and a directive is that in a directive the subject is usually missed out—but not always:

'You just put that down at once!'

direct object *see:* OBJECT

page 220

etymology The study of the history of the words of a language. The word 'etymology' is also used to refer to the origins of a particular word.

page 134

euphemism A 'gentle' word or expression which is used in place of one which may offend some people. Sometimes the use of a euphemism is thoughtful and sensitive, as in the use of euphemisms for 'death' and 'died' when talking to people who are grieving the death of someone they loved. Often it is fussy, as in 'Do you want to spend a penny?' for 'Do you want to use the lavatory?' And it can even be confusing, as in 'Do you want to wash your hands?' for the same question.

page 193
finite verb A clause normally has to contain a finite verb. That is a verb which:

1 AGREES with the subject in number and person
2 shows tense

So, for example, this is not a proper simple sentence:

'To visit Paris in the spring—one of the great experiences of youth.'

because the only verb in it is an infinitive, 'to visit'. It doesn't agree with the subject (because there isn't one) and it has no tense. Compare:

'I *visited* Paris in the spring—one of the great experiences of youth.'
'I *shall visit* Paris in the spring—one of the great experiences of youth.'

full verb *see:* VERB PHRASE

pages 184
grammar The study of how words are changed to fit into sentences (morphology) and how they are ordered to construct sentences (syntax). *See also:* DESCRIPTIVE GRAMMAR, TRADITIONAL GRAMMAR, PRESCRIPTIVE GRAMMAR

indirect object *see:* OBJECT

page 192
infinitive The 'to——' form of the verb:

to be, to go, to understand

Many languages have a one-word infinitive form (as French—être, aller, comprendre), but English does not. If you remove the 'to', you are left with the verb stem, which is used in certain tenses:

'She will be unhappy.'

The infinitive itself is used with verbs like 'want' and 'love' ('I'd love to go to Paris.') and can be used in sentences as a part of a noun phrase: '*To lose* one parent, Mr Worthing, may be regarded as a misfortune; *to lose* both looks like carelessness.'

page 281
intonation The 'tune' with which we speak. This sentence, for example, can be spoken in more than one way: 'You saw her yesterday.' If we say it so that the voice rises at the beginning of 'yesterday' and then falls through the rest of the word, the sentence is a statement of fact. If we say it so that the voice *rises* towards the end of 'yesterday', the sentence becomes a question and should be written with a final question mark.

page 233
jargon Many subjects have a specialist language, which non-specialists find difficult or impossible to understand. This means that when specialists speak to each other they may accidentally or deliberately exclude any non-specialists who happen to be present. Any such technical language can be described as 'jargon', but the term is often used as a criticism—especially when technical or specialist language is used either to show off, or to exclude other people, or both.

page 196

linking verbs A small group of verbs (sometimes called copular verbs) that are used to link a subject and its complement:

'Mrs Brown *is* a teacher at the local school.'

Other linking verbs are:

appear, seem, become, feel, remain, sound

page 205

main clause In a COMPLEX SENTENCE one clause is grammatically more important than the other *subordinate* clauses. In the sentences that follow, the main clauses are underlined:

A

'<u>She told us</u> that she had to go home.'

B

'When I arrived, <u>all the food had gone</u>.'

C

'<u>Mr Jones was the teacher</u> who taught me most.'

In each of these sentences, the subordinate clause can be replaced by a single word or short phrase, and the main clause will then make a grammatically complete simple sentence:

A: 'She told us *the truth*.'
B: '*By then* all the food had gone.'
C: 'Mr Jones was the *best* teacher.'

You cannot do the same with the subordinate clauses—they depend on the main clause.

page 200

minor sentence It is possible to construct a kind of 'sentence' without a finite verb. Such utterances have a clear and complete meaning but they are grammatically incomplete:

No entry.
Car park for customers only.

Such sentences are called 'minor sentences'.

multiple sentence A multiple sentence is one that consists of more than one clause. Multiple sentences are either COMPOUND or COMPLEX.

pages 156–60

narrative One of the four traditional modes (types) of discourse (writing and speaking). Any text which relates a series of events which happened over a period of time is a narrative. The simplest form begins at the beginning and relates events in the order in which they happened, but this approach is frequently not followed; newspaper reports, for example, are narratives, but they often begin with the most striking element of the story and then fill in the background later. Other examples of narratives are short stories, novels, the minutes of a meeting, the record of a legal trial, and many jokes ('There's this fellow who goes into a pub, right?').

non-defining relative clause *see:* RELATIVE CLAUSE

non-restrictive relative clause *see:* RELATIVE CLAUSE

non-standard A term used to refer to language uses that differ grammatically from standard English.

noun Traditionally nouns have been described as 'words that refer to people, places, things, and ideas'. Grammatically we can say that most nouns:

- can be modified by an ADJECTIVE ('the red *house*')
- can be preceded by an ARTICLE ('the *house*')
- preceded by an article can stand as the SUBJECT or OBJECT of a clause
  '*The house* has been sold.' (subject)
  'We have sold *the house*.' (object)
- can follow a preposition ('All the illustrations were done *in house*.')

page 209

noun clause A clause which forms the subject, object, or complement of a complex sentence:

SUBJECT
'<u>What I want to know</u> is the answer to my first question.'
OBJECT
'You still haven't told me <u>what I want to know</u>.'
COMPLEMENT
'That is <u>what I want to know</u>.'

page 190

noun phrase A phrase which is based on a noun. It can have words before and after the noun:

'The highest *mountain* in Scotland'

Noun phrases can form the subject, object, or complement of a sentence; they can also form part of other phrases.

page 193

number The subject of a sentence can be singular (one) or plural (more than one). The verb must agree with the number of the subject. *See:* AGREEMENT

page 195

object The object in a clause normally comes after the verb. The objects in these sentences have been underlined:

'I nearly lost <u>my temper</u>.'
'I nearly lost <u>what I most treasured in the world</u>. '

In the first example the object is a NOUN PHRASE; in the second it is a NOUN CLAUSE.

Certain verbs can have two objects, a *direct* object and an *indirect* object:

I gave the dog   a bone.
INDIRECT   DIRECT
OBJECT   OBJECT

These sentences can be turned round like this:

I gave a bone to   the dog.
      DIRECT   INDIRECT
      OBJECT   OBJECT

The indirect object is the one which needs 'to' placing before it.

page 194

person PRONOUNS can be 1st, 2nd or 3rd person:

1ST PERSON: I/We (and my/our, etc.)
2ND PERSON: you/your, etc.
3RD PERSON: she/he/it/they

The form of the verb changes according to the person:

I like/she likes.
See: AGREEMENT

pages 277-80

phoneme Phonemes are the speech sounds of a language. In RECEIVED PRONUNCIATION there are 44 phonemes. See CONSONANT and VOWEL.

page 188

phrase A group of words which forms a part of a clause, but which, unlike a clause, does not contain a finite verb. Phrases are named after their headword. In these examples the headword is in bold type:

- a noun phrase ('the **leader** of the gang')
- a verb phrase ('would have been **going**')
- a prepositional phrase ('**to** the edge')
- an adverbial phrase ('very, very, **slowly**')
- an adjective phrase ('really rather **unusual**')

Plain English Literally, 'plain English' is speech or writing in English that is clear and straightforward to understand. Since 1974, it has also been the name of a movement in the UK, the Plain English Campaign, founded to persuade government and business to communicate simply and clearly with the general public. Books such as *The Plain English Guide* (Martin Cutts, OUP, 1995) set out rules which can be followed by the writer who wishes to write 'plain English'. This campaign and its establishment of the 'Crystal Mark' have achieved a great deal to make government and commercial communications clearer and more straightforward. There are, however, limitations to what such an approach can achieve. It is not possible to communicate effectively in the widest possible range of situations just by following a set of rules; you need also to be sensitive to the demands of audience, subject, and purpose, as suggested in Section B of this book.

prefix *see:* WORD STRUCTURE

preposition A class of words which are used with nouns, pronouns, noun phrases, and some verb forms. As their name suggests, they come before the word(s) that complement them. In these phrases the prepositions are underlined:

> <u>in</u> time
> <u>with</u> us
> <u>behind</u> the green baize door
> <u>without</u> thinking

Prepositions may consist of more than one word:

> <u>up to</u> you
> <u>except for</u> the French

page 184 **prescriptive grammar** Grammar which sets out rules about how language should be used. For example: 'You should never end a sentence with a preposition.' A large number of the rules of prescriptive grammar either have exceptions, or are just plain wrong (as with the example quoted).

primary verb *see:* VERB PHRASE

pronoun A word which refers back to a noun, noun phrase, pronoun, or another group of words or idea already mentioned in a text. Examples are:

> I/me/my/mine/myself
> they/them/their/theirs/themselves

page 283 **received pronunciation (RP)** An English ACCENT which used to be regarded as superior to other, regional, accents. It was also known as 'BBC English'. Until recently, and even to some extent today, people believed that you had to learn how to speak with an RP accent if you wished to advance in the professions, national government, and other areas of employment. It is certainly true that many regional accents are still widely regarded as inferior to RP.

page 209 **relative clause** A clause that modifies a noun, noun phrase, or pronoun. In these examples the relative clauses are underlined:

> **A**
> 'Mrs Rowen, <u>who was born in France,</u> loved good plain cooking.'
> **B**
> 'The person <u>she most admires</u> is the Duchess of St Pancras.'

Relative clauses may be introduced by a relative pronoun, as in sentence A. Other relative pronouns are 'whom', 'whose', 'which', and 'that'. Sometimes a relative clause has no introductory relative pronoun, as in sentence B. Some relative clauses define or restrict the word or words they refer to. In sentence B, for example, 'she' obviously admires more than one person; the relative clause is there to define the person we are referring to. Such relative clauses are described as defining or restrictive relative clauses. Other relative clauses do not define, but simply add extra information, as in sentence A: there is only one Mrs Rowen in question and the clause tells us more about her. Such non-defining or nonrestrictive relative clauses should be enclosed in commas, as in the example.

RP *see:* RECEIVED PRONUNCIATION

page 232 **slang** Language that is much less formal and less socially acceptable than standard English. It is subject to changes of fashion and is often connected with membership of a particular social group. Slang expressions for *eat* include:

 feed your face
 tie on the feed bag
 grab a bite
 get amongst the groceries

standard English *see:* DIALECT

stem *see:* WORD STRUCTURE

pages 280 **stress** In any spoken sentence, some SYLLABLES will be spoken with more emphasis than the others; they are said to be *stressed*. English has two kinds of stress. In any word of more than one syllable, there will be one syllable that is stressed more than the others. For example:

 des**pair, hap**py

Longer words may have two stressed syllables, but one of them will normally be stronger (primary stress) and the other weaker (secondary stress).

  In addition to word stress, there is sentence stress. If you say that last sentence aloud, you see that two syllables are stressed:

 In addition to **word** stress, there is **sen**tence stress.

Sentence stress combines with INTONATION to give spoken English its distinctive rhythm and tune.

page 190 **subject** The subject of a statement clause normally comes before the verb. It frequently, but by no means always, gives an indication of what the clause will be about:

 Our success in the match was due to excellent teamwork.

Sometimes, however, a clause may have a 'dummy subject', with a grammatical purpose but not a lot of meaning:

 It is raining this morning.

subordinate clause *see:* MAIN CLAUSE

subordinating conjunction *see:* CONJUNCTION

suffix *see:* WORD STRUCTURE

page 282

syllable A syllable is the smallest unit into which spoken language will break down. It can be just one vowel, or a combination of consonant(s) and vowel. All these words have one syllable:

I, my, mine, mind, dined, grind

(Notice that we are dealing with spoken language here; 'dined' may appear to have two syllables on the page, but when you say it you can see that there is only one.) These words all have two syllables:

any, many, timid, grounded, happened
See: STRESS

page 231

taboo Certain informal words and expressions are generally considered to be unsuitable for 'polite society'. These are often concerned with human sexuality and excretion. They are described as 'taboo', or 'taboo slang'. Which words and expressions are taboo is a matter of opinion, and people's ideas about this shift as society changes.

page 192

tense One of the ways in which time can be indicated in a sentence is by the use of verb tense. Confusingly, this term is used in two different ways by people who write about language. In its strictest sense, tense means changes to the form of the verb to show a difference of time. In this sense, English has two tenses:

PRESENT: I walk, she walks, etc.
PAST: I walked, she walked, etc.

So it is correct to say that 'English has no future tense'. But, people argue, what about 'she will walk'? The answer is that the term 'tense' is also widely used to describe all the different forms the verb phrase can take to show time. In that meaning of tense, all the following are different tenses:

I walk, I am walking, I have walked, I walked, I was walking, I shall walk, I shall be walking, I shall have walked, and so on
See: VERB PHRASE

pages 125

tone Sometimes a person speaks in such a way that their voice makes clear what their attitude is to the person they are addressing. We may say, 'I knew she didn't like me the moment she opened her mouth; I could tell it from her tone of voice.' It is often possible to detect the same thing in the way a person writes: we can tell from the tone of their writing their relationship with and attitude towards their audience.

page 184

traditional grammar In the past all students of language were educated in a system that laid great emphasis on Greek and Latin language and literature. When they came to study English they based their systematic analysis of this language on what they knew of the great classical languages. The result was a grammar that often regarded English as inferior to Latin and sought to improve it, often by bringing it closer to Latin. This process involved distorting the true nature of English and imposing 'rules' which did not reflect linguistic reality.

See: **PRESCRIPTIVE GRAMMAR, DESCRIPTIVE GRAMMAR**

verb A large class of words which are used to refer to actions, states, and conditions. For example:

to run   to decide   to love   to be

To check whether a word is a verb add 'to' to it and see if it makes an INFINITIVE. If it does, the word is a verb.

page 191

verb phrase Every clause must contain a verb phrase (sometimes shortened to 'verb'). In a statement sentence, this normally comes after the subject and before the object or complement. The verb phrase may consist of one word or more than one. The verbs that make up a verb phrase are of three types:

FULL VERBS

These are verbs with a 'dictionary meaning' and they can be the only verb in the verb phrase: 'I *love* ice cream.'

AUXILIARY VERBS

These work with full verbs: 'I *should* love an ice cream.' They cannot stand as the only verb in a verb phrase, unless they are referring back to an earlier verb phrase. (As in 'Would you like an ice cream?'—'Yes, I *would*.')

PRIMARY VERBS

There are three verbs that can act as full verbs or as auxiliaries: 'to be', 'to have', to do'. So we can say, 'I *have* a golden labrador' (full verb use) and 'I *have* taken the dog for a walk' (auxiliary use).

pages 277

vowel There are five vowel letters in English: a e i o u.

Vowel sounds are those speech sounds made with the mouth open and the flow of air unimpeded. Each of the following words has one vowel sound sandwiched between two consonant sounds:

beet, bit, bet, bat, but, part, pot, port, put, boot, hurt, bate, bite, boil, bowl, howl

The second sound in each of these words is a vowel sound:

the, here, there, poor

The vowel sounds represented in the words listed comprise all the vowels of RECEIVED PRONUNCIATION.

page 224

word structure All words have a stem, and some words consist only of a stem. For example:

paper, example, comfort

Other words have a stem with a section before and/or after it:

un   comfort   able

PREFIX   STEM   SUFFIX

The general term for prefixes and suffixes is *affixes*. Prefixes are used to add meaning to the stem or alter its meaning. (For example, adding 'un-' to a stem gives it the opposite meaning to what it had before.) Suffixes are used to form new words from existing words. This often involves moving them from one word class to another. So the noun 'comfort' gives us the adjective 'comfortable'.

'You Try' answers

Chapter 2

It would be difficult to argue that this letter is a success. It is expressed in an awkward, pompous, and jargon-ridden way. Using a layout in which each sentence is presented as a separate paragraph makes it difficult to read. It would be much more successful if it were rewritten along these lines:

> Dear Mr & Mrs Green,
>
> Your letter of 13th October has been referred to me. I should like to apologize unreservedly for the mistake we made.
>
> It seems that our letter of 1st October, about insurance cover on your overdraft, was sent by mistake. I can assure you that your account has not been charged with any insurance premium. You should by now have received an amended letter, confirming that the overdraft arrangement has been renewed.
>
> You mention that you would like to explore the possibility of our setting up an automatic transfer between your Current Account and your Deposit Account. This is sometimes arranged for our customers. You would need to arrange it with one of our Managers. If you would like to do this, please ask one of our staff.
>
> I apologize again for any inconvenience caused by our letter of 1st October. Please do not hesitate to contact me if I may be of any further assistance in this or any other matter.
>
> Yours sincerely,

Chapter 10

page 122

Extract 'A' is from an introduction to Egyptology for the general (adult) reader. Extract 'B' is from a book for children aged 7–11, and Extract 'C' is a more specialized book for adults.

Extract 'A' is clearly aimed at a very low level of knowledge—not just about computers, but about life! (For example, most adults *should* know that it is safer to lift heavy objects by bending at the knees, rather than the waist.) Extract 'B', on the other hand, assumes quite a high level of knowledge. For example, the reader is expected to know what *drives, files, data*, and *software* are.

This writer has a good vocabulary, using words such as *ironically, epicentre*, and *philanthropy*. Unfortunately he is under the impression that in order to make his point he has to sound pompous and write long sentences which run away with him. The first sentence, for example, is so convoluted that it is impossible to work out what it means. The moral is clear: imagine that you are talking to one or two people of a similar intelligence to yourself, and address them in straightforward sentences that are not too long. If in doubt, try reading your text aloud to yourself and check that it sounds right. Writers such as the author of this letter fail to have the effect they would like and just make themselves look foolish.

Chapter 11

Extract 'B' is certainly much easier to understand; it is journalism and journalists who fail to communicate clearly are soon out of a job. Extract 'A', on the other hand, is part of a pension policy, a legal document. The writer decided to choose what could be defended in a court of law in preference to what might be easily understood by the lay person. As the Plain English Campaign has shown, however, these two need not be so obviously in conflict. Extract 'A' *could* be written more clearly. The sentence beginning 'The Benefit Value...', for example, is clearly too long and needs punctuation to make it clearer. It could be rewritten like this:

> The Benefit Value will be applied to secure an annuity. GA Life's immediate annuity rates current at the date Investment Units are cancelled will be used (taking account of any relevant charges). The annuity will be paid during the Member's lifetime by monthly payments in arrear from the Pension Date without proportion to the date of death.

There is an element of jargon here. Some of the expressions used would certainly put off many general readers and some professional ones: *organizational culture* and *the feedback principle*, for example. This is made worse by the length of some of the sentences, especially the last one quoted, which is convoluted and difficult to disentangle.

Chapter 13

A: to entertain

B: to inform

C: to regulate

D: to influence (although it also informs)

Chapter 14

page 159

Clearly the first paper has given a lot more space to the story than the second, so it must believe that it is of greater interest to its readers. The headlines already suggest a difference of emphasis, with the second account making use of the derogatory word 'booze' to ensure that its readers know what was involved—and what to think of it. The same word is then repeated in the story. The first account uses the more neutral phrase 'banned for drink driving' and keeps it out of the headline.

The first account carries a lot more detail about Alexander Bonsor's lifestyle and we get the impression that the whole affair was a bit of a prank and not to be taken too seriously. The second story does not appear to take such a lenient view of the affair, although it does not go so far as to openly criticize the subject of the story.

The first extract is taken from the *Daily Mail*, the second from the *Mirror*.

page 163

Extract A is from a travel writer's account of a stay in Delhi. Extract B comes from a guidebook. Extract A pulls no punches and gives us a personal account of the writer's earlier preconceptions and later disillusion. Extract B does not attempt to pretend that the romantic view of Chandni Chowk is entirely true to life, but it does still give a qualified recommendation: 'It's a fascinating area, but ...'

As might be expected from a guidebook, the second extract contains a mass of detailed information. The first piece, on the other hand, is more concerned to paint a picture and so selects detail with this in mind.

page 171

A, although historical, is essentially exposition. B is description. C is narrative. D presents an argument.

Chapter 15

page 179

You try 1

Your response to this will depend on who you are and when you make it. At the time of writing it looked like this:

bratpack	rather dated
card swipe	current
networker	current
pressing the flesh	dated but usable in a slightly ironic way
wuss	still current at the time of writing
crumbly	in the sense of 'an older person', dated
moral majority	a useful historical term
infomercial	reasonably modern
des res	only in ironic use, anyway
mega	slightly dated

You try 2

These words were taken from the excellent website devoted to new words, <www.wordspy.com>, and I am grateful to Paul McFedries for allowing me to use the following definitions:

baby-lag
n. Extreme fatigue and disorientation due to the sleep deprivation associated with parenting a baby.

flirtationship
n. A relationship that consists mostly of flirting. [Flirt + relationship.]

mansplaining
pp. Explaining in a patronizing way, particularly when done by a man who combines arrogance with ignorance of the topic. [Man + explaining.]

selfie
n. A photographic self-portrait, particularly one taken with the intent of posting it to a social network.

omnishambles
n. A situation or person that is a mess in every possible way.

page 182

Again these are personal judgements:

1 informal
2 informal
3 standard
4 standard
5 informal
6 informal

1 People disagree about whether *different to* and *different than* are acceptable. They have been widely used by many famous writers for centuries. The argument is that if you can say *similar to* there is no reason why you can't say *different to*. The use of *different than* tends to be American. If you don't want to be criticized by people who fuss about things like this, use *different from*.

2 A split infinitive. Nothing wrong with it. If you put *fully* anywhere else in the sentence it sounds awkward.

3 Some people object to a preposition at the end of a sentence, but for no good reason. If you avoid it by saying ... *to whom I sold* ... it sounds a bit strained.

4 Some people say that it should be 'I shall ...' for normal future time and that 'I will' is emphatic, but this is clearly dying out, especially in speech.

5 The *Oxford English Dictionary* states that 'none' means 'no persons', so this sentence is correct. Some people, however, argue that 'none' is a shortened form of 'no one' and so is singular.

6 Technically 'media' is a plural and should be followed by 'are', but few people follow this rule these days, except in very formal writing.

7 Some people object to -ize forms like 'finalize'. Certainly, 'finalize' says nothing that 'complete' or 'conclude' does not.

8 'Spaniards' is a countable noun, so 'fewer' would be better.

9 Standard English is 'interested in'.

10 The centre is the mid-point of something, so 'centred on' is correct.

Chapter 16

SUBJECT	VERB
1 Making good coffee	is
2 The occasion of my last visit to see my Great Aunt Annie	could have been
3 I	shall have been living
4 the composer	had become

1 are
2 were
3 have
4 were

1 adverbial
2 complement
3 object
4 verb
5 adverbial

1 **a** means that Harry forgot everyone's birthday
  b means that everyone forgot grandfather's birthday
2 little difference
3 **a** means that it was fortunate that Peter gave the book back
  b means that he was happy to give it back
4 **a** means that Sales are the only department to want this
  b means that Sales want every other product painted a different colour from pink
  c means that they want pink to be the only colour to be used on the new product

Chapter 17

1a describes a possible situation in the future. **1b** describes a situation in the future that could happen but is unlikely. **1c** describes a situation in the past that did not happen.

2a describes a situation in the past that did not happen. **2b** describes a general situation that already exists and will continue to do so.

3a and **3b** describe much the same situation, although **3b** is clearer. **3c** refers to a situation in the past.

4a describes a possible situation in the future. **4b** describes a possible but unlikely situation in the past. **4c** describes a situation in the past that could have happened but is improbable.

Chapter 18

Words that could be included in each of the other diagrams are:

large	sail	sailor	wait
enlarge	boardsailing	sailoress	await
enlarged	cross-sail	sailoring	awaited
enlargement	disailment	sailorizing	dumb-waiter
enlarger	fore-sail	sailorless	outwait
largely	fore-spritsail	sailorly	overwait
largemost	fore-topsail	sailorship	quarter-waiter
largeness	gaff-topsail	sailplane	unawait
larger	head-sail	sailsman	wait-list
over-large	lug-sail	sailworthy	waiter
re-enlarge	mainsail	sailyard	waitership
unenlarged	main-topsail	spritsail	waiting
unlarge	outsail	sprit-topsail	waiting-maid
	plain sailing n.	square sail	waiting-man
	sailable	staysail	waiting-room
	sailage n.	topsail	waiting-woman
	sailboard	under-sail	waitress
	sailcloth	unsailable	
	sailed	unsailed ppl.	
	sailer	unsailorlike	
	sail-fish	unsailorly	
	sailful	windsail	
	sailing		

page 230

The definitions that follow are taken from the *Oxford English Dictionary*

geocentric Referred to the earth as centre; considered as viewed from the centre of the earth.

geochronology The chronology of the earth; the measurement of geological time and the ordering of past geological events.

geodynamic Of or pertaining to the (latent) forces of the earth.

hydrogeologist An expert in, or student of, hydrogeology, that part of geology which treats of the relations of water on or below the surface of the earth.

geophysicist An expert in, or student of, geophysics, the science or study of the physics of the earth, esp. of its crust.

theogeological Of or pertaining to geology as accommodated to theological tenets.

geometrize To work by geometrical methods, to form geometrically.

geoscopy A kind of knowlege of the nature and qualities of the ground, or soil; gained by viewing and considering it...

geochemistry The chemistry of the earth; the study of the chemical composition of the earth.

bioclimatic Pertaining to the study of climate in relation to the seasonal activities and geographical distribution of living organisms.

bioluminescence The emission of light by living organisms; also, the light so produced.

biomechanics The study of the mechanical laws relating to the movement or structure of living organisms.

biosphere The regions of the earth's crust and atmosphere that are occupied by living organisms; occas., the living organisms themselves.

bioscope 1. A view or survey of life. Obs. **2.** An earlier form of cinematograph (cf. biograph n. 2); retained in South Africa as the usual term for a cinema or a moving film.

---

page 233 This is, to some extent, a matter of personal experience and opinion, but this is one possible grading. In each case the lists run from formal to informal.

intellectual	insolvent	relax	flee
guru	in difficulties	rest	run away
highbrow	short of money	snooze	hurry off
intellect	hard up	take a breather	decamp
boffin	cleaned out	take a nap	split
egghead	strapped	have forty winks	beat it
culture-vulture	skint	take five	skedaddle
knowall	boracic	kip down	scarper
pointy-head		hit the hay	vamoose
clever clogs			
smartarse			

---

page 235 A simpler version of the text might be:

Surveys showed that it was possible to stabilize the land in a temporary or a long-term way. The Town Council preferred a long-term solution, although it would cost more.

The Town Council did not have enough money to undertake the work, so it welcomed an offer of help from West Dorset District Council. We then applied to the Ministry of Agriculture, Fisheries and Food to receive additional funding as part of the Coastal Defence Programme.

The first set of definitions that follow are quoted—for both enlightenment and entertainment—from *Jargon* by Walter Nash. The author does not necessarily follow the suggestions about language use contained in this Guide.

agenda, hidden In the political mode, the hidden agenda means the complex of sensitive issues that make up the potentially unaccept-able items of someone's ideology—meaning what they don't tell you about what they intend to do if they get half a chance. Old phrases like 'ulterior motive' or 'concealed purpose' might do at a pinch, but somehow lack the clout. This is a very modish expression. Do not say 'Some parish councillors are trying to get rid of the old fish-and-chip shop on the sly'; say 'The progressive streamlining of local catering facilities is evidently an item of high priority on the council's hidden agenda'.

ballpark figure Book-keepers' and statisticians' shop: a general, round figure estimate of a large number. Originally used to denote the prob-able size of the crowd at a baseball game, this American expression was subsequently extended to any estimate of population, expenditure, bud-getary outlay, etc. 'How much is this project going to cost?—I don't want it down to the last penny, just give me a ballpark figure.' Britons tend to confuse 'ballpark' and ballgame'—but that is a whole new ballpark.

cold calling Salesman's jargon: the practice of calling on a prospective client or entering a potential market without a preliminary introduction or recommendation. 'Before arriving' (at the Cannes Film Festival) 'she researches the trade papers, discovers who will be here and what proj-ects they are keen on. Then she braces herself for some "cold calling" at the luxury Majestic and Carlton hotels'—*Independent*.

de-skilling In industry, through technological advances, rendering the skilled worker unnecessary. 'It is now in the US and UK, where the implementation of the style [= the technology] is proving difficult, that it is doing most to increase inequality; destroying whole industries, de-skilling occupations, weakening unions ...'—*Guardian*.

hands-on Adjective, meaning 'practical', 'direct', as in hands-on experi-ence. The original hands-on experience was the trainee's first touching of the computer keyboard; now the expression can apply more diverse-ly—for example to a medical student's first attempts at the clinical examination of a patient, or a learner-driver's practical training in han-dling the controls of a car. The epithet hands-on may also be used in application to persons; 'The question hardly anyone dare ask in Washington ... was whether the crisis could have been averted in the first place by a more hands-on president'—*Observer*. From hands-on follows hands-off: 'Mr Lilley ... has traditionally taken a hands-off approach to industry'—*Guardian*.

The following five are somewhat more recent, and the definitions are my own:

core competencies	in company-speak, 'the things we do really well' (i.e. properly)
disintermediation	the process by which a seller gets rid of the middle man. So for example, self-publishing is a form of disintermediation, because it does not involve a commercial publisher: the author does it alone.
facetime	an opportunity for two (or more) individuals to sit down or stand together (by the water-cooler?) to talk about things rather than communicating by email or phone.
touch base	like facetime, an opportunity to meet personally to discuss something, often the current status of a project.
wetware	a rather unpleasant term to refer to human beings (by contrast with, for example 'software' and 'hardware').

page 238

clergyman : *priest, minister*
craftsman : *craft worker*
layman : *lay person* (in religious contexts), *non-expert*, or *ordinary person* (where the word is meaning 'someone without special knowledge or qualifications')
man-made : *synthetic, artificial, manufactured*
policeman : *police officer* (or give rank)
salesman : *sales representative, sales assistant*

page 239

This is another occasion where the choice is based on personal experience. One possible grading would be:

A	B	C
stocky	brawny	heavy
well-endowed	gross	hefty
well-built	elephantine	thickset
beefy	well-upholstered	obese
comfortable	fat	
burly	paunchy	
chunky	lumbering	

Chapter 22

Guide for Business Guests from Hangzhou

Subject matter

- Introduction to Cheltenham and its Regency history
- Montpellier
- Pittville Park and Pump Room
- Promenade
- Council Offices – role of the Council
- Business opportunities in Cheltenham

Readership

- Chamber of Commerce Chairman and members
- Visitors from Hangzhou
- (Council members)

Purposes

- Present town at its best
- Emphasize business opportunities
- Make visitors feel welcome

Schedule

- To Chairman of Chamber of Commerce: 1 May
- Revised for CCC meeting: 24 May
- Cheltenham Design & Print: 1 June
- Visit: 10 July

Format

- A4 trifold leaflet
- One mini-page per topic (see above)
- 50/50 text/illustrations
- Full colour

Chapter 25

page 325

All three extracts come from books about France and the French. **A** indicates that it is going to be about people. By starting with a reference to national stereotypes it perhaps implies that it wants to dig beneath the surface and find out what the 'real people' are like. **B** clearly has a business and commercial focus, while **C** is obviously concerned with the landscape of the country and how it appears to visitors.

A comes from *The French* by Theodore Zeldin

B is from French Entrée website and introduces an article entitled *New auto-entrepreneur system for small businesses*

C comes from the *Rough Guide to France*

page 331

Sentence 1 presents us with a situation (the waitress showing us to a table in a restaurant) and a puzzle (what is going on inside her head as she does so?). The second sentence provides an amplification both of the situation (by describing Thérèse's manner in more detail) and, by implication, of the puzzle (if she is so self-possessed and 'all energy', what is she doing waiting at tables?). Sentence 3 develops the last two words of the second, by giving an example of her 'friendly solicitude'. Now that Thérèse's situation and manner have been established, the fourth sentence returns to the puzzle by providing a key piece of information: that she has an MA in Art History. Sentence 5 provides a kind of coded solution to the puzzle. Thérèse is highly competent because she is intelligent and well-educated; she works in this apparently lowly job because she gets something special out of it. It gives her a 'purpose in life'. And thus the writer sets up the succeeding paragraphs: they will explain just what that 'purpose in life' is.

Chapter 26

In the first part of the **manuscript,** most attention is focused on the relation between the first paragraph and the two bullet points that follow it. The changes are intended to make this as simple and clear as possible. The later changes are mainly a question of tidying up, but in the middle of the extract an important later addition is made to the point about correcting punctuation.

In the **word-processed version** the main change is that the order of the second set of bullet points has been changed. Other changes are quite small, but there is an attempt to rephrase the last sentence so that it is more accurate.

The ways in which I thought the text still needed improvement can be seen in the final version on page 276. You may not necessarily agree with me.

One important set of changes concerns the way in which the writer addresses the reader. In the previous draft I used 'we' throughout. This has now been changed to 'you'—in keeping with the general tone throughout the book. (There was a gap of nine months between the two drafts, during which the style and tone of the book had 'settled down' quite a lot. Revisions of material written early on had to take this into account.) The other main change is that the order of the original three bullet points ('Changes to the structure', etc.) has been rationalized by placing the biggest first and the smallest last. These three short sections of text have been upgraded from bullet points to short paragraphs, to make them easier to read.

Index

Note: entries in *italics* indicate references to the usage of those words.

Acknowledgements

Thanks are due to the following for permission to reproduce extracts from copyrighted material in this book.

ACAS: copyright © ACAS Work *Research Unit 1988.*

Ashford, Buchan, & Enright: from *Groc's Candid Guide to Crete and Mainland Ports.*

Blackwell Publishers: from Walter Nash, *Jargon, Its Uses and Abuses* (1993).

Bloomsbury: 'Sage' from *Bloomsbury Thesaurus* (1993), edited by Betty Kirkpatrick.

The British Red Cross: extract from a newspaper advertisement, 'Urgent Appeal: Crisis in Lebanon'.

Butterworth-Heinemann Ltd: extract from R. E. Jackson, S. F. Ray, G. G. Attridge, *The Manual of Photography* (Focal Press, 1988).

Cobuild Ltd. Institute of Research & Development: definition of 'Sage' from *Collins Cobuild English Language Dictionary* (1987).

Daily Mail: 'Driving ban for nine-in-car ...', Daily Mail, 21/3/97.

Judy Daish Associates Ltd: extract from Harold Pinter, *Pinter Plays: Two* (Eyre Methuen, 1977; orig. publ. Methuen 1961, © Harold Pinter 1961).

Driver and Vehicle Licensing Agency: extract from Vehicle Registration document.

Encyclopaedia Britannica International Ltd: 'Sensory Perception', p. 181 from *Encyclopaedia Britannica Macropedia.*

Faber & Faber Ltd: extract from 'Night Mail' by W. H. Auden, from *The Collected Poems of W. H. Auden,* edited by Edward Mendelson (1976).

Fisons plc: extract from instruction leaflet for Intal Inhaler, © Fisons plc 1989.

Forestry Commission: extracts from 'Developing Off-road Cycling in Woodlands in the South West – a Feasibility Study'.

4-Sight UK: extract from an advert in *MacUser 7,* March 1997.

Google: for a screenshot. Google is a trademark of Google Inc.

HarperCollins Publishers: extracts from William Dalrymple *A Year in Delhi* (1993); Peter de la Billière *Looking for Trouble* (1994).

Heinemann Educational Publishers, a division of Reed Educational & Professional Publishing Ltd: 'Sage' from *Heinemann English Dictionary*; extract from Anita Ganeri, *Pharaohs and Embalmers* (1997).

The Controller, Her Majesty's Stationery Office: extract from the new Self Assessment form. Crown © 1996.

Ilford Imaging: from Richard Platt, *Ilford Multigrade IV RC DeLuxe*.

Lonely Planet Publications: extracts from 'Climate' and 'Refugees & the Dispossessed', Geoff Crowther and Hugh Finlay, *East Africa—A Travel Survival Kit* (1994).

Met Office: extract from the Met Office website, © Crown Copyright 2005 Published by the Met Office, UK.

Microsoft™: screenshots reprinted by permission from Microsoft™ Corporation.

Mirror Group Newspapers: extract from the Daily Mirror, 21/3/97.

Penguin Books Ltd: extracts from Alan Gemmell, *The Penguin Book of Basic Gardening* (1975), and Joy Richardson, *What Happens When You Look?* (Hamish Hamilton, 1985).

Quintet Publishing Limited, London: from James Putnam, *Egyptology*.

Random House UK Ltd: extract from Theodore Zeldin, *An Intimate History of Humanity* (Sinclair-Stevenson, 1994).

Rough Guides Ltd: 'Old Delhi (Shahjahanabad)' from *India the Rough Guide* (1996).

Thames & Hudson Ltd: from N. Reeves and R. H. Williamson, *The Complete Valley of the Kings*, © 1996 Thames & Hudson Ltd.

Weidenfeld & Nicolson: from Alan Clark, *Diaries* (1993).

Western Daily Press: from Stephen Hayward, 'Lee's a high flier', *Western Daily Press*, 25/2/97.